Going Where My Pig Is Headed

By the same author

Liontooth: the story of a garden

Going Where My Pig Is Headed

SARA SHARPE

BEAUTIFULBOOKS

First published 2006.

Beautiful Books Limited
117 Sugden Road
London SW11 5ED

www.beautiful-books.co.uk

ISBN 1905636040 / 9781905636044

9 8 7 6 5 4 3 2 1

A catalogue reference for this book is available from the
British Library.

Jacket painting by Julian Borra
Digital photography of painting by Ian Pickard
Jacket artwork by Two Feet South Limited
Typesetting by Mel Strauss
Printed in Great Britain by T J International

Acknowledgements

The author and publishers would like to thank Dave Calder for
permission to quote from his 1975 collection of poetry,
Fingerbook of thumb, Faber & Faber for permission to quote from
The Unbearable Lightness of Being, by Milan Kundera; Anvil Press
for permission to quote from *Denial*, by George Seferis; The
Overlook Press for permission to quote from *Alexander's Path* by
Freya Stark; Henry Holt and Co for permission to quote from
Jerusalem Walks by Nitza Rosovsky; HarperCollins for permission
to quote from *The Towers of Trebizond* by Rose Macauley.

Author's note

I've always collected heroes. Three crop up in this book – Freya Stark, Rose Macaulay and Mustafa Kemal Atatürk. I'd like to think they'd met each other in the course of their extraordinary lives.

Mustafa Kemal Atatürk (1881-1938) is the father of Modern Turkey. After thwarting the British in the Dardenelles in 1915, he became leader of the Turkish liberation struggle, ended the six hundred year old Ottoman dynasty and – in the space of 15 years – took Turkey out of the Middle Ages and into the 20th century. Every small dusty Turkish town sells postcards of him. My good friend Gus Economides, now sadly dead, was the son of his Istanbuliot tailor.

The infant Freya Stark (1893-1993) was carried over the Dolomites in a basket by her father. She subsequently became a legendary travel writer, explorer, mapmaker, ethnographer, war correspondent and amateur archaeologist. She learnt Arabic, crisscrossed the Middle East and wrote 30 books. My favourite is *Alexander's Path*. I quote the blurb on the back of my paperback. She found 'no part of the world is more beautiful than the western and southern coasts of Turkey'.

'Tall in figure, informal of manner, careless of mere appearances, a gay and spirited conversationalist', Rose Macaulay (1881-1958) wrote my favourite book in the whole world, *The Towers of Trebizond*. Like Stark she was an inveterate traveller. I came on *Told by an Idiot* first published in 1923 as a teenager and was entranced by the life of the Garden family and their doubting clergyman father. As well as novels she wrote poetry, essays and criticism.

for Jenny Marsh

Preface

In late 1976 I had a well-paid job in advertising, a house and garden on the Suffolk border, wonderful friends, a lover who lived in Paris – so infrequent sex was always good – and a secure pension. It was a pleasant pattern, stitched together from the usual ups and downs of a life just arriving at middle age. A pattern neither dull nor predictable. The future, when I thought about it, looked intriguing. Four summers of sitting on the verandah with a gin and tonic, the smell of new-mown grass mixing with whiffs of night-scented stock, seemed likely to stretch to 20 years. Maybe the lover's wife would run off with her lover? I would write a novel, have a baby, wangle early retirement, weatherboard the eccentric house and indulge my passion for gardening; all within the pattern. I liked my pattern.

In Milan Kundera's *The Unbearable Lightness of Being*, the protagonist is keen to find out what happens when 'a person rejects what he previously considered his mission'. So what irresistible force, that November evening, burst from its cave and changed my life; a force so potent I never questioned it? Taken at the flood, blown off course and whoosh, nothing was ever the same again. Not so much a question of unpicking the pattern as tearing it up. Rejection of a perfectly good life, without a thought for the consequences. Most peculiar of all – for one prone to doubt – absolute certainty.

The following year I sold the house and furniture, left the job, chucked the pension over my shoulder and – on a blue September day – went away with my pig.

They tried to persuade me not to cross the curious hills,
finally, shrugging, called me foolish, stubborn;
that's how it is, I said,
I'm going where my pig is headed.

Dave Calder
from *Fingerbook of thumb,* 1975

Contents

Introduction

It's November 2004. The sea is lapping round the island like a saucer of milk. Look at me it croons. How sweet and gentle I am. See, I can even turn a silly pink at sunset. The island knows better. Over the centuries great holes have been torn from its sides. In 1940, one winter's night, my friend Angelica's house was taken. Sitting in the room above the sea wall, looking at the wrinkled satin of the deceitful one, I wonder when the first storm will come.

After years away I've come home to Likos – a small island to the north of Athens and south of the Sporades and Gates of the Wind. On a clear day you can see the coast of Turkey. Likos, pronounced like the Welsh vegetable, is Greek for wolf; and the landmass looks like the shaggy beast couchant, its nose concealing the port and the tail a promontory of jagged rocks. Many a caique has foundered on that tail, not that you would think it today. Not much has changed. Old friends look older but are still alive, still loving in their hugs and flatteries. The handsome teenage boys I remembered are now married with children of their own. There are new tavernas, bars, even a new, beautiful hotel. None of this has eroded the politeness of the people, their kindness and genuine charm.

It was on a January night in 1980 that I first came to Likos. A force 8 blew; and as we nudged round the tip of the nose, the local steamer bouncing and bucking, the Captain said: 'Now Sara, you must proceed to the taverna of Kyria Effie. There you will find good food and a welcome. Say that Captain Spiro sent you.' Three men and a truck stood on the murky quayside. Dodging lumps of sea I walked toward the town. No lights. No life. The wind howled. A plastic bag flew by. Then – somewhere to the left – I heard a distant twittering. Following the twitters I saw light from

1

steamed-up windows, pushed open a door and entered a room in which five old men sat at separate tables. Two other, younger men drank at the bar. Behind it, regal and startled, stood Kyria Effie. I cleared my throat:

'Good evening. I am a traveller come in from the storm. I bring greetings from Captain Spiro. He told me to come here so I have come.'

Modern Greek induces a formal yet poetic style in the speaker. Cries of welcome exploded from the old men. Kyria Effie smiled. Small fish, morsels of liver and a salad appeared as if by magic as I sat at the bar, shyly explaining my business to Elias the tailor and Panagiotis the carpenter. These two courteous men and Kyria Effie were to become my firm friends. Next morning, with a hangover from the bottled retsina, I walked up into the hills above the port. A flagged way meandered past orchards and stone bothies, little fields and olive groves. The air smelt of herbs and blossom. I fell in love...

'Purposeless travel for fun and adventure,' as Graham Greene put it, brings out the irrational. You spend uncomfortable days and nights getting some-where and then wish you hadn't got there. Or you arrive somewhere and start worrying about leaving – before you've even found a room. Or, most bizarre of all, you become attached to your means of transport – ferry, bus or train – and dread leaving it. What planted the travel virus in me I don't know. I've always had it. It might have been the smell of Burma remembered by a child refugee; or moving, always moving after the war; or the adventure stories I devoured. Perhaps, later, it was the dread of waste – to be old and infirm and regret the years not seized. All I know is this: that, sitting in front of a log fire in 1976, I decided to go and live in Greece, learn Modern Greek and wander about with a pack on my back. It took four minutes to change my life. It took years to understand the consequences.

The wind is getting up. I sit in my room above the

sea wall looking at the bag of my diaries, the laptop, the days and months of work ahead. When I start reading, sifting, sorting, what will it be like? Will the voice be familiar? Will I recognise the writer? Or will she turn out to be a disconcerting stranger, this middle-aged adventuress who doesn't do what she's supposed to do and hasn't the faintest idea why? The sea has turned into a ravening beast and fills, not only the small white room but my head with its roars. It's time to open Pandora's Box. It's time to go back 27 years, almost to the day...

Greece: a beginning 1977 – 1981

With what spirit, what heart,
what desire and passion
we lived our life: a mistake!
So we changed our life.

***Denial* by George Seferis**

Chapter One

A winter in Piraeus – New Year in Salamis – Mykonos – Delos
1977 – 1978

Nov 4th, move into the boat

The boat is dirty and damp. Make an inauspicious start by hosing the decks and leaving the portholes open. Pour myself a glass of wine and find Bach on Greek Radio 3 to blot out the noise of those things at the top of the mast. What with them going tching, tching, tching and the gangplank groaning I shall go mad. Yesterday I met Peter and Roger and their sidekick Taki and a small Scot with dreadful teeth who was sunk by killer sharks a few years back in the South Seas. Peter and Roger look after the boats on this quayside. Last night, my first night on board, quite awful. A southerly blew into the harbour. I thought I'd suffocated all the creaks in the warps with J-cloths but I woke to find a thing going AARP and then WIRRP by my left ear – a creature grumbling on. Finally went on deck with another packet of J-cloths and choked it to death. Roger says the harbour is so full of shit it's inadvisable to fall in. If you do, they either shoot you before you climb out or send you to a typhoid clinic!

Nov 8/9th, Piraeus

Two sets of Greek classes a week are killing me. Have borrowed an electric fire from a Canadian woman called Molly McKenzie. Went to lunch with her last week and met an alarming old bird who turned out to be Glubb Pasha's sister. Also Maud who lives in Salamis. I am to visit her soon. The electric fire is attached to some mysterious source of energy on the quayside. Will it fly apart in the night and electrocute me? Am deeply depressed by my Greek though cheered to find three lunacies in my *Teach Yourself Demotic Greek* book: *The lemon is neither white nor black, it is yellow. He who has brains does not always have hair. Where is the baby? I don't know, it was here yesterday.* Have made a friend in my Greek class, a Swede called Ingrid Mura. They'd only just arrived from Iran a month ago when her husband died. She has two kids. Am getting better at washing in the galley sink. Look forward to a HOT bath like a castaway dreams of steak. Have just found another gem: *My uncle is humpbacked but he is a very nice man.*

Letter to a friend Nov 10th, Piraeus

Dearest Bel

It's eight o'clock in the evening and I don't know what to have for supper. This morning I went to the Tuesday market so the choice is huge – cauliflower dressed with oil and lemon and masses of garlic or eggs or slices of *pastourmas* which is a kind of cured ham covered in garlic fudge, or celeriac? Guide me, O wise one. On what shall I wax fat and windy? Incidentally, no-one ever stops eating in the Piraeus. Sticky cakes and fruits, hot pastry parcels full of cheese or spinach, nuts, nougat, chestnuts, little kebabs and savoury doughnuts are devoured by men in suits, students, children and enormous women. Some of the children are grotesquely overweight, worse than American ones. Greek radio is telling mothers not to stuff their families.

You will be disappointed to learn that I have not been ravaged by Lascars. There are gloomy gangs of them in Boubelinas Street which climbs from the clock in Zea Marina over the hill and down into the main port of Piraeus. Also hookers. I've walked it at 1am and felt a lot safer than in the Earls Court Road. This is the route I take to my Greek classes in the Y in Athens; along the quaysides where the big boat for Crete lies, past tugs and tiny ferries to Salamis and bigger ones to Aegina, Poros and Hydra, over the road through the manic rush-hour traffic and onto a train. Some of the old trains are wooden-slatted. Do you remember when we came with Murison Small in '61? It was all country between the Piraeus and Athens, little farmhouses, fields, olive groves, market gardens. Now it's skein on skein of suburb linking the two cities. Sadly, the old, wicked Piraeus was demolished years ago by a reforming mayor. He built a silly tower which is still unoccupied and knocked down all the shacks of the refugees from Smyrna in 1922 and the clubs where they used to play *Rembetica* (not sure what this is but think it's Turkish-born Greek refugee music) and the hashish dens. No wonder the Lascars in Boubelinas look gloomy. He also knocked down Venetian and Turkish and Othonian houses, streets of them, and built ghastly apartment blocks. May his legs drop off.

I get out at Thission which still has the air of a country station and there, on the other side of the road, is the Acropolis. Looking at it, golden in the early morning mist, is miraculous. Athens is awful. So far, I only like three bits of it: Pangrati where a Canadian who lent me an electric fire lives; the street of Athinas near Monasteraki and the flea market, a wonderful bedlam of do-it-yourself shops, little bars and the old fish and meat markets in their Turkish halls; and the street of Black Michael in the university quarter under the Hill of Lycabettos which contains the oldest corset in the world. And of course the Plaka which the city fathers would like to knock down. What is the matter with them? Don't they realise that people come to see the old and the charming, not concrete blocks?

Good things are chicken and egg shops (why is this so funny when it's so logical?), the Green Ones – buses with no springs which bounce along at 100mph between Athens and Piraeus – and a local ancient in a shack who sells draft ouzo. I like Piraeus and its streets and squares and big ships that come and go and the unfathomable mixture of smells – jasmine, diesel, the clean musti-ness of Greek clothes, hot pine trees, cinnamon cakes, aftershave and sewage. Adonis is the cook on the gin palace at the top of the quay and a dignified man. When he calls by, he always makes sure that the saloon door, hatch, whatever it's called, stays open. So I am not compromised in the ever-watchful eyes of the Greeks working on the quayside. Yesterday he brought cakes the shape of small cucumbers and very sweet and lectured me on the foolishness of being single: 'What's going to happen to you when you're old and ill and haven't any money?' His eyebrows are like bars under his woolly cap. One day, I might understand half of what he says.

8

You asked me how my Greek was going. Don't. I try and do about six hours a day. We have so much homework, I can hardly keep up.

This morning it was bedlam on the quayside. Boats came and went. A carpenter sawed a door in half. Motor bikes, small boys, vans, officialdom surged up and down. And the drill which started at 7am is still whining now, seven hours later. Suddenly, I feel very homesick writing to you. It was lovely to get your letter. Every afternoon I walk for two hours; along the mole past the gin palaces or up Odos Themistokleous or down the long straight road which runs from Piraeus to Kazanova Street and the Naval College. In the Kazanova district you find little old country houses which the reforming mayor missed. And here people stare at a foreigner. Another pleasure is Kastella, the hill above the harbour. Sometimes I stand there in a lavender and apricot sunset, watching the planes fly west.

Am sleepy and full of celeriac. Love to David and the children.

Love Sara

Nov 20th, Piraeus

Dougal, the small Scot, drinks far too much whisky. He tells me I yell when I speak Greek. Over the two weeks I've made three HORRENDOUS mistakes with this bloody language. Reading a poem by Seferis in my Greek class I was puzzled by a line and asked Sarah, the teacher, why *tonsils were blooming*. The class fell about. Take away one i and tonsils and almond trees are the same word! Then, because I was sleepy and pronounced an m as an l, I asked the baker for a *nice hot fresh penis*. The same day I alarmed the greengrocer who shouts at his wife. 'It is but November,' I said, very slowly, 'but last night there were cauliflowers flying round my bedroom and biting me.' A cauliflower is *kounoupidi* and a mosquito is *kounoupi*. I think I shall kill myself.

Dec 3rd, Piraeus

Weather gloomy and drizzly. The Tourist Police are pigs. Am

getting fat from too many lunches with Roger and Peter and Douglas at *Il Mare*. Greek went badly today. Felt miserable so walked out onto the last, long breakwater of Zea Marina and stood, huddled in my donkey jacket, looking at the sea and the hulks that rot in the lee of Salamis and the planes flying to England. Something has gone wrong with my bridge and gluck is oozing out of it. When it rains the boat leaks, but now I know where to stuff the J-cloths and position the plastic bags at the end of my bunk. A boat on a nearby quay blew up yesterday when its owner lit the gas. Inexplicably he is alive and well.

Letter to a friend Dec 19th, Piraeus

Dear Hugh

So many thanks for your letter. Great dramas here. My bridge came loose and my gum oozed pus and I saw myself toothless and mumbling within a few months. Greek dentists are notorious for pulling everything out. However, Roger sent me to a physician in Kolokotroni Street, one Dimitri Panagiotou. What a nice man. He works at the hospital all day so appointments are from 9pm onwards. For the last week he has been poking needles into my root, drilling holes here and there and measuring me for a new bridge. He is an artist. Three times a week I've been walking at dead of night to his surgery, emerging, exhausted, after midnight...It's like a love affair.

Dimitri says Greek dentists don't deserve their bad reputation. It's the patients who are the trouble, either fainting or falling on their knees or swallowing handfuls of Valium. Last night a large woman in black was moaning in his waiting room. A friend dropped by to visit. 'Come and look at this,' said Dimitri. My bridge was admired and much chat ensued. Imagine that happening in an English dentist's surgery? The other night, after a particularly long session, I felt emotional and shook his hand and said how grateful I was to have found such a dentist. He smiled. 'And I, to have made such a friend.'

Christmas is here. In the big square up the hill loudspeakers play carols – *O noble stem of Jesse, Hark the Herald, Adeste Fidelis.* The snow falls on orange trees covered in oranges and a neon Virgin is pinned to the bosom of the Town Hall. There are tinselly Xmas trees with candles and below and around them clash the colours of bougainvillea, hibiscus, geraniums and pyracantha. Everyone is very excited by the snow. They are not used to it. These Greek flowers and shrubs don't seem bothered. Isn't that odd? There is a splendid, life-size Nativity on the quayside beside the clock. The shepherds are frozen in awe beneath arc lamps, seven white angels stand at attention and a Dolly Baby Jesus is in the crib. There are also three kings with three ENORMOUS camels. Yesterday a dozen or so Santas were drifting about with balloons. Fat children in fur coats grabbed at them. One young one stood near me scratching his balls.

I must go. Dougal has bronchitis, not surprising since he smokes 80 cigarettes a day. I have an amazing soup for him called *Bombay Broth* which I have invented. It consists of: oil and butter, potatoes, cabbage, onions, garlic, beef stock, salt and pepper, cayenne pepper, turmeric, rice, porridge oats, marmite, parsley and milk.

Send me news of the office and all the scandal when you have time.

Love Sara

Dec 28th, Piraeus

The snow has gone. The end of December is blue and beautiful, shirt sleeves weather. Yesterday made my last visit to the dentist's chair. Adonis gave me a bracelet and Dougal confided his love for an artist in Staffordshire. The gang of Piraeus stray dogs has lived through the cold snap. In this country animals gang up to survive. Children stone kittens, skeletons cringe over spilt garbage. The Orthodox Church teaches that animals have no souls; so if you torture a cat or dog or misuse a mule or donkey your immortal soul remains untarnished. It breaks my heart how polite and affectionate the skeletons are. Good luck to the eight wolves who sleep under the clock in Zea Marina, their rumps tucked into the flower borders. They fear no-one.

Jan 6th, New Year in Salamis

On December 30, I crossed by small boat from Piraeus to Palookia, lugging spit-roasted chook, yoghurt, veg and fruit. A bus dropped me at Kakkivigla. From there I walked. The day was boiling, a near-heatwave. What a mad country! A rough track wound over the hills through thorn and sistus, broom, oregano and clumps of rosemary. I stopped to rest under a gnarled carob and admired the lush base leaves of the autumn sea squills. Got lost, found the track again and finally reached the ridge. There, below me, was Maud's paradise – a valley enfolded in olive-dotted hills, with higher, wilder ranges behind. At the bottom of the valley lay the bay, a sandy crescent, its dunes backed by bamboo and pampas. I could see in the distance an old stone farmhouse, white with yellow windows. Smoke rose from the chimney. A red dot hung out washing. Arriving to cries of welcome and a kitten with large feet, I felt myself – for the first time – in old Greece.

What a week! Each day we breakfast outside on the old threshing floor under the olive tree, munching toast and honey and yoghurt and sipping strong coffee. The house is one big room with dirt walls and floor and a fireplace. There is a small room for visitors and another tiny one at the back where the meat safe lives. Maud has no light, no water, no loo. The well is twenty minutes' walk over fairly rough ground up the hill. Guests are handed a trowel with their towel. You go to the gully, *remma,* to shit, then catlike dig a hole with the trowel and bury your turds. At night olive branches crackle in the fireplace; oil lamps cast their soft light. M cooks delicious meals on a baby two-ring gas attached to a cylinder and we drink strong wine, drawn from barrels by a woman called *the moustachioed one,* and brought back in gallon flasks over the mountain.

The kitten grows daily bolder. It's learning to climb the olive tree but only gets a quarter of the way up before falling off. It's called Shimsu, a delicate name which doesn't suit its big feet. To M's annoyance, I call it Gymshoe. Sitting in my dressing gown, supervising its futile efforts, I can't keep my eyes off the view of the

12

bay below and its two headlands and the fishing boats and steamers which appear and disappear as if pushed and pulled by invisible hands. Down the hill, in-between the sea and the house, is Spiro's market garden, vivid with the green of young lettuces and dill. Spiro and his brothers and sisters, about eight or nine I think, grew up in Maud's one room. He is a wonderful man with tombstone teeth in a melancholy face, transformed in a flash by his smile. We drank wine one evening with him and his wife Fanni, nibbling at her honey cakes called *melomacarona*. When Spiro started singing *kleftika tragoudia*, the old freedom songs from the last century, and banging the table she got cross with him. They are clearly devoted. I wish I could understand what they say. Maud and they gossiped while I sat, bemused by the sound of water rushing through the neat irrigation channels and the bleating of goats and the tinkle of the sheep being driven into the hills by two girls and a raggedy dog. The valley has four houses and a tiny church. There are mulberries, date palms and young cypresses; at the side of the road figs and pomegranates grow fat. Best recipe yet for pomegranates: gouge out the seeds and soak overnight in Metaxa brandy and sugar.

M and I walk and talk and I learn about old customs and traditions and what to say when. To *kalos orisate* meaning *welcome,* the reply must be *kalos sas vrikame, good that we have found you.* Yesterday the wind veered to the north, lifting the pressure and turning the sky bright blue. We climbed high into the centre of the island through woods of wild cyclamen to a plateau and a ruined village and a church so small you could have wrapped it in a handkerchief. On one side the land tumbled in folds and gullies, their contours furred by pine and carob, the line broken here and there by a sentinel cypress, to the sea. An Edward Lear painting.

Jan 14th, Perani. Amazing Rat Tale

About a week ago, Maud discovered mouse or rat shit so we set two traps: a mouser where the meat safe is and a ratter in the big room – fleeing in sudden panic from the latter in case it sprang at us. Shimsu, being witless, was dispatched to a painter friend down the hill out of harm's way. Three nights running the *rat-mouse* sprung the trap in the big room and ate the bait. On the fourth night it had the temerity to fling the trap in the air. A fatal mistake. Maud, enraged, went down the hill to borrow the painter's cat, a large tabby tom seemingly made of wood. We christened him Captain Teak. This slayer of dragons settled in, purred a lot and went to sleep. 'He doesn't look very aggressive,' observed Maud. 'You'd better bring a camp bed in here for tonight in case he needs help.' Later the hole under the door was blocked with three small rocks. The cat watched, still purring.

The olive wood fire burnt to its embers; we yawned goodnight and slept. Some hours later I was awoken by the unmistakable smell of catshit. 'The bloody animal's got diarrhoea,' complained a voice. I heard soft cursing and the swabbing of cloths. The smell receded. Then I woke again. CRASH! Another CRASH! M's torch flickered excitedly. 'Yes, yes, it's something!' Then came the scream, a dreadful despairing cry, then silence. Isolated in the middle of the room on my camp bed, I felt uneasy. Another CRASH and then CRUNCHINGS. 'The bloody cat's eating my lizard!' Maud's voice quivered with outrage.

Next morning we found a huge rat tail and a spherical Teak. Reverently, M and I tiptoed outside with our coffee.

We retrieve Shimsu from the painter – a slight woman, with a low, enchanting voice and the manner of a nervous faun. She looks at me in alarm. 'How large and noisy you are.' I haven't been told that since I was fired by Unilever in 1959. 'I suppose I am,' I reply. This alarms her even more. She backs away. 'O, don't say that.'

What a magic valley. We gather Fat Hen, boil it and dress the green mess with oil, lemon juice, salt and pepper. It is delicious. The locals call it *Lamboti*.

Jan 22nd, Piraeus

The blizzards return, filling up the cockpit with snow. One morning

I have to dig myself out. Athens in despair and convulsed with flu. Everyone's flats are freezing as central heating systems collapse. Feel superior lying in my warm boat lagged with sweaters, watching the snow fall – a Nansen in my Fram. Being cocooned makes me want to mend things. I repair my grey sweater. It takes me hours and results in a re-born, chic garment with short sleeves. The darn down the right hand side looks like an appendix scar but you can't have everything. Decide to patch my cords and go out in a blizzard, passing two optimists selling bananas on the bonnet of a car. There is a marvelous shop in Piraeus full of elderly gents snipping through bolts of cloth. I was told about it by Lefteri of the button and braid shop to whom I was sent by Sokrati, the Istanbuliot tailor. Found dark brown fake leather stuff and am now happily patching. One evening, fearing that the boat would be an igloo in the morning with me trapped inside, I shoveled out the cockpit, then sprinkled salt. Next morning, aha, Thyateira is the only boat without a snowed-up cockpit. I hope it snows forever. I have a comfy bunk, Espresso coffee, oil, garlic, eggs, cheese, apples from Tripoli which smell like Jonathans and a big blue jug full of parsley and dill. And a fire to keep me warm.

Jan 30th, Piraeus

Now there are floods everywhere. Ingrid and the children and I drive to Levadia to find an ancient oracle, a name ending in *onos*. It's pissing with rain. A depressing landscape of mountain, soggy plain and mist. We lunch beside a river in spate with swans whizzing down it like Ferraris – hope they know where they're going – then return gloomily to Ingrid's flat to drink tea and whisky. Drive down to the boat through pink and purple thunder and lightning. Just in time. The drainage holes in the cockpit don't work so it's awash and about to spill over into the saloon. Worse, rain is rushing down the electric fire lead which snakes through the window into the saloon and smoke pouring from the connecting bit. HELP! The wind howls, the gangplank dances like a dervish. We are clearly about to explode. There is nothing for it but to rip the electric coils apart, getting a shock which knocks me over. Am saved by my wellies. I don't understand electricity!

15

Feb 6th, Piraeus

Janni (a local scoundrel) has fixed me up with a billiards teacher in the nearby billiard hall. It's like something out of Conrad, down dirty steps in a basement full of swarthy men who stare. The curious looks and sniggers soon stopped when the manager took me under his wing. He's the brother of Janni's wife. My teacher, a polite, mild-mannered man is supposed to be the champion of Jordan but Janni tells such whoppers, who knows? Billiards give me cramp. My hands shake and I don't seem to be able to extricate my left little finger and my fourth finger from their mother lump. My teacher massages my left hand in his large brown paw then tactfully leaves me to practise alone. I fear that billiards, like carpentry, is full of angles, so I shall never be Minnesota Fats.

Feb 14th, boat to Mykonos

A grey, drizzly day. I woke up in a bad mood not wanting to go anywhere and caught the boat jam-packed with National Servicemen going somewhere – not, I hoped bleakly, to Mykonos. The Aegean behaved like the North Sea and at Syros we hung about while two dwarfs in oilskins danced round the anchor chain. The man beside me sighed, crossed his legs, opened his briefcase and offered me a chocolate biscuit. 'The anchor which is down does not wish to come up.' He sighed again. An hour later the dwarfs triumphed and we were away, finally arriving at Mykonos at 3.30pm. The steamer lay off and a tiny boat came out of the harbour to take a few of us off. Much kerfuffle with parcels, a bicycle and two sea-sick old ladies, then lo, we were on the quayside. I am in Mykonos. Hurray!

Letter to friend, Feb 18th, Mykonos

Dearest Minnie

This is to make up for all the letters I haven't written you. It is February, I am in Mykonos and I simply don't believe my eyes. It is BEAUTIFUL. White houses circle a scoop of harbour, with more sugar lumps behind climbing the hill in a maze of little streets. Balconies drip with geraniums, jasmin, plump fresias in

16

pots. Everywhere the mimosa blooms. When I arrived I thought I had the DTs because the first thing I saw was a pink pelican. A Dutch girl and I were approached by a shy woman offering rooms. She is a darling called Kyria Maria and her house, an old one, is at the back of the town near the windmills. Her sheets smell of wild flowers. Margaret, the Dutch girl and I share a room for 80 drachs each. Only two or three kafs are open. Our first evening M and I found one of them which we'll never find again and ate *fasolada*, the winter beansoup, and bread washed down with vinegary retsina. Mykonos is rich in good-looking old men with huge moustaches. Two of these walruses sat in the corner of the kaf. After beaming at us, they sent over another bottle of vinegar. Very liverish we were the next morning.

The weather was awful when I first got here but now a hot sun takes the edge off the wind. The people are extraordinarily friendly. They seem able to disassociate themselves from the summer madness when cruise ships disgorge thrice daily and a colony of thugs under some dope fiend (paid to keep out of his country, they say) rampage. A man in a bar talked about it. 'In the summer if you're ill and need a doctor quickly, you'll die. No one can get through the crowds.' He laughed. 'The locals quite like the thugs. Sometimes they get violent and break up places. Next day the German sends his heavy to find out how much the damage is and whatever price the owner names, he pays it. Most of the bars can't *wait* to be done over.'

There's a dotty old lady with swollen legs in the fishermen's kafenion in the harbour. Outside it, like washing, hang octopuses. When she opens up in the morning, cats fly through the door along with plastic bags of rubbish and dead fish. She yells at everyone but has a heart of gold. The other morning I sat on a bollard sucking a sweet given to me by a passing walrus and watched the fun. Two men pretended to set fire to a friend's load of fodder, three-wheelers breezed past, fishermen mended their webs of rust, ochre, purple and plum-crimson, donkeys brayed, dogs howled, the sun shone. I decided Mykonos wasn't real but a kind of Cycladic Brigadoon. One evening, a walrus who claimed to be an intimate of the Shah's first wife, Soraya, tried to kiss me by a windmill. 70 if he was a day! Margaret, bored by Greek, had

17

gone to a bar. We'd been discussing the cost of living when he pounced. 'No, no, Sir,' I said. 'I am virtuous.' (I'd just learnt the Greek word *enaretos*). Depressed, he left. Imagine saying 'I am virtuous' to a groper in the cinema! Every day I explore the sugar lump maze of the town, a penguin among the icebergs, slipping in and out of the blue shadows. Guess what? Mykonos has 365 churches, one for each day of the year. They are red, white and blue.

I've only just recovered from walking 26 kilometres there and back to Ano Mera on the other side of the island. A heatwave struck. Apparently it can happen in February. Armed with the baker's spinach pies, chocolate biscuits, a bottle of wine and my Greek dictionary, Margaret and I took a dusty road which wound past little churches, baking like meringues in the sun. After an ouzo in Ano Mera, we wandered on, up and down the hills, past fields of flowers and fat sheep to slabs of rock. The sea had bitten holes in them, leaving scarred, eyeless contours. Margaret sketched while I chanted Greek and pigs ran around on the beach. I talked to the swineherd, a smiley boy. 'It's hot,' he said. 'They like to cool off in the sea.' The pigs frolicked and paddled and I wondered again whether the place was real.

Write to me soon. I'll be in and out of Piraeus this spring, but Barbara's Kazanova address will always find me.

Much love Sara

Feb 22nd, Visit to Delos

A small caique leaves for Delos at nine. Five of us board it – a Japanese girl with an expensive camera, a couple of Americans and a charming Dane. Are there nasty Danes? I've never met one. The boatman looks like a hamster. Delos is Apollo's birthplace. My God. Ever since Delphi all those years ago I've had Apollo in my head. Such a strange mixture of art, order and violence. The guides of Delos, guardians they're called, are the only people allowed to stay on this sacred island. We arrive. A desire to get away from the others sends me climbing huge steps cut out of the hill thousands of years ago when Naxos was lawlord. On the

18

top is a shrine, to Hera I think. It's wonderfully peaceful, like being on top of the world, and you can see other Cycladic islands floating nearby. I eat my cheese pie and fall asleep, waking when the two Americans trip over me. 'Oh my, pardon me.' Together we hurry back down the steps to find the lionesses. Three guardians spot us. Immediately they spring to life like dogs offered a walk. Lionesses? Certainly. But first we must see the great city where 40,000 people lived in 4,000 BC. Nikolaos, the senior guardian, shows us the shells of noble houses with cisterns, cool courtyards, wonderful mosaics. My favourite is a tiger's head, a wily, smiley tiger. Down the main street, past hotels, markets, brothels, a theatre, a stadium – all gone, all ghosts – we pass a dead pelican floating in a cistern. There is so much left from so long ago it makes my thumbs prick. Nikolaos has bad feet. The Americans and I bicker amicably about dates. My leaflet says barbarians from the sea destroyed the city in 2,500 BC, their guidebook disagrees. Who cares? This city is one of the most extraordinary things I have ever seen.

Larks tweet high in the sky as we pick our way through downtown Delos and skirt the base of the Colossos. The swamp where the God was born is to our right. When his mother gave birth to him, holding a tree, it was a lake. Now rush and bamboo choke it. It is *terribly* hot. Small lizards pant on marble. And there are the lionesses, sublime, making tears prick my eyes.

But the place is oppressive. Too old, too knowing, too much. A frisson of angst makes me sweat. It's a relief when we start back to the boat. Outside one of the guardians' cottages a flock of hens scratch in the dust. I stop to croon and caw and they reply in kind. The Americans look embarrassed, Nikolaos alarmed. I decide to make a joke. 'I am a hen,' I say in Greek. Nikolaos looks serious. 'No, you are *not* a H-E-N, you are a W-O-M-A-N.'

Back in Mykonos I eat octopus stew and enjoy good draft wine from Crete. Am horribly sunburnt.

March 2nd, Piraeus

On the boat from Mykonos to the Piraeus I sat on the sundeck and watched two old gentlemen munching Turkish Delight. For two hours non-stop they chattered. At Syros, they started on their second box of Turkish Delight, and when that was finished fell on a bag of rusks. The afternoon chilled into evening and everyone went on deck to look at Sunion. That temple to Poseidon is a beacon for Greeks returning to their mainland. Next day, I went to see Ingrid in Athens. We lounged in wicker chairs on her balcony sipping ouzo, while from the house across the narrow street a piano tinkled Chopin and the little girls in the ballet school rose and fell on their points. March is here and the days are blue. The fig trees in the Piraeus are showing green shoots, the big ships hoot over the hill and the old men in panama hats sit in the sunshine, making that gesture with their right hand as if winding up a clock.

The orange blossom is nearly out. Alas, my billiards teacher has gone back to Jordan so now I shall never beat Minnesota Fats. Dishes in Greece seem to go with the seasons. This month's delicacy is artichokes cooked in some lovely gravy of onions and carrots and celery and dill. Dougal is sailing away soon. My first winter in Greece is over.

Likos, 2004

Last night it thundered and rained, the sky exploding pink and purple and forks of lightning stabbing at the sea. Likos' twin peaks, the ears of the wolf, attract storms. My small white room, found for me by Angelica, is all that I dreamed of a year ago in London. It's up a flight of steep stone steps a few yards from the sea. Sitting at my laptop in front of the big window, all I see are bits of Italian coffee pot drying on the sill, the rusty railing of the balcony, a small boat painted blue inside beached at the edge of the road, a low, whitewashed wall, sea, a rump of distant land and sky. The top of the door hinges back and opens. Every morning I unlatch it and stand like a horse contemplating the weather. Sometimes, if it's just dawn, Ilias the tailor is passing. He is old now, a ghost of the cheerful, hard-drinking man I met in the taverna 24 years ago. But the twinkle is still there and he chuckles as he remembers teaching me unsuitable words.

Up a step from the bedsitting room is a bathroom, beautiful and modern, with bath, basin, loo and a window with bright yellow shutters. A tank almost as large as the bath provides hot water and Stammatis, the agent, who works in the bakery round the corner, has gouged a summerful of tourist hair out of the basin's waste pipe so now the water runs away. My workroom has two beds, one of them acting as a horizontal filing cabinet for papers, books and diaries, two bedside tables, one of which I sit on to type, two purple chairs and a wardrobe. An ancient lamp whose only function seems to be as a flypaper hangs from the ceiling; but the bedside light is fine and bright and makes the room cosy in the evenings. Below on the terrace, cats of all shapes and colours gather to wail and fight and make love.

When the gales blow from the Gates of the Wind they come straight at me, screaming and yelling and whipping the sea into paroxysms of rage. Then everything gets

21

bolted and barred and shuttered and no steamers come. The last force 9 blew for three days and taught me what an alarming neighbour the sea is, how invasive her voice. With sea inside your head, sleep is impossible. Only one steamer made it to the island that week so there was a mad rush for vegetables and fruit. Just as on another island, in another winter, twenty five years ago...

Chapter Two

An island in the Cyclades
1979

Jan 9th, to Amorgos with the steamer Miaoulis

Get up at 5am, muttering darkly, and walk over the hill to the main Piraeus harbour. The steamer is leaning against the quay and doesn't look as if it's going anywhere. A dark-skinned man in uniform paces up and down.

'Is this ship sailing?'

'No.'

'Why the hell not, I've got a ticket?'

The man smiles apologetically, extending his hands in that Mediterranean gesture which absolves one from all blame.

'Fancy having a ticket and no boat.' I'm so cross I'm talking to myself. I confront him again.

'How do you know anyway?' This is not very polite of me.

Gleaming white teeth flash in a broad grin.

'Alas Madam, I know because *I* am the captain.'

Mortified, I apologise profusely. He is still quivering with laughter as I stalk off to murder the ticket office.

Next day the ship is well and we leave on time, steaming through a harbourful of French letters. One is enormous! Sitting on the top deck out of the wind I consume an unforgettable breakfast – spit-roasted chicken, bread and wine. The Miaoulis though battered is charming. Her decks of seasoned wood sweep aft, her colours are dark green, orange and red with white paint-work. Greek boats are always green and orange. They invariably smell of diesel and hot mince. While we run before the north wind I eavesdrop on a burly man who's going to Amorgos. He's Greek, looks rich, about 53-ish. 'What's there?' he asks nervously. Poking about the steamer, I come on all kinds of oddities. Someone in the crew loves birds because the ceiling of third class is hung with them: budgies, canaries and frightened little red, white and brown things. Maybe the crew eat them? What a dreadful thought. Back in second class is an even stranger sight. A man feeds his falcon. The speckled bird takes the lumps of raw flesh then hops onto his shoulder. We passengers are not so lucky. No meat, raw or cooked on the Miaoulis. The crew are surly, the service non-existent.

It's dark when we arrive at Amorgos, jostling through a hole in the ship's side. M waves from the quay. A drama holds us both captive: a car unable to negotiate the ramp. Finally the captain loses patience and six large crew manhandle the vehicle and its hysterical driver onto dry land. The port of Amorgos is called Katapola. Under a tree is the oldest bus in the world. Everyone for the top village, the *hora*, piles on and we are off, rattling down an avenue of gum trees. It is a pitch-dark night without stars and the driver looks as if he's had a few. The road up the mountain is dirt and potholed, a veritable serpent of Z-bends. Rock faces and prickly pears loom and recede in our headlights; gears grind and clash. This is no journey for the fainthearted, especially as the driver gives only 30 per cent of his attention to the road. The woman in the seat behind him has the other 70. She looks like a hen and holds a glassy-eyed baby. Sucked into quagmires, skidding, hanging over precipices, thrown about in our seats like dice in a shaker we finally make it to the top.

A small silent square outside a village. No sound. A few shadows. Tired out, I eat an omelette and salad washed down by strong draft wine and fall into a dreamless sleep.

24

Jan 15th, Amorgos

Am entranced by the *hora* and its inhabitants. Built on a bluff under an enormous rock, the houses of the high village, maze-like, form a buttress against the hunting wind. So successful is this blocking device that, even when a force 10 screams from the North, you can't hear a sound in the taverna. Outside the village is a saddleback. Here the wind can blow you off the cliff. For two days I explore the white jigsaw of little streets, finding squares shaded by jacaranda and acacia, peering into mysterious walled gardens. There are no cars to disturb my peace; only the soft plod of mule and donkey. The land tumbles away in terraces, now largely uncultivated. Cliffs guard the southern approaches. I encounter my first mandrake and am fascinated. What a bizarre plant – a cross between a salad and a hat. The asphodel and almond blossom are out, the sparrows fight and wagtails dip and flit. At sunset the sky turns piebald, a gash of pink. Small owls wail like cats.

The centre of our universe is the taverna: for food, wine, gossip, fixing things and finding out things. There sits Nikitas, jovial husband of the ever-restless, sharp-eyed Aspasia who cooks like an angel. The Murderer – who murdered someone ages ago in Thessaloniki – is one of the regulars. He stares and cackles but is harmless. In the pale sunlight of a winter morning Nikitas sits in the window reading his newspaper. He is the kindest of men and has dreadful arthritis. Food depends on what's available. I must have put on half a stone since arriving here, due to a diet of soup and rice, pumpkin and rice, potatoes in garlic sauce, pitta parcels of greens, rice pudding, sometimes just rice.

In cold weather, as it is now, the taverna is freezing. For some reason, no wood perhaps – there are no fires in the *hora*. Instead, the inhabitants crouch over things called *mangalia*: large woks with legs, full of charcoal. These smell, give out minimal heat and kill you if the door isn't open. Quite Irish really. Most evenings Aspasia spins wool beside hers or knits away at a kind of woolly Quatermass. The gossip ebbs and flows: the school-teacher is mean; the mayor is a good man; the painter Adonis must marry – but who? The helicopter from Piraeus has come for the boy dragged by a mule. 'He will die,' they say, shaking their heads. During the winter there are no doctors on the island. If you're dying – and you're lucky – the helicopter or a navy ship might come for you.

At the moment we're all living in Molly's house. This is a very grand affair, almost Georgian in its proportions, facing south-west over the hills to the sea. A Scottish view. There's a large living room, a bedroom, a dark kitchen and an outside loo. In the loo-bathroom lies a magnificent bath, as yet unconnected to pipe or water source. The mayor makes wild promises to install it. I am in love with his moustache. Below the house and its wide stone balcony is a barn, and in front of that a garden.

Maud's house is a gem. You enter by a door tucked in an archway of the old castro and climb steep steps to a courtyard in the air. Jasmine and fuchsia spill out of pots and there's a vine overhead. Leading from the courtyard are two doors – one into the living room, the other into a diminutive kitchen. The ceilings are wooden-rafted and painted flax blue. All the inside rooms join up with one another. The chaos in the top house is impressive. Every morning Maud and I dig small holes in it, only to produce more chaos. We unpack, sort, rub down old chairs, paint, whitewash, fill holes with putty and haunt the mayor who is also the electrician. For a large man he moves fast, especially when he sees Maud coming. I love him more each day. Most of his installations explode. Molly fumes in the house below. The bath remains a stranger to water.

Jan 23rd, letter to a friend

Darling Charlie

I'm spending January in Amorgos. My friend Maud had to leave that dream place in Salamis. Karamanlis passed a vote-catching law allowing people to build shack-holiday homes and now the place is ruined. Her valley is a nightmare of excreta-smeared paper and blaring transistors – the most obscene spoliation I've ever seen. I can't bear it. Neither could she. Her new home is a stone eyrie in which I play carpenter's mate to her foreman. Those hands that once ruffled your hair are now callused lumps!

I have two stories for you. One concerns the mayor with whom I am seriously in love; and the other M's landlady, Diasino, a saint who gives everything away. Her husband Georgi plays the violin. One afternoon after an enormous lunch – boiled potatoes and garlic sauce, I think – Maud and I heard bangings on the door. Giorgi and Diasino had arrived to remove the sofa. This is an old piece, about ten foot long and uncomfortable. Gingerly we inched the monster out onto the balcony, preparatory to tobogganing it down a flight of steep steps to the street. As we stood poised for this manoeuvre, a host of visitors flowed up the steps: Aspasia to prune the vine (she's queen of the local taverna) and a man to clean the chimney in the kitchen. M took the chimney sweep and his thorn bush to the kitchen; Aspasia fell on the vine; and Diasino, Georgi and I set off with the sofa.

It was clear to me that the sofa would *never* get down the steps, simply because it was wider than they were. Diasino however was made of sterner stuff. Down we went, the sofa moulting planks and struts at every step and branches of pruned vine falling from above. Chunks of masonry and earth fell too. By the time we got it to the street our cargo was kindling. No one seemed to mind. Its remains were stored in a cavernous barn and we all said what a magnificent sofa it had been. Diasino vanished, only to reappear with a present of a cabbage leaf of herby rice, enough for at least twelve people. The kindness and the manners here are exquisite. *Our* soi-disant civilised society could learn a thing or two.

January 17 was the Feast of Adonis. The island is full of Adonises. The painter is one. So is the mayor. When someone has a *name day*, everyone visits their house to be fed goodies. So off we set that evening, purple rain lashing the cobbles, in our best clothes. The mayor, as usual, looked wonderful. We were eight: the priest, Maud, Molly and me, a woman with a squint and a couple with two children. After some minutes, the mayor's wife treated us to a piece of chocolate cake, a glass of green liquid and home-made bars of sesame seed and honey. Greeks in small communities are very respectable. They abhor nudism and are horrified by topless foreign tourists. So I was fascinated by the pictures on the walls of the parlour, most of them females in one or other form of undress. A naked woman caressed her nipples straight in front of me. The clock ticked. No one spoke. Then I noticed that Maud had sunk her front teeth (recently capped) into her sesame and honey bar and couldn't get them out. The green leaf, on which each portion of the delicacy rested, stuck out of one corner of her mouth. The eyes above the immobilised teeth registered a mixture of puzzlement and panic.

The two children and I became convulsed. Was it Adonis who plucked the thorn from the lion's paw?

Outside the village is a windy saddleback. A flagged way zigzags down from it to a dirt road built by the Army. Here you turn left and are soon on a dizzy path round an alarmingly vertical cliff. This leads to the monastery – an extraordinary sight; a slice of feta cheese stuck to red rocks. The ikon, so they say, refused to be put somewhere else and, when taken away on a ship, jumped off it and flew back up the cliff. We visited last week and an old monk gave us coffee and *kitron*, a delicious liqueur, and teased M about her age. The monks have land and animals. Sadly their number dwindles each year.

I hope you miss me as much as I miss you. I'm wandering this spring and summer but hope to pick up a letter from you in-between.

Much love, Sara

Jan 25th, Amorgos

The confusion continues to grow and we still have one, final, horrific challenge: the pipes for the stove in the living room. These rusty things fit into the petroleum burning stove at one end and vanish through a hole in the wall at the other. They come in sections, are supposed to fit together but never do, and, being second-hand, are full of soot. Guess who's cleaning them? I grumble to Aspasia at lunchtime. She ignores my wails and fixes her beady eye instead on an old, darned dress I'm wearing. I call it *Taxidi*, the travelling one. Every time it springs a hole, I darn it. A's incredulity at its sorry state has finally got the better of her manners. 'Sara, have you no other dress?' When I suggest a bet on whether it will last or fall to bits before I leave, she collapses into giggles. She is a darling behind that hawkish fierceness.

Jan 27th, Amorgos

There are two fishermen in Amorgos – handsome Dimitri and his old father. They bring their catch to the village from a bay at the bottom of the cliff. To summon the customers, the old man blows a conch shell. A strange, unearthly sound. Everyone gallops down the street. About 30 cats are always first in the queue. Last night Maud bought a Moray eel and Aspasia cooked it. Dear God, what a fearful creature. A sea serpent with monstrous teeth. Apparently, they lurk in caves under the water and when their fangs sink into a passing swimmer's arm, the only way to get them out is to chop off the arm. Also, if you hook them on a line, they'll come up it to tear you to pieces. Quite lost my appetite due to these horror stories. The flesh had a subtle and delicious flavour but to extract it from the minefield of bones proved almost impossible.

Jan 29th, Amorgos

It is the feast of Basil, Gregory and John the Golden-tongued. The mayor's fuses continue to explode and so do I, due to a diet of cauliflower, cabbage, wild greens and eggs. Met a handsome Dutchman called Henni. He says he doesn't want to learn Greek in case he wouldn't like the old men in the taverna so much, once he understood their conversations. What a romantic. The barrel of wine is empty. What on earth are we going to do? 'Is there meat in England?' asks Aspasia. She is astonished by my affirmative answer, just as she was astonished the other day that I could ride a mule. We galloped down the mountain. I've come to the conclusion that Greek astonishment is born of a national sense of superiority.

Yesterday, the pipes for M's stove were fitted. The night was black, the wind howling, and suddenly everyone decided that *this* was the moment for the *boo-ree-ah* as the pipes are called. First Dimitri the fisherman, married to Maria one of Aspasia's daughters, appeared. Then Adonis the painter. While Dimitri on a ladder coaxed the *boo-ree-ah* through their exit hole and Adonis on another ladder grappled with the sections rising from the stove, Maud stood in the middle of the room, holding up the central structure with a broom. She looked as if she'd fallen off a merry-go-round. Molly offered advice and Aspasia, Maria and a plump, unmarried lady said to be fabulously rich settled down in chairs to watch the fun. The good news is that the boy dragged by the mule will live.

Feb 2nd, Amorgos

Odd dogs in this village. I saw one riding a donkey and waving its tail, the dog not the donkey. Another had fallen asleep with its head stuck through some green railings. It was a ginger and white head so made a nice colour scheme. M tells me horror stories about the Miaoulis. It is apparently notorious for crashing into quaysides. Both Simi and Nisyros, islands down in the Dodecanese, have been dented by its impromptu arrivals. Another eccentric, a human this time, is Mr Green who works for the schoolmistress. He comes to Maud for English lessons and delights me by speaking of *fried pots* and the *Virgin Mary's thighs*. He is a philosopher. M's home is now ready, cosy with rag rugs, a white furry one in the bedroom, pictures on the wall and a jug of flowers on the blue table. The other night, to celebrate the new house, we commanded Aspasia to cook us pigeon. The village was electrified by this extravagance; and when we arrived at the taverna, dressed up in honour of the occasion, we found an audience assembled. Sadly it was much too cold to take off our scarves, macs and coats so our finery remained hidden. The meal was lovely. Though ancient, the birds had been conjured into the most tender of casseroles. Spinning wool over her *mangali*, the chef watched our every mouthful. So did the audience. Two hours later, bursting with food and wine, we praised

Aspasia's genius and tottered off to rumbles of approval from the watchers.

I shall miss this village. Who knows when or if I shall ever return? The people in the port, Katapola, are charmless; but up here among the rocks and the wind and the soft white jigsaw of houses survive good old-fashioned values: courtesy, a wisdom, a love of laughter, kindness to the stranger. I shall never forget the high village of Amorgos.

Likos, 2004

No one can remember the real name of the port. Centuries ago someone – perhaps a crusader with a sense of humour – nicknamed it nose *and that's what it's been called ever since: Miti. The houses ramble up from the sea to a ruined Venetian castle, here and there circling orchards of cherry, lemon and fig and finally petering out where the terraces start their climb. Lettuce, spring onions, garlic, courgettes, beans and potatoes are cultivated. Small crofts dot the hills but few people live in them now, preferring to return to a house in the port with electric light, loo and bath after their day's work on the land. The cows are large and sleek, the pigs enormous. I once saw a black and white sow the size of a sideboard.*

The island has two other villages – a fishing village called Psara and Mavro Klima meaning 'Black Climate' which nestles in a fertile patch between the two mountain peaks. Near to the top of one peak is the church of the prophet Elijah. There's a distinctly mega-lomaniac whiff to this prophet because his church is always nearer to God than anyone else's.

Unlike the Amorgos of 1979, Likos has excellent roads and the bus, modern and well-serviced, purrs up and down them taking children from the villages to school in Miti and back. Sometimes I hitch a lift with it in the afternoon, getting off halfway up the mountain and walking back on an old flagged way. Due to last week's downpour, wild cyclamen and autumn crocus are sprouting in the grass and even a sistus flower or two is in bloom. The air is sweet enough to eat.

My great love is Psara, the fishing village. Two summers spent here in the early eighties made me an honorary inhabitant. One of my needs is to be still and do nothing and Psara nourished it. Lulled by the gurgles of the sea, I would sit by a jumble of rocks and fish crates outside a taverna, and speculate on eternity, watch a crab sidle over a rock and take pleasure in the play of light on water. One morning two old ladies in shifts and bathing hats came down to the beach and waded out up to their bosoms in sea and rested, bobbing like seals, softly chatting. One spring day, full of wine, I slept the afternoon away under an olive tree behind the village, my head cushioned on daisies and poppies, corn marigolds and lupins. When I awoke, drugged and disorientated, I thought for a minute I was back in the Peloponnese...

Chapter Three

Spring in the Peloponnese

1979

May 27th, journey to Kalavrita

The day before my train journey I got an attack of *foreigner's rage*, a disease well known to all travellers and enquirers into foreign customs and language. It is a rich mix of ennui, exasperation, rebellion and fatigue from trying endlessly to *fit in*. 'Fuck Greek,' I said, bought an incredibly expensive pot of Marmite and went to see *Gone With the Wind*. I felt like Mark Twain, halfway down Italy in 1867: 'Oh, the rare happiness of comprehending every single word that is said, and knowing that every word one says in return will be understood as well.'

Woke next day feeling better, shouldered my pack, locked the boat and made my way to the Peloponnese Railway Station. It's not a town station at all, drowsy with the dust drifting in rays of sun and old things in black sitting among bundles. The train when it arrived turned out to be a musical train and almost empty. Off we went. Someone strummed a guitar. Someone else sang. At Athens a few more people got in but the carriages still weren't crowded. A holiday atmosphere prevailed. Sun and small sleepy stations and the Corinth Canal; then the train perked up and we bustled clattery jack, clattery jack along the southern shore of the Gulf of Corinth. I dozed off and on, then awoke to eat cakes pressed on me by a kind woman. Diakopto arrived. From here a miniature railway bears you up the mountain to Kalavrita. Sitting in the sun, waiting for the train to arrive, I drank ouzo with three friendly men and thought how Italian the Peloponnesians seemed – dark and charming and outgoing.

The train was yellow and wooden and took us past and over the most fearful gorges where we hung in mid-air. A fat Cretan, who made a lot of noise and smelt, said he was going to Kalavrita to bathe. Clearly batty. The ticket collector was more disconcerting. A randy 75-year old, he kept clutching my knee and whispering: 'It's not too late. We can still make beautiful babies together.'

Kalavrita was burned and/or bombed in the war (and probably knocked about in the Greek Civil War) because it's largely new. Find a nice room for 100 drachs with Kyria Panagoula, then stroll to the memorial – a huge cross on a hillock – which commemorates the deaths of all the men and boys (12-year olds counted as men) shot by the Germans in 1943. They lined the women and children up and made them watch. Life is weird. One minute I'm in a terrible rage, the next I'm comforting two young Germans who are in floods of tears. 'Look at what England did in the Boer War,' I find myself saying. Dear God, they weren't even born in 1943.

The roses in the town must be the biggest in the world, the surrounding mountains are snow-capped and rivers rush about. Next day, Sunday, lots of Greek trippers appear so I trip too, to the nearby monastery where Bishop Germanos raised the first flag for Greek independence and started the struggle against the Turks. Kyria Panagoula looks fierce but is soft as a tippet. Despite my protests she feeds me morsel upon morsel. The nights are cold, a great relief. It was too hot in Piraeus.

May 29th, to Langadia via Vlacherna

The bus leaves at 9.15am and bounces over dirt roads, making my teeth chatter and a plump lady behind me shriek. As the road becomes more precipitous, quite a few people throw up. We are descending into Arcadia, absurdly Poussin-like and carpeted with wild flowers. Get off in the back of beyond and walk a few kilometres along the Tripolis-Olympia road to my next bus stop. My rucksack is overloaded. Bloody books. You'd think I'd have learnt by now. Decide to climb to a nearby village and drink tea. On the way a beefy-looking woman asks me to hold her donkey because her mule has bolted. I wish I hadn't. I wish I'd let the donkey go and the mule and murdered the woman. When she

35

brings the mule back she beats both animals with an iron bar. I shout at her but she takes no notice and rides off. There is blood on the mule's neck. I feel sick. Plodding on towards the village, in despair about the animals, I am hailed by an old lady behind enormous roses. In the house she bursts into tears and says her son, her youngest, is in the merchant navy 'in strange lands, poor boy!' She feeds me cakes and a potent colourless liquid and when I tell her that her son will receive the same kindness in strange lands as I, a stranger, receive here, she bursts into fresh floods and feeds me more of the colourless liquid. Arrive, completely plastered, at Langadia 2-3pm.

Langadia is a spectacular village halfway down the side of a steep mountain on the edge of a gorge. I descend from the bus into a dusty space between the gorge and the houses. A few old men sit outside a kafenion and a small boy pirouettes on a wall. 'Hullo, aunt,' says the boy. This means he thinks I am pretty old but is being polite. The men goggle. I approach them and try out one of my jokes:

'Good day, gentlemen. Perhaps you can guide me to a good woman who has clean rooms which are not too expensive? I am a writer without a publisher, therefore I need to make economies. I'm also half Scottish which, according to you Greeks, means that I am only half a miser.'

Roars of laughter greet this feeble jest. First I am bought an ouzo, not a good idea as I am still full of the colourless liquid, then the doctor leads me to a surly man who gives me a room with an unmade bed for 80 drachs. Don't need sheets anyway as I've got a sleeping bag. It is now mid-afternoon, and everyone has taken to their beds. Not a bark, not a cry, not a cheep of birdsong. Little terraces smothered in clover rise from the village; so I climb up into one of these and lie down in the soft green stuff surrounded by trees of dog roses. Can't believe I'm in Arcadia or that Arcadia looks like I thought it would look. Fall asleep. That evening, *mezzedakia* are brought to me under a giant plane tree near the edge of the gorge. With my ouzo come three kidneys, five pieces of potato, three chunks of cheese and half a loaf of bread. The barrel wine is wonderful – the rosé of the Peloponnese called *kokinelli*. Fancy falling asleep with wild flowers closing over my head! Old men chatter and a child plays nearby. No one interrupts me because I'm writing up my diary.

Next morning, unexpected goodies appear at the bus stop. The woman in the tourist shop takes me into her house and feeds me a breakfast of brandy and coffee, rusks and marmalade, boiled eggs and cake. Nervous about the bus, I bolt this feast, then long to fart but have no privacy in which to do so. On my way back to the bus stop, I'm intercepted by the woman's husband, who, finger to lips, presses 200 drachmas into my hand! This is FRIGHTFUL. The village must have taken my joke seriously. Decide that it would be more awful to refuse the money so, muttering thanks, I stuff the notes into my pocket and climb onto the bus. Do I look that much of a tramp? Taxidi and her darns will have to go.

May 30th, to Olympia

It's a beautiful road. En route, two things make me laugh: the first is a priest in his hat driving a tractor; the second is an old man waving an umbrella chasing a dog down an empty road. Pines and more enormous roses. We arrive at Olympia just before midday. A small hotel has a room so I dump my rucksack and make for the ruins, armed, o fresh embarrassment, with a packed lunch of bread and cheese and hard-boiled eggs provided by the kind woman in Langadia's tourist shop. The ruins are tranquil and the pines make that sea noise, their needles filling my nose with the smell of church candles. Munching my lunch in the shade of a massive pine, I am struck by a blob of resin, clearly a libation from the Gods. It is black and sticky and sounds the death knell for my beloved dress. Later that evening, a man in a jewellery shop annoys me. Am I Norwegian? No, I am not. Nor do I care for the arm of a strange man round my waist who wants to share my shower. 'You are not at all polite,' I say in Greek and am interested when he removes his hand as if a snake had bitten it. Perhaps my terrible Greek is of some use after all? Eat in my room. Scribble, read, drink nasty bottled wine. Peloponnesian doors don't have handles.

May 31st, to Andritsena via Pirgos

It all gets better and better and more and more beautiful. The bus leaves at 7.15am for Pirgos – a place famed only, so I am told, for earthquakes and sex maniacs. Untroubled by either of these, I while away the morning until the 2.30pm bus for Andritsena leaves. On arrival, am stunned by its beauty, even lovelier than Langadia. The crumbling charm of the Hotel Bassae and its pro-prietor's sweetness make me decide to stay a few days. The room is a delight and smells of old wood and gives the impression of hanging in space like the train to Kalavrita. The balcony is very rickety. Kyrios Nikos, the proprietor, tells me the Italians built the hotel before the last war. The loos have gone off a bit since Mussolini's time but the rest is a joy. Unpack contentedly, then go for a walk and get drenched by an Arcadian thunderstorm, solid water and lots of lightning. My room seems as rickety as its balcony and will probably fall into the ravine in the middle of the night. Who cares? After changing into an eccentric mixture of dry clothes, I descend ravenous to the hotel restaurant and eat *briam* and fried eggs and decide to spend the rest of my life here.

June 2nd, Andritsena

It is *bliss* not to have to go anywhere. Didn't sleep much due to the lumpy bed, thunderstorms and a car rally going past so dozed till 10.15am. The village turns out to be full of surprises: carpet makers, a library full of ancient books about Byzantium and the editor of the *Andritsena News* who accepted a poem I'd written in Greek – a simple thing about sitting on the top deck of a boat and looking at the seagulls while they looked at you. What a thrill to have it printed! That afternoon I talked to several locals, then walked along damp paths flecked with flowers under plane trees and elders. Later in the evening, sipping *kokinelli* at a corner table in a restaurant, I eavesdropped on three well-bred

Englishwomen and a French couple; listening more to the music of the languages than their meaning. My conclusions were a kind of tone-graph: English drones on with a dying fall at the end; French seesaws to a querulous upbeat; and Greek resembles nothing so much as linguistic melodrama. All foreigners think Greeks are having terrible rows when all they're discussing – with complete amiability – is the price of socks.

Today has been the kind of day which makes up for all the miseries and frustrations of travel. Kyrios Nikos had spoken to the *filax*, the guardian of Apollo's temple at Bassae, high in the hills behind Andritsena, and arranged a lift for me in his taxi to the site. Arise at first light and am picked up outside the hotel at 7.15am *precisely* by the *filax* and two of his archaeological colleagues. Such punctuality is most unusual. Greek time runs one to two hours late as a rule. When necessity – or lunatics – dictate *real* punctuality, Greeks refer to this aberration as *English time*. It's about 15 kilometres to the site and we negotiate the dirt road in silence. Greeks are not good in the morning and neither am I. The early morning light plays tricks with colour, turning green into ochre and splashing the rocks with pink. Bassae, like Delphi and Delos, is numinous. It lies inside a saucer of hills under a silent sky. Even shored-up with scaffolding as it is at the moment, it stops the heart. Approaching the temple quite alone – the others have vanished over the hill to look at a dig – I trip over a dog asleep in the grass. The old thing rises up, dusty and apologetic, from its bed of flowers and a cuckoo calls. Overcome by homesickness I burst into tears. The old dog sympathises which makes me cry even more.

I don't want to leave tomorrow. Kyrios Nikos, my gentle protector, looks old and frail. This evening we sat together under the great plane tree at dusk and he told me about his friend in Sparta: 'He has a nice hotel, Sara, you must stay there most cheaply.' Swallows flitted in and out as he carefully wrote the address. He has also arranged for me to share a taxi with someone to Megalopolis – 'the same price, Sara, as the bus would have been.' …Ah, my bear, what shall I do without you?

June 3rd, to Sparta via Megalopolis and Kalamata

A thick mist at 7am as we drive off. It blots out the countryside and most of the road for several miles, then parts miraculously on a bend to reveal, way below, one of William de Villardoun's keeps. The Peloponnese is full of crusader castles. I wonder how many knights turned into property developers? A castle in the mist and knights riding out to hawk and hunt, lances a-flutter. Lulled by these thoughts, I drop off and wake up in Megalopolis, a drab little place. Fall asleep again on the way to Kalamata. There was a fearful earthquake here – in the '30s I think – which flattened the place and killed hundreds of people. Kalamata is now mostly new buildings and full of hats and olives. It's midday and I'm starving. The shabby yet dignified frontage of the Hotel Gallia catches my eye. Everything about it, down to the shade of green of the paint is perfect. It *didn't* fall down in the earthquake. The waiters are gloomy; and the feta, green beans and draft rosé delicious. Ah, contentment.

The bus for Sparta leaves in a thunderstorm and takes a spectacular route across the spine of Tagetos, the mountain whose ribs run all the way down into the Mani. Wish I didn't have to be in Crete by June 13th, leaving not enough time to go right to the bottom. They say mermaids haunt the waters between the southern cape and Kithera, rising up before ships and crying 'Where is Alexander the Great?' The correct reply is 'Alexander the Great lives and reigns!' and the ship is allowed to pass. Mariners who don't know the pass-word are sucked down into the mermaids' embrace…The hotel in Sparta costs 276 drachs a night and I can't beat them down. Too tired and cross to look elsewhere so decide to spend my 200 drach present from the man in Andritsena on this extravagance. Sparta is not only HIDEOUS but without restaurants.

June 4th, Sparta and then to Gytheion

What an ugly place. The beauty of the plain and the glory of Mistra only increase the horror of modern Sparta. At 7am I gaze through barred gates at glimpses of Byzantine marvels but Mistra doesn't open till 10am and I don't think I can stand another night in Sparta. Flee on an afternoon bus to Gytheion after a quick poke round Old Sparta, horrified at myself. Perhaps she who turns down one of the wonders of the world and says 'Thanks so much but another time' meets a dreadful end? The journey to Gytheion is pleasant, enlivened by a schoolteacher called Thomas who reminds me of an old lover.

Gytheion is a pretty town with a harbour and an isthmus – can that be right? – to an island where Paris and Helen spent their first night of love en route for Troy. Prowl and find a clean pleasant room with Kyria Georgia who is an intellectual snob. She and her husband have sacrificed everything for their daughters' education and the result is two slobs who despise their parents. Wander out of town down a road with a squashed snake and find market gardens and lemon groves and a deserted beach. An old man sits at the sea's edge untangling a fishing line. His eyes are bad and he asks me to help him. As I fumble with the snarls and knots, he speaks of the war and the English they hid in a cave and the bad time they had from the Germans. I ask about the Italians. He laughs: 'Oh, they were alright. They just stole everything.'

June 5th-10th, Gytheion

This is a good centre for jaunting: to the underwater caves at Pirgos Dirou, to Kardamili and out into the countryside to help Kyria Georgia's farmer cousins pick their tomatoes. They are good people, strong and stockily built, with beautiful manners and broad smiles. I like the farm, the old house, the lines of warm, wet polythene sheds. We pick and pick and pick, the cousins and Kyria Georgia and me, that is. The two daughters flop about giggling and reading Mills and Boon. 'Aren't they going to help?' I enquire. Kyria Georgia looks apologetic: 'They're reading the classics, you see. They work very hard.'

Later, over a lunch of hot pitta bread, eggs, cucumbers, cheese and wine, I get my revenge. 'This,' I say contemptuously, picking up one of the books, 'is trash.' If looks could kill…Apricots fresh off the tree are bliss.

A fisherman discovered the underwater caves at Pirgos Dirou at the end of the sixties. They are deep, dark, damp and very, very old – to be lost in them a living death. Ten of us float in a small boat. The stalactytes we pass assume human forms, turn into gargoyles. Monsters loom and fade. Here dwell the dwarf lords in their halls of stone. The guide is enjoying himself: 'Look,' he hisses, 'there is the hand of Dracula, beware!' The child behind me bursts into tears and whimpers for the rest of the trip. Going home in the bus I brood on why very old things are alarming. Is it their indifference? Kardamili is idyllic, tucked beside a glittering sea and backed by mountains and gorges, woods and distant, tumbling hamlets. The village itself is full of vines, sweet-scented creepers, flowers, gurgling streams. Another Brigadoon. A genial hawk gives me a room for 80 drachs and I spend a happy day poking about in the clematis and bougainvillea of the acropolis, swimming and drinking brandy with a nice lad who runs a kafenion. Flee later in the evening from a bore in a panama hat.

My last day in Gytheion is full of regret there isn't another fortnight free to investigate the Mani. It sounds a forbidding place – tower houses and feuds and murders. An old Maniot in the café of Small Basil tells me that Maniot girls caught sleeping with a lover are still shot by their brothers or fathers. God knows what happens to the lover. There are quantities of poisonous snakes so you have to watch out camping. 'Rocks, olives and moustaches, that's all it is,' says Small Basil. 'Barbarians,' he adds, pouring me another ouzo. The early North Wind that the sailors call the *Cherry Meltemi* is blowing. I sit and do my accounts and find that I've spent a fortnight in the Peloponnese for about £50. The exchange rate is 76 drachs to the pound.

Likos, 2004

Yesterday, November 21st, we celebrated the feast of the Virgin Mary's birth in a church in Mavro Klima. 'I'm sorry we're going so early,' said Angelica's daughter Maria, negotiating the hairpin bends up the mountain, 'but Mama insists.' An icy wind blew round the sugar lump village and into the church with its chandeliers, ikons, flickering candles and beautiful male chanting. Two elderly vergers bickered sotto voce about where the money for the candles should go and how the bread should be piled. Propped in a tall wooden stall, frozen to death, I watched a woman in an apron. She wore knee socks, a check dress and sneakers. In and out she went, berating the vergers, rearranging the money, bread and candles, vanishing into the priests' sanctum, then popping, gopher-like, from another exit. What she was doing I never discovered. One of the chanters had a moustache the wing span of a kestrel.

I dozed and froze and wondered whom the school-master on the bus from Sparta had reminded me of – and then I thought about Spiro. Ah, Spiro. One winter night in 1979 a local boat rescued me from a gloomy island where I'd been checking up on facts for a friend revising a guidebook. Driving it was a pirate. He was big, barrel-chested with a wicked smile and a gap between his two front teeth. He had a moustache like a stoat. 'You are invited to the crew's Christmas party,' he beamed two hours later, took me by the hand and led me to third class. There, at the table closest to the engine, Kefi had exploded. Kefi is almost untranslatable but roughly speaking means joy. The captain, the second officer, the cook, and five crew members were drinking beer and bellowing at one another. A transistor radio, unable to compete, squeaked Theodorakis. The keeper of the engine, an ancient in a balaclava, watched us disapprovingly. The ship, the Boubelina, appeared to be driving herself.

'Where are you going Sara?'

'WHAT?'

The table tottered under its tidbits. The captain and the cook were dancing on an area the approximate diameter of a beer mat.

'WHERE ARE YOU GOING?'

'Skyros.'

'We will take you to Evvia tomorrow.' Without a cheep of protest I went.

It took me two years to get over Spiro. I wish I was like other people and could just fall in and out of love. Spiro wasn't just gorgeous, bearlike and sweet-smelling. He was funny and very kind – the only Greek male I've ever seen carrying bundles for an old lady. 'Frank Sinatra no 99!' he would cry as he burst into song. After our first night of cuddles and rather absent-minded sex, he confided: 'Young girls are no good Sara. Too much serious. I thought you looked the right age and clean.' That's when I fell hopelessly in love…

Emerging from my reverie I found the service was over. Old friends not seen for years embraced me. At midday it was time to feast. There must have been about a hundred of us at trestle tables, gorging on course after course: small fried fish with a cabbage, anchovy and garlic salad, then a rich bean soup followed by salt cod with garlic sauce. Greek feasts are happy bedlam. Wine flowed, music played, the voices got louder and louder and suddenly a man leapt up and started to dance and people joined him – fat ladies, small children, handsome boys, the taxi driver. Later I found one of the priests. He was gossiping with friends in a side room, devouring chunks of bread dipped in a saucer of wine. He beamed. 'Does it please you?' 'Oh yes,' I said, 'and what a beautiful service.' A crust of wine-soaked bread was promptly popped into my mouth. 'Guess what?' I said to Maria, 'at last I've been confirmed!'

Today the rains which obligingly stopped for the

Virgin are back. A grey sea with heaving spume. A bitter wind. A freighter from Thessaloniki is slumped against the quayside, its hull scarred and rusty, the R of ALEXANDROU missing. Staring at it, I let my mind wander back to the north of Greece, to the old kingdom of Alexander and a golden July beside a lake...

Chapter Four

A Macedonian lake

1979

July 3rd, to Microlimni via Kozani and Florina

Left Athens two and a bit days ago – the bus station bedlam. Leaving buses blocked arriving buses and crowds milled in a panic of bus-finding, doubt and weeping children. The journey to Kozani took eight hours. After Lamia the bus, radio blaring, sailed north-west through lion lands furred with corn. Longed to stroke, comb, clip the fur. Kozani, alas, is horrible. If there was ever an old Turkish quarter it's vanished under acres of reinforced concrete. People either stared, shouted or were rude. 4,000 Russians work in the electrical installation to the north of the town so they should be used to foreigners. Next morning, with another surly driver, we crossed big country under bigger skies. Very Balkan. Very exciting. At Florina another illusion crumbled. My fondly-imagined Turkish town is on the way to being a concrete jungle, there's not a room to be had under 300 drachs and everything is wet.

Mooch about crossly. Decide to sleep out in the woods on the other side of the river. It's getting dark. I find a spot under acacia trees, spread my bag and groundsheet, light my mosquito coil – the air is thick with the little buggers – and wriggle into my bag fully dressed. Soaking wet jungle. Everything steams. There's a track nearby and during the night voices and footsteps come and go, murderers or bears or both. At 3am a dog falls over me and flees, wailing. It should be in its basket, not waking sleepers in woods. Teeny things rustle and one grinds its teeth. Perhaps I'm asleep on its front door? Luckily snakes didn't occur to me. Arise at dawn, stiff and damp but unbitten. What a noble coil!

It's a wonderful drive from Florina to Microlimni. Up up into the mountains we go. The air is cold, the sky rinsed clean. July is on the edge of winter. In Pisoderi you can smell the woodsmoke from the chimneys. On we sail, a nice driver this one, to our left the blue jags of Albania, to our right the ridgebacks of Yugoslavia. Marvel and brood about frontiers going backwards and forwards and whether anyone can really know whether they're Macedonian, Greek, Albanian or Yugoslavian. Am half asleep when we bump along a track to a few houses beside a lake. Please God let the taverna still be there. Down I climb into the pale sunlight. The bus roars off. Silence. Three old men on rickety chairs stare at me. July 3rd in the back of beyond.

Now it's evening and I'm writing this after eating fish from the lake. The owner of the taverna is Pantelis Hassos. He has a clever, wary face, a reserved manner and walks with difficulty. His handsome wife Aleiky talks so fast that if I lived in Greece for another ten lifetimes I wouldn't understand a word she said. Georgios, the son, is 30 with a wife Lena and a small Aleiky. My welcome was courteous but unsmiling. This is the North, a far cry from the easy charm of the Peloponnese, and I am a stranger and *on approval.* My host and I settled on 150 drachs a night for a month.

'A month? You will stay a month?' A flicker of amusement crossed his face.

My bedroom smells like Aunt Daisy's house in Sutherland and there are two blankets on the bed. What bliss.

July 4/5th, Microlimni, first impressions

Presspa Small Lake with Albania on one side and Yugoslavia on the other is a birdwatcher's paradise; also a bear lover's. After two days I am bewitched, footsore and *even* more frightened of snakes than I was before.

The lake is a protected area for the 60 or so pelicans who nest on it – extraordinary birds with their pouches tucked under their chins. My first morning I rose at dawn and crept out to the lakeside. The fishermen sorting their catch under the poplars were surprised to see me. Several cows ruminated and hens clucked in the dust. I looked at Albania on the other side of the lake and the mountains rising all around, furred with oak, elm, beech, pine, plane, chestnut and thought the land lovelier than any I'd ever seen – even Sutherland. The lake is fringed with forests of bamboo and to the right of the village a dyked marshland meanders in and out of neat, cultivated crop patterns. Coots bustle round the pelicans like tugs. Everywhere there are wild flowers.

I poked around the village and the lake and met several dogs, shaggy monsters with English names like Jack and Fox. Then I set off to walk in the hills. Bears live in them. Black and white and yellow ones. A covey of old ladies in black shouted at me from a sunny doorstep:

'Who are you? Where are you going? Are you not afraid to go alone?'

'I'm going to the mountains to say hullo to a bear.'

They cackled and tittered and rocked to and fro over their knitting.

Large tortoises patrol the woods: I followed sheep paths which hemmed a neat way along terraces and in and out of gullies. It was hot in the sun. Wild flowers grew waist-high, the dwarf elder and Old Man's Beard giving off the sickly, drugged smell of English meadowsweet; a thistle eight feet tall was covered in butterflies. That afternoon I sat on the balcony above the lake and started *The Riddle of the Sands*. Ate eggs and salad for supper. The family polite, still reserving judgement. The old men in their chairs as glum as ever.

Today was snake drama day. Along the lake from the village runs a beautiful track; up and down, past the birdwatchers' house on its rock and then round to the left, dipping into a kind of Hardy village green before straightening out and heading for Albania. 'Be careful if you get to the shepherds' camp,' said Pantelis, 'their dogs are fierce.' There are fig and apple trees by the ruined village. Cows ruminate and pelicans float nearby. Intent on them and not watching my feet I'm suddenly aware of hissing. A few inches away an enormous snake is standing on its tail and flickering its tongue. Scream, leap back. The monster slithers off. Jesus! It's about six foot long and thick as a draft excluder. Probably gone to tell its mother what a fearful thing it's seen. Armed with a large stick and permanently damaged heart I go onto the shepherds' camp. It's like something out of the nineteenth century – ramshackle tents, squalor, black-eyed children and a woman in brilliant colours, a kingfisher matron, who laughs at my bad Greek and snake story. Horses graze under an oak tree. The dogs are sleeping wolves.

Tonight I detect a thaw. Maybe I've passed the test?

July 8th, Microlimni

Come back from a walk on Sunday morning to find lunchtime frenzy of packed taverna, shouting customers and the family run off their feet. Lena, the daughter-in-law doesn't like me but when I offer to help she grudgingly sticks me in the sink. 'No, no!' screams Kyria Aleiky, 'take those beers to that lot over there.' For two hours I carry beer, take orders, wash, stack and wipe. Supper that night is on the house, Kyria Aleiky pats my arm and Georgios confides his longing to emigrate to Canada.

The local doctor is young, dark and beautiful and comes from Patras. He's up here doing his National Service, two and a half years in the wilds of Macedonia, and his patent affection for the people and theirs for him is a delight. We talk of the Civil War which raged here, the depopulation of the villages, the children 'saved' or 'kidnapped' depending which side you were on by the *andartes* – the communists. Most never came back. Now the villages are largely populated by the old and infirm, some with 60 souls, some with less. A kind woman who lent me a shirt when I got caught in a thunderstorm lost her children. They were taken in 1947/48. She weeps as she tells me her story. Her husband is old and ill, the house cold.

'They send no money.'

She sobs.

'It were better we were dead.'

July 12th, Microlimni

The other day four American landscape architects, Douglas, Andrea, Irenka and Sandy arrived. They're staying at the bird-watchers' house and working on a project which aims to revitalise the district, bring back the young and create new local industries. They're nice kids, all in their early twenties, but the two girls wear tight shorts which is idiotic. Douglas, a pleasant reserved man, is the leader and lover of beautiful dark Irenka; Andrea is jolly and a bit dim and Sandy a New York Jew, miserably homesick for bagels, lox and Mama. Why haven't they boned up on the customs and moralities of isolated communities? Dressed the way they are they won't get anywhere. 'Prostitutes,' whispered a scandalised ancient. It's quite funny, but also sad. Caricatures of well-meaning Americans abroad. The doctor thinks they're twits.

July 15th, Microlimni

It's suddenly very hot. I've started to write a short story so work in the morning and walk in the afternoon. Sometimes I take green tracks through the woods, cool and shadowy, needles of sunlight slanting here and there. On other days I walk the marsh, home to two of the doziest storks in the world. At my approach, they lumber into the sky like transports, then land again immediately, just in front of me. Again they take off and so it goes. Purple herons, golden-bodied egrets, eagles, wild duck, snipe, partridge, dippers, turtle doves, hoopoes breed in or visit the marshlands. I'm bad at birds. Wish my mother was alive to see this.

The village cows are magnificent. There are furry moley ones and black and white Fresians. Every morning they gather outside the taverna and wait for a conductor to take them to the first valley and the ruined village. In the evening they bring themselves back and are picked up by their owners like children coming out of school. A few beasts are recalcitrant. One old girl chases her cow about with a stick under my window – a nightly performance I much enjoy. Wish-wash go the waves on the sandy beach. That's where the women make fires and boil their wool in the great pots.

Every evening after supper I climb with my glass of sour red wine onto the balcony and watch darkness fall over the Albanian mountains. I have an admirer, a dog the size of a bear who looks like a sheep. It belongs to a woman whose son paints ikons in Athens. It curvettes idiotically whenever we meet. There are starving dogs here and children are taught to throw stones at them. When I talk to and feed the wretched animals, they think me mad.

July 20th, Microlimni

Bit Lena's head off the other day which has made her more civil. What a bore bullies are. In the early morning the fishing nets hung to dry between the white-socked poplars look like mist. A hen eats small fish under them. Her eggs must taste horrible. Harvest time is here and the village full of contract tractors and tractor boys, some of whom live in tents by the poplars. Doom doom doom go the threshers and cutters and binders. Went to Florina for the day before all this row began and when I got back was greeted by cries of, 'Sara, Sara! You missed a bear! It came down to eat potatoes and we shot it!'

'You WHAT!'

'I shot it,' said a man whose face I knew. Proudly. I felt like smashing my fist into his grin.

'You idiot! It's against the law!'

Sick with rage and upset, I turned on my heel and stormed off.

51

Stupid bloody peasants. It was a coffee-coloured bear. All it did was eat potatoes.

Am cheered up by some pleasant Germans from Stuttgart. We walk together in the marshes. By a stream minuscule frogs sit and hop. To hold in the hand they are cool. Nearby a baby tortoise is eating a piece of wood. Sitting in the kafenion one morning, taking a break from writing, I see a weird thing. Two identical patches of sun fall on the inside section of the window. On each patch sunbathes a fly. Their positions correspond precisely, as if someone had arranged them with a set square and ruler. Pantelis' and Aleiky's daughter Artemis arrived the other day. She is lovely and adores her father. We all jaunt off to an ancient church to christen her baby Polyxeni who does not enjoy the three dippings and roars. Afterwards, under a huge pear tree, we feast on lamb, *kokkeretsi* (guts), salad, cheeses, fresh crusty loaves. Pantelis, splendid in a Chicago hat, reclines against a tree trunk looking happy. Poor man. His leg was smashed in the war, he's got one kidney, high blood pressure and a rotten heart. He's a Vlach, originally a tribe of shepherds like the Sarakatsani. Vlachs are renowned for their intelligence and fine music and have their own language and traditions. Five languages are spoken in these parts – Greek, Vlach, Macedonian, Serbian and Albanian.

July 24th, visit to Zilla at Agios Germanos

A painter friend is staying in a nearby village. One morning I get up at 5am, devour Kyria Aleiky's rice pudding and catch the early bus. Zilla is living with 'Gran' – an elderly tyrant with bright eyes and a rat pigtail. I'm staying the night in her house, my bed an astonishing arrangement of springs and rag rugs. The plan is to walk in the beech woods, look for wild strawberries and gossip. Zilla is a darling. Her watercolours are excellent. Before setting off we drink coffee with Gran; outside her kafenion because the inside is full of corn. Agios Germanos seems mostly ruined houses and very old people; but there must be thwarted customers who have nowhere to go? Do they sit on the corn? Gran shrugs her shoulders.

Our lunch and wine packed in Zilla's knapsack, off we go – following a river which rushes brownly over smooth stones, jungled about with juicy water plants, brambles, cherry trees, willows and honeysuckle. Here and there are horses, a stone or wood dwelling, a party of people harvesting. Ahead, above the tree line, is a pass through high green hills into Yugoslavia. It's such a treat to talk to a friend, and in your own language. Suddenly ravenous, we fall on lunch, spreading our bread, salami, tomatoes, cucumber and wine beside a brook, in a spot so idyllic we might have invented it. Heavy flower heads, hanging boughs and damp, lush undergrowth cocoon us. Dappled shade. Chuckling water. Occasionally a puff of wind goosefleshes our legs. Zilla sketches and I count flowers: 14-foot mulleins, heavy-headed hemlocks, euphorbia, camomile, chicory flower, a creamy pink vetch-type thing and an especially wonderful plant of long sprays clotted with red berries. There are little pink thistles and a kind of bluebell/campanula.

Afternoon blur of greens and shadows. Zill is asleep. Her feet are enormous. How touching people are when they sleep. Just before my eyes close, something emerges with great caution from a dark tunnel of weed opposite. It is a slim gentleman in a fur coat – a stoat. Transfixed, I stare at him. He stares at me. He stares at Zilla. He stares at me again, nose twitching, full of curiosity. Then a twig cracks and he's gone. Later we find the wild strawberries, carpets of them, under the bracken below the copper beeches.

Back in Agios Germanos, Gran watches us fondly as we eat a huge salad and drink more wine.

'Zilla must marry,' she says.

'Who will have her with feet that size?' I reply. The offending organs, truly huge, repose grubbily in their flip flops.

Fly papers like cemeteries hang in Gran's kitchen. We munch plums under an almond tree and go to bed.

July 30th, Microlimni, letter to a friend

Dearest Zeenie

You told me to come to Macedonia and yes, you were right, it *is* the loveliest place in the world. The Hassos family are well and send greetings. When I arrived they looked me over for a few days, then decided I would do. What a month it's been. Now alack it's over and the only bear I might have met appeared at Microlimni the day I went to Florina and some fool shot it. You didn't tell me about the snakes! They are python-sized and keep getting in my way and frightening me to death. I've done some writing, my Greek's a little better and walking the mountains has reduced my Piraeus boots to tatters. Everything that grows here is so enormous and exotic. I've seen tigerlilies literally springing from boulders.

Pantelis had his *name day* last week and I was touched and honoured to be asked to the family dinner in Pisoderi. That's their real home, a mountain house with stone floors and a log fire blazing in the main room. Georgios and I left the lake at about 9pm, the roads full of drunk tractor drivers, presumably all Pantelises! Dinner was magnificent, melting lamb and crispy chops and greens and potatoes and a seven-year old rich dry red wine, the equal of any Margaux or Lafite. Oh my. I felt happy and relaxed and even understood about 50 per cent of the conversation. Afterwards we sat round the fire and P, looking rosy and festive, sang old Vlach songs. He has a strong, mellow voice. What bliss to sleep in crisp cotton sheets and soft blankets and listen to rain drumming on the roof. Next morning Artemis, P's daughter who lives in Athens (God knows why), showed me the village and some famous inhabitants – her aunt, a delightful character, and the resident author, Kyrios Liakos. He is a true Macedonian, tall, upright and courteous with laughing blue eyes. We spoke French together and to my astonishment he gave me a book he was instrumental in getting published – the travels of a Victorian English Miss in Macedonia and Albania, Turkey as it then was! Isn't that extraordinary? He's 85 and an old soldier but his real passion is the derivation of language. He has a riveting theory that Ancient Macedonian evolved from a mix of Gaelic and Latin. Afterwards Artemis took me to Bear Rock where bears used to come and told me about her childhood and how she and

Georgios ran wild in the hills.

Next excitement was a wedding in Agios Germanos. Zilla, a painter friend of mine, knew the bride so we were both invited. They still hang the blood-spotted sheets out of the window the next morning as proof of virginity! While the bride was being titivated in her parents' house we – best man, relations, friends, hangers on and the band – went to fetch the bridegroom. He looked a right prat in his tuxedo, black bow tie and white suit ('He's very rich,' said Gran, Zill's landlady); frightful that he was marrying the fragile, exquisitely pretty Eleni. Anyway, drums beating, violin wailing, clarinet shrilling, accordion squeaking, we conducted this fat little man to his bride. God, it was hot. Zill and I got our ritual greetings wrong which was mortifying. Then we sat down in the salon, a rather stiff occasion, and ate lumps of lamb and raisins and cheese and Turkish Delight; the bride was being prepared, like a chicken for the oven, in a side room.

At last she appeared, weeping. One dark brother, a mirror of her, also wept. She danced the farewell dance with, in turn, father, brothers, uncles, cousins, and they all pinned notes to her dress ('Her dowry,' hissed Gran). Her dark brother continued to weep. When they danced together they looked like Romeo and Juliet. Not exactly a joyous occasion. By this time I had a splitting headache and felt distraught. The girl was clearly marrying the wrong man, even if she had been given three chances to say 'no', and certainly didn't want to leave her parents' house. When we went into the church the brother sat outside with his head in his hands, sobbing. You might have warned me that Macedonian weddings are Classical Greek tragedies!

The day after tomorrow I go south to Paxos via Kalambaka to look at the Meteora. See you in Athens in a month or so. Hope all is well with Richard's legs. I loved that remark of his doctor that he had the torso of a buffalo on the legs of a greyhound.

Much love Sara

July 31st, Microlimni

My last day and full of goodbyes. I hate goodbyes. Start with the shepherd and his wife and small Vasoula who's followed me around like a dog for a fortnight. We drink retsina. On the wall hangs a bizarre memento of the oldest daughter's wedding in Australia: a heavily-artworked photograph of the husband's head in silhouette with a pic of his bride in her finery where his brain should be. Say goodbye to Michael the doctor who takes my blood pressure and says it's perfect; also to the owner of the flirtatious sheep and to poor Stavroula who weeps again for her 'stolen' children. An old thing gives me a cucumber and my crones on the doorstep embrace me.

Now it's evening. The cows are coming home and the pelicans flying, chins tucked in, to some mysterious pelican destination near the Albanian shore. Two swans appear from nowhere. Slowly, imperceptibly, the lake settles into its dusk. My last sunset.

Likos, 2004

A north-east wind called the Tramoundana *has been screeching for four days and everyone's nerves, including mine, are in shreds. Miltiadis, Angelica and the cat Fred who looks like a pillow sit huddled over their* mangali. *They tell me frightful tales of snowfall in the old days, and how one woman living up the mountain was buried alive for 22 days. She survived. This information filters through to me over two other conversations going on with three people about spoilt voting papers in the recent elections for mayor. Greek indifference to noise is endemic. If God turned them into birds, they could only be starlings. One lunchtime, in an attempt to find peace from the gale, I tried a taverna, sunny and dusty, tucked away in a web of alleys. For ten minutes silence soothed me. Then the door burst open and six men came in, turned on both TV and radio and bellowed over them. The tailor appeared, seeming smaller than his fur hat, and told me of a poultice for strains and sprains – white of egg, ouzo and soap. Another man chipped in with his mother's remedy for inflamed tonsils: first rub the outside of the throat with olive oil, then apply a mash of finely-choppped olives and hold it in place by a cloth wound round throat and head. The patient must look a cross between Edith Sitwell and Lawrence of Arabia.*

The day after tomorrow is December 1st. Reading and editing my diaries has been giving me nightmares – mythic ones with black bulls and monstrous heads. There is no defence against dreams. Always in nightmares I lose things – my bag, my luggage, my money, my clothes. Loss, leviathan supreme. 1938. On the very night my mother and I sailed in a troop ship for Burma my brother died. A little boy of five with a throat infection. If my mother had known he was ill she would never have left. My sister Susan was seven. Army rules said the baby could go but school age children stayed with relations. My uncle flew to Marseilles to tell my mother her son was dead. What to do? On to my father, distraught in Rangoon, or back to Susan? My mother went on. For two months, in a cabin with a broken-hearted woman, I, pre-verbal, two years old, inhaled loss. Only years later, doing Jungian work with an extraordinary psychotherapist, did I begin to understand why I missed skins.

Looking for consequences in large grey exercise books. That's what I'm doing, I say to my complaining inner world. Fuck off! Hunched over my electric fire, I turn back to the diaries and curse the Anatolian plateau for filling the wind with ice and turning my idyll into a fridge. Tonight I might try a sprig or two of rosemary under the pillow.

Thank God for food and drink. Pulses must anaesthetise the nervous system for I often feel calm after a bean or lentil or chickpea soup. Eggs, cheese and potatoes are plentiful; chicken done the old way in the oven, with roasted potatoes in a savoury juice is delicious. One evening Popi in the harbour made patsas, *a winter soup of tripe or heads or feet; and munching through it I remembered another time I nearly froze to death and wondered what I was doing...*

Chapter Five

The YWCA in Thessaloniki – Xmas in Kavala – Philippi – New Year in Samothraki
1980 - 1981

Nov 28th, Thessaloniki

It's 7.30pm and here we are. I'm reluctant to leave my Brussels bus – basket, nest, home. It overtook Mercedes in the outside lane through Germany and crossed Yugoslavia, still a desolation of cabbages, in five minutes. Thessaloniki is wet. Taxi drivers pretend not to know where the YWCA is but I am in no mood for jokes. Arrive to find the admin section as charmless as the cows in Athens and the place full of staring girls. I'm too cross to care. My room has a dim light, three hospital beds – so far I'm the only occupant – and costs 170 drachs a night. The loos smell. Finish off my Belgian salami and cheese and plod about for a bit. Egnatia Street reminds me of Oxford Street and there isn't a kafenion to be seen. My head aches. Drinking coffee by the sea in a place full of students and fat women, I'm cheered by the memory of 1978 and the brown dog who came to a patch of shade in a park and fell asleep with its legs straight up in the air. We stayed one night and just missed the earthquake. I've always worried about that dog. Back at the Y giggling girls rush to and from an incessantly ringing telephone. It's usually for someone called Karalavidou. The lift whirrs from the basement, cabbage smells float up from the restaurant. But the sheets are clean, the bed soft and the woman who showed me my room seems kind.

Dec 1st, Thess

Having got the curse feel better and decide Thessaloniki is good news. Up in the district of the seven towers are acres of Roman wall. Every Byzantine church is shut for repair due to the 1978 earthquake so that takes care of that. I once teased Molly in Athens by saying: 'Once you've seen one Byzantine church you've

59

seen them all.' The feel of the city is good – lots of students, a few old Turkish houses left and a *real* Turkish bath, with clouds of steam puffing out of the blisters on its roof. Then I discover the museum. The treasures from Vergina, Pella and here, 500-300 BC, are incredible. There are ducks' heads on snakes' bodies, dolphins curl into the handle of a vase and a ram's head embellishes the handle of a Vergina omelette pan. Only genius makes beauty of this order. My guide book tells me that the district of the seven towers was built in 500 AD by the good Theodosius. I sit among them in the sun and learn Greek vocabulary.

Dec 3rd, Thess

The Y is growing on me. I like the circular staircase, probably twenties or thirties, which wraps round the lift like a marble scarf. My room is that peachy colour of old-fashioned bloomers and a Margaret Tarrant Jesus prays above the bed. The beds are painted blue to match the furniture and the Fablon on the chest of drawers – chunky green, blue and white flowers – is in surprisingly good taste. The inmates are mostly girls from the villages training to be hairdressers. They giggle and squawk and spend hours standing about in their dressing gowns doing their hair. Occasionally they burst in, then flee quelled by my fierce looks. Kyria Sapouna is a hoot. Can she really be called Mrs Soapdish? Blowing smoke from her tortoiseshell cigarette holder she tells me she is the *directrice*. She has a telly.

I begin to slot into the streets and squares of the city. Find the British Council, the Goethe Institute, a zoo with two bored bears and a restaurant called Patris, a fine place full of Serbs talking Serbian. A waiter puts me at a table under the stairs and brings me a plate of delicious brains dressed with lemon juice and flanked by little heaps of cabbage and salad, radishes and tomatoes. Hot fresh bread and a glass of the local red wine complete my contentment.

'What beautiful brains,' I say to the waiter.

'You are beautiful,' he replies politely.

As I leave, a tiny, exquisitely dressed man, probably the proprietor, asks me where my husband is. He's scandalised to learn that I don't possess one.

'I'm staying at the Y,' I say apologetically.

This pleases him. He beams. 'A most fitting place.'

Lo, I am respectable.

Dec 5th, Thess

The other day I found the market – fruit and veg, cakes, sweets and red alleyways of meat. I peered into dark pannikins and saw mussels in rice. The day after, the Majestic café fell into my path. A treasure. A pearl to be examined day by day, at leisure, with love. It has mock-wood panelling and above, brown paint. A black stove squats in a corner, its pipe rising and travelling miles across the ceiling before vanishing. The crossest waiter in the world works here. He dislikes everyone; if possible desires to serve no one with nothing. The clientele are well-dressed, delicately gesturing old men and students. Often customers sit and talk without even bothering to order. When the smoke gets very thick, someone will scream at someone else to open a door but no-one takes any notice. Talk, talk, talk over tiny coffees, glasses of lemonade or hot milk. Some of the students are so engrossed in their debates they might be on Mars. One absentmindedly empties an entire sugar bowl into his Nescafé. Crik-crak go the backgammon pieces.

A bear called Aristidis has a bookshop near the university. Drinking coffee, we discuss the Achilles tendon, the kindness of the English, the abominable rudeness of the French. I tell him of my plan to go to Samothraki for Xmas. 'Oh, I would so love to go there!' he exclaims, 'but there is no time, no time…' Later the National Tourist Office tells me that a boat may or may not leave from Kavala for Samothraki every Sunday at midnight. It sounds romantic. It's raining. The sea has gone a weird green colour.

Dec 6th, Thess

The Collector by Fowles is on at the theatre but I opt for sexpot Redford in *The Electric Cowboy* and make friends with an usherette in a small '30s cinema on the front. She is talking to a fat policeman. Down a side road beside the cinema are cars full of policemen. It must be a stake-out. Two hours later as I drift past, wishing I was Fonda kissed by Redford or me kissed by my sea captain, *there* they still are. They look like dark green parcels inside the small Fiats.

'How was the film?' It is the fat policeman. Clearly a Greek stake-out is like an Irish funeral – jolly and public.

'Wonderful. You must see it!'

We part, noisily, with goodnights and how nice to have met you's.

On my way to the Majestic to have a brandy and watch the sunset, I see a crowd and join it. A hideous sideboard is being winched up to the fifth floor of a block of flats by a crane. The crane is gigantic. It should be on an oil rig, not in a side street in Thessaloniki. Pious music floats from a nearby church and an audible sigh of disappointment from the crowd as the sideboard arrives at its destination. Fog from nowhere has crept onto the quayside. I sit in the Majestic drinking coffee and looking at nothing. The waiter has put sugar in my coffee. I bet he did it on purpose. *Thermandiko soma* is a radiator of steam. The one in the Y showers has just exploded into a lake of boiling rust.

Dec 8th, Thess

A diverse collection of room-mates comes and goes. Noelle was French and wore a little Trilby hat which she used to put over the ashtray at night. Sad Nella with the massive thighs has just left. Her legacy is a pair of enormous knickers. Now Darian from North California has appeared. Work hard writing poetry and reading bloody Janni Mari's novel which has taken me three years to finish – only 30 more pages of impenetrable Greek to get through. After mornings beavering in the British Council library – not only sunny but centrally heated – I prowl. Latest finds are the street of Crete, old fashioned and charming with a shop full of marvellous embroidery (this city restores my faith in educated middle-class Greeks and points up, not for the first time in several centuries, the abject quality of the Athenians). Also the street of Tositsa where the antique and junk shops are. Crones sit among their cobwebbed knick-knacks – lamps, clothes, copper, bronze, silver. A helmet nests beside a hubble-bubble; all is chaos and most restful.

Above a store in Egnatia Street is one enormous silvery-white court shoe, dotted with little lights, which slowly revolves. The Turkish Embassy is shut. I bang hopefully on the door and a man appears.

'I wish to see the house of Atatürk,' I say in Greek.

He doesn't understand Greek so we switch to German. Sorrowfully he shakes his dark head.

'Very sorry. The house is shut up.'

'I'm staying three more weeks,' I say hopefully. 'Perhaps if I come back in two?'

'Return in five days.' He gives me a smile of extreme sweetness. 'We shall walk together in the house then.'

Bemused by Middle Eastern logic, I plod on, walking miles through little streets where cottages and hens co-habit with ugly apartment blocks. Poor Thessaloniki has been knocked flat so many times through the centuries, I'm surprised anything survives. Fancy Atatürk being born here and how like the Greek Tourist Office to ignore the fact. A tiny, neat, pretty and very shy Japanese girl now shares with Darian and me. She keeps bowing. It must be a culture shock sharing with a retsina-drinking, middle-aged Englishwoman and an American who eats taramasalata and fresh tomatoes, salted and peppered, in bed for breakfast.

63

Dec 11th, Thess

The weather is mad, swinging from April to Siberia without warning. At the Majestic my hot breakfast milk is brought to me before I order it. Hah, I am a regular. To sit there, the sea before me, the ships, the light, the snow-capped mountains in the blue distance, is a daily treat. Fortunately the water system at the Y has packed up so I can't do my washing. Decide on culture and go to a lecture in the School of Philosophy, *Anaïs Nin, Nathaniel Hawthorne and the pursuit of happiness* by Anna Balakian – a comparison of the adulterous dilemmas and diverse fates of Hester and Sabina. Also check out the city's symphony orchestra which needs a bomb under it. I sat near the front of the hall surrounded by very old people in fur coats who coughed and clapped in-between movements. George some-body played that well-known Beethoven concerto with fine flourishes (forgot to get a programme); but the orchestra was so dire I left.

One evening Darian and I went for a blow-out of Greek haggis called *Tsigerosarmas,* soup, cheese and three tumblerfuls each of the potent local red wine from the barrel. I like Darian. She tells me bloodcurdling tales of Eastern European bureaucracy, gives me tips for India and says that the Sudan won't let you in if you have an Israeli/Egyptian border stamp. Back at the Y where the central heating has broken down, she throws me a Ching. The Ching doesn't like me. It reproaches me for character flaws, most of them true, like wanting everything to happen instantly; then adds condescendingly that I shall have some small successes. Darian now replaced by Di and Deb from Melbourne.

The tourist office changes its mind and says that the boat to Samothraki from Kavala goes on Wednesday, not Sunday. I've got dry patches on my hips. This evening the sunset is extraordinary – a raspberry sun taking a golden path into a green sea. As I walk home past the white tower where the Janissaries were murdered, a man hails me. He's sitting on bench with another man.

'Have you got a dog?'

I look round. Not a dog to be seen. 'No,' I say.

Decide I'm going mad so am not surprised when an elderly Greek poet bursts into my room at the Y and insists on reading her poems. She's called Mella, has a long nose and close-set eyes and I don't think I like her. The Aussies are hilarious. Di is tall, bent and thin, Deb squat. They are cousins. Di spends all her time putting on and taking off her black tights. Sometimes she wears gloves to stop them laddering but they always do. Deb is her minder. They go to bed at 2am and don't get up till noon.

Dec 15th, Thess

The Y is disintegrating. The central heating has collapsed again, the lights are fused and a wretched girl is stuck in the lift. Mrs Soapdish is phlegmatic. 'The showers still work,' she purrs, vanishing into her room in a cloud of smoke. Kyria Alexandra, the hatchet-faced admin boss who melted at the mention of Inverness, is now a pal. She explains the problem of the crippled central heating. The Y is owned by the bank and it refuses to cough up for a new system. Christmas is only a week and a bit away. It rains and rains and all the drivers are furious and so are the pedestrians. Beggars sit beside puddles being effectively reproachful. One old lady is sitting in a puddle. Priests with rat-tail hair-do's dodge past. The big square of the city glitters with stalls and festivity: cheap felt dogs, rag dolls, calendars, candles, diaries, more woolly dogs with horrible eyes, Chinese yo-yos, embroideries in unspeakable taste, puzzles, paintings of God, pillows. I gaze at little packets in a kiosk labelled *Scandal, Amour, French Ticklers* and wonder what they are – cigars or exotic foreign chocolates? It's the *French Ticklers* that does it. Fool that I am, they are condoms. Now it's snowing. Men wheel small carts along the pavements with tin kettles in them, also salt and pepper. In the kettles is something called *Tsalip*, good for the throat in cold weather. Thessaloniki is full of pigeons and sparrows. Little russety-bosomed birds sit at the top of cypresses in the woods behind the city. They are called *Floros*. One swings backwards and forwards on a minuscule twig, like a fly on a strand of hair. The turkeys in the market are pathetic. They lie on their backs under bright lights with their heads in plastic bags, black and dishevelled like ravaged widows.

I've become fond of Thessaloniki and the Y. The little girls are beginning to leave for their villages; and yesterday Mrs Soapdish gave me a piece of the oldest cake in Greece. Her cigarette holder was having one of its Garbo moods. 'Ah, Sara, you are one of us,' she growled.

Dec 22nd, Thess

On this, my last day, I find a wonderful restaurant. Its wall decoration is an enormous photograph of three recently-hatched yellow chickens, each chicken raised into a three dimensional bulge. They eye me balefully as I study the menu. *Frigid Fish, Scuttle Fish* and *Lamp,* lots of *Lamp.* The most intriguing item is *Grill Millers Thumb* which I should have tried but, cravenly, don't. Rain induces melancholy. Lying on my bed after lunch, fed up with writing down Greek vocab which I won't remember, I wonder what the point of my life is. Do NOT want to go to Samothraki tomorrow. Buy Deb and Di some farewell cakes in a coffee house on the front. I shall miss the sea view. This morning Olympus, mountain of the Gods, peered through a quilt of cloud while black ships glided a lettuce sea. This evening the colours of the sunset are too subtle to describe – moss rose pink, old man's grey, veils worn by elegant women in Budapest.

Dec 23rd, Kavala

The best laid plans of mice and Greek timetables...the boat which originally went to Samothraki at midnight on Sunday, then switched to 5am on Wednesday, changed its mind for Xmas week and left at 10am this morning, Tuesday. So I missed it. Radiating resignation I dumped my backpack in the boat's booking office – cheerful they were and quite unrepentant – and went to look for a hotel. The Acropolis I remembered from two years ago, an old-fashioned Greek hotel with the feel of a family concern – clean,

welcoming and cheap. The great Venizelos once stayed there.
Sadly, despite charm and jokes, they wouldn't budge from 350
drachs a night, £2 over my budget. Living on £2000 a year makes
me a skinflint – I'd rather splash out on boats, buses, trains, food
and drink. Prowling a side street, my eye fell on the seedy
frontage and elderly aspect of the Pangaion; in I went and there
was that pre-war smell of old wood and a beaming grandfather
who gave me a room for 200 a night. It is an E Class establishment and entirely unheated!

Walked, read, found a friendly taverna and am now tucked up
with a book in my tiny room. It has a washbasin with real soap
in it – the glass shelf as usual is broken – a cupboard, a chair, a
rather large bed and, wonder of wonders, a reading light. The
nearby mountains are snow-covered, the room is arctic; but my
Freeport Maine sleeping bag with two layers of musty blanket on
top makes a fine igloo. I am a strange sight in my woolly hat and
donkey jacket, turning the pages with fur gloves!

Xmas Eve, Kavala

Kavala is not what it seems. Centuries ago the road between Rome
and Constantinople, the *Via Egnatia*, ran through Thessaloniki
linking the emperors in the West and the East. It passed through
Kavala. The place looks like a city and behaves like a city yet to
me has the heart and mentality of a market town. I should read
up about it but am more interested in looking at it. The docks are
busy and smell of cereals, grain, fish and dried grass; there's an
oil rig out in the sea which wasn't there two years ago and the
town is full of nasty bars. It's often the way arriving in a new
place – you can't find its centre and you wander and wander,
usually mapless in my case, and find nothing and no-one and
then suddenly, round a corner, there it is, bang, and you wonder
how you missed it. The modern blocks are empty and lifeless,
affluent window-dressing. They're going up so fast from the
mountains of sand and cement in the street they're treading on
one another's tails. Near the Roman viaduct beats the present
heart of the town; bustling markets with fruit stalls and fish stalls,

grocers crammed with goodies and last minute shoppers, the bar-relled vaults of the wine shops and two old hotels, the Rex and Parthenon. Small shacks on cobbles rub shoulders with workers' houses of the '30s or '40s, perhaps some remnant of Communist idealism. The people are friendly and don't stare. Even three years of solitary travelling haven't inured me against bouts of self-consciousness.

It's Xmas Eve; and could be St Agnes Eve it's so bloody freezing. The snow lies on Pangaion to the west, the wind blows and the cliff path, almost obliterated in places by impenetrable thorn, is not the best way to go and see the white cross above the town. See it I do, freeze to death and rush back into the town to find somewhere to eat, or better still, an *ouzerie* to put the blood back into my feet. The statue of the Father Christmas in the main square waving his three balls and a bell looks familiar. It would be just like the ingenious Greeks to tart up an existing statue. Could a hero of the War of Independence or Alexander the Great be sulking under the cap and bells? Kavala, unlike Thessaloniki, does not have a taverna on every corner; but I find a small place with fat cooks and a communal table where old men are eating bean soup. The young waiters are sweet and help the ones who are very tottery. I *do* like Kavala. This afternoon I picked a sprig of heather, still in flower, from the hills. It shall be my Xmas Tree.

Xmas Day, Kavala

Drums and the blowing and bleatings of fife and trumpet seep through my blankets at 8am, break into ragged march time, then suddenly, as if the ground has swallowed them up, fade and vanish. A brilliant blue day, not a cloud in the sky and there are icicles on the inside of the window. This is no day for washing. With a roar I leap from my bag into my clothes, brush my teeth, wash my face and sally forth. Past the tourist beaches are quiet corners of cliff, pine tree and rock mislaid from a Greece of 20 years ago. Out of the wind the sun is hot. My head is empty, rinsed of thought. The sea flops about in the rocks, the waves are green, the sky lilac. Old men walk with their grandchildren and I

68

wonder where I'll spend my next Xmas. There are the melancholy remnants of an ancient city, Antisaras, on the way back from the cove: eighteen or so boulders, in a neat pile, occupying the garage space of an unfinished modern block, their only companions plastic bags and dogshit. *Sic transit gloria mundi.*

Every decent restaurant is shut; but the hotel has put a plate of fruit and cakes in my room. Am touched by this kindness and retire to bed with a bottle of wine and the plate. An awful-looking place on the sea front is open. In the evening I enter its portals. Some kind of Xmas dinner *must* be had. Alas, the inside lives up to the outside. The waiters wear dolled-up jackets with dirty, red satin collars; the clientele are ugly and fat; and the food, cold greasy meat soup and cold greasy aubergines, is disgusting. On the plus side, the central heating works and the Chinese Circus is on the telly. What deftness and delicacy Chinese bodies have. Also a group of men off a ship or rig interest me. They speak English and some other tongue quietly, eat colossal quantities of food in the wrong order, and drink wine very fast. Am tempted to go and talk to them but don't.

Dec 28th, Kavala

Culture time: Mechmet Ali was so frightful he got thrown out of Kavala and went off to Egypt to found the Farouk dynasty. His lovely old Turkish house is fascinating. Nearby is the Imam's palace which is falling to pieces and ought to be restored. Bugger the Greeks and their Turkophobia. The cold wastes of Kavala's archaeological museum contain fine bits and pieces from the temple of Parthenos and Amfipolis (I think the lion sitting by the main road came from there) and there is a terracotta face of Aphrodite circa 500 BC which is exquisite. It maddens me that I can't get to Ecossifinitza, a 400 AD monastery, wedged in a ravine 20 kilometres from a bus stop. The winter days are too short, the snow too deep.

After culture, food: the patsas in Kavala is a joy if you like a soup made of tripe and parts. There's a place by the bus station that does nothing but this winter food. By the door is a basin three feet in diameter, bubbling over a fire. Flanking it is a wooden board on which, night and day, tripe, guts, feet, heads are smashed and chopped. Bang, bang, bang is the background music to a *patsas* place. You can ask for a fine, medium or rough-chopped helping. To the steaming bowlful which arrives, just add vinegar or lemon juice, salt and a really hot rough pepper; and order a glass of local red wine to go with it. The light is dim, one wall pretends to be an Italian lake and presiding over the establishment is a stuffed, albeit undernourished lamb. What a professionally-run business. Also worth mentioning are *mezze* I was served with my ouzo in an old-fashioned *ouzerie*: a large ouzo arrived and with it a chunk of sausage, a vine leaf, *tsatsiki*, three olives, an egg, a slab of cheese, three hot peppers and crusty bread. You pay only for the drink.

One day, on a whim, I took a bus to Drama – just because it's such a dotty name for a small country town. It rained, then sleeted, then snowed. The old town is charming, the new the usual tasteless mess of cement blocks. The girls have moustaches and olive eyes. There was *no* drama anywhere.

Dec 29th, Trip to Philippi

The water is so cold out of the tap I've given up washing. God is a hot bath. God is a log fire. God, where are you? Philippi is a patchwork plain with two little hillocks on it. Kosta, the guide, says they were crucial to the battle between Octavian and Brutus because whoever took them was going to win. Cliffs with an acropolis, Macedonian and Roman ruins, ghosts, leafless trees standing about like old soldiers. There is a spot high on the cliffs where poor Brutus ran on his sword. I wish someone had brought me here when I was reading Julius Caesar. Macedonian pomp (the French excavated the bits now on show in the thirties), Roman plumbing and Saint Paul – the site is strange and sad. It's odd how some places hold the life that was and others lose it. What a grand Macedonian city it must have been; and what a marvel of design and plumbing the later Roman loos. It's a pity the Greeks never grasped the concept. Depressed by the cold and fallen glories, I look round the museum. It's colder inside than out and the curator has only one eye.

Dec 30th – Jan 2nd, to Samothraki

Here Philip of Macedon fell in love one drunken night with Olympias, the mother of Alexander the Great. Here the rites to the Dioscuri, Castor and Polydeuces took place. One myth has it that these twins were hatched from the same egg as Helen of Troy, Leda their Mama having been ravished by Zeus disguised as a swan. There is a moon mountain (Leda was deified as Nemesis, the moon goddess). The French dug up the Winged Victory and took it back to France. And that is the sum of what I know about Samothraki. It sounds a strange and magic place so I thought I'd go and look at it. The Skopelos is a neat, well-appointed boat with a dreary crew. The day is blue, calm and clean and the profile of the island as we approach dotted with little pads of white – as if it had cut itself shaving. The Moon Mountain is beautiful, white with snow. 'Don't sit on the table!' barks the bad-tempered bosun.

An old boy needs help with his suitcase off the boat. I meet Sophia who is waiting for him and she offers me a nice room. At first blush, Samothraki seems to consist of rubbish and goats. After a couple of ouzos and a mound of *mezze*, I wander up the road to the top village, through ploughed fields, olives and acres of arable crops. The olive picking season is on, as late as that of Crete. It's early afternoon and roses bloom on dead twigs. Tractors bounce past me in the dust and army trucks hoot and cry hullo. 40 minutes later, up in the *hora* – so cunningly placed behind a hillock that not even Barbarossa would have spotted it – a handsome youth in stained fatigues hails me:

'Good day, welcome, come and join us.'

I do. They're nice, bored youngsters doing their National Service. 'Oh God, it's so quiet here!' they wail. After a look at an old fortress, probably where Philip ravaged Olympias, I dawdle back down the hill to fried eggs, wine and an early night.

Dec 31st, Samothraki

Three winters in Greece have made me hate the North Wind; the older you get, the more you hate it. It roars in my face as I plod to the ruins at Paliopolis, about six to eight miles down the coast road from where I'm staying. It's a site to visit at the death of the year, as magnificent as Delphi and as full of ghosts. The Moon Mountain towers behind the great walls of the city – none of it as yet excavated and the ruins go underneath the mountain, so they say – and the spot where the sacred rites were held; hillocks, dells, olive trees, thickets, a kind of idyllic eighteenth century rural scene. God knows what human sacrifices were strung up in pre-Hellenic times. The guide, Theodorus, is over-sexed and leaps like a goat from boulder to boulder. He shows me a lump of stone with pre-Greek writing on it (probably Pelasgians who came out of Palestine in 3,500 BC, so Graves says), where the Winged Victory was discovered by French archaeologists, a pre-historic hotel where they used to put up visiting dignitaries, the ancient harbour, the towers, walls, graves and temples.

Over-sexed Greek men are a pain. The museum and its contents are fascinating; but I duck drinks and lunch from the heavy-breathing, thigh-clutching nitbag and go home with a headache. Fall into bed at 4pm and the next thing I know it's the middle of the night and 1981.

Jan 1st, Samothraki

Walk to Lakoma, a village six or seven miles away. Samothraki's a fertile island with wide plains of wheat, corn and oats. There are sheep, goats, orchards and forests of olives on the south side. Today I meet a man on a tractor – a cook in Manhattan for 15 years – and a plump woman who invites me into her house. It's an old place set among groves of olives and plane trees. Her father is a retired priest and they speak and weep of a recently dead son and brother. Tears of grief in the Mediterranean are innocent. Katina laments her unmarried state and her weight and offers me a chicken leg made of blotting paper and a glass of glorious wine. 'The chicken is ours,' she says proudly.

'That explains why it is so tasty,' I say cravenly, prising morsels of sawdust out of my teeth.

The father-priest is a darling. He's pensioned off, has a bad leg, grieves for the dead son yet radiates kindness and peace. 'Do stay here,' he says. 'Stay as long as you like.' Katina shows me an ancient olive press and confides her despair as to the pressures of Greek society on one who is unmarried. 'It's alright for you, you're daring, I am a coward.' She looks almost pretty when she smiles. On my way back, a black-eyed boy driving goats in the pale sunshine stops to chat, telling me about his National Service with Customs and Excise on the Yugoslavian border and how, if you're late back from your leave or do something wrong, the authorities stick another 20 days on your service. Some hapless recruits end up doing three years or more.

Jan 2nd, Samothraki

The weather has changed; rain and wind whip the sea into a foamy stew and opinions vary as to whether the boat goes this evening or this morning or tomorrow or not at all. A nightmare has made me gloomy. I dreamed I was possessed of the devil and no-one would talk to me; women with ugly sneers knocked me about and a lover's ex-wife spat at me. Am cheered and restored by the sweetness of the people in the post office who actually *know* that the boat goes at 3pm. Someone has green fingers there. A plant called Dragon looks set to devour everything in sight. Another, flaunting fronds, is called Desire.

Several grannies are sick during the crossing and I finish Kerouac's *On the Road*. Paul Theroux has a sad story about Kerouac. Years later, fat and alarming-looking, the Beat ikon tried to retrace his exploits but failed to get a lift out of New Jersey. He returned, embittered, to New York. He forgot the rule. Never go back.

Likos, 2004

It's early on a December morning. By the low sea wall the waves caress the jumble of rocks with hardly a murmur. Sunday and silence and a solitary cormorant fishing in the straits. Likos is wrapped in sleepy enchantment, from the tip of its wicked tail to the mist between its ears. It's going to be a warm day, a halcyon one. The wind and depression of eight days ago has slid off the edge of my memory, its only relics the quantities of sand under one of my beds, a washing line pole at a drunken angle and a deep gash in the middle finger of my right hand. It is imprudent to open a tin of corned beef when your nerves are shattered by wind.

'Never go back,' I wrote on the boat from Samothraki in 1981. There are exceptions to every rule and this island is one of them; although six weeks ago my heart was beating overfast as the steamer ploughed her furrow up the wolfish left flank. Fires, alarmingly frequent on Greek islands, could have destroyed the dense woodland, mass tourism descended, death carried off my friends. Against the most calamitous of these – mass tourism – the island has one unassailable defence: pebbly beaches. It may seem heartless to call mass tourism worse than death but it's true. After a death, however dreadful, life continues. After mass tourism, no place nor its people are ever the same again. It's as if it rotted the society in the parts which gave it a purpose, leaving it looking the same on the outside but cancerous, eaten away inside. Five years wandering in Greece showed me many such corpses.

For the time being, Likos with its fringe of jagged rocks is safe. There are greenhouses and market gardens, fishing and the obsidian quarry and enough summer tourism to keep the hotels, tavernas and kafenions flourishing. People come here who enjoy swimming, walking, poking about in rocks, snorkelling, sailing in small boats and spending time in a beautiful place which has managed to keep its integrity without turning into a museum. They are made welcome and treated with kindness. Most cherish the experience, many return year after year.

Centuries ago, someone tucked the tiny monastery of St George into the pleat of a hillside. Last Tuesday, December 6th, was his feast day. Everyone came in cars or lorries or the bus or on scooters to the bend in the road where a sheeptrack meanders down between olives and oaks to the valley floor, then weaves up three flights of terraces to the white splash with its rough green cross. A sweet-smelling rose, still in bloom, sprawled over the courtyard wall. The mouse-sized church only held the priest and a few worshippers; so people came and went and chatted outside and when the talking got too loud, the devout hissed reprovingly. I left, not in the mood for noise and feasting, and walked through the hills to Psara. An old friend was asleep in a sunny corner, his fly swat in one hand. We talked of the scandal of the incumbent mayor of Miti who was refusing to leave the Town Hall despite losing the election, a death, the weather. Over to the East, the ghost of a shadowland stole in and out of the haze: Turkey.

The Ottoman Empire at the height of its puissance reached the gates of Vienna and but for torrential rain which – I think – interfered with the battering rams might have surged on to who knows where. Four hundred years of subjection to another power is a long time; but there is an unreasonable quality to the professed Greek hatred and distrust of the Turk. Actually, many Greeks are fascinated to know what Turkey and its people are like; and by now both bloods are so mixed – certainly where the landmasses lie close – that neither country could lay claim to any purity. It was one long summer spent in Psara that finally lured me into Turkey. That tempting shadow to the East drew me, especially in the calm of dawn when it 'showed itself' as the Greeks say. Sitting once with some cross old men outside a kafenion which hadn't opened, I watched an apricot sun shoot up from behind the dark shape as if a foot had kicked it. Touchingly or infuriatingly, depending on my mood, the Greeks still call Istanbul 'the city' ie Constantinople, city of the emperor Constantine and founded by him in AD333 on the site of Byzantium, a Greek colony since BC667.

The wind has gone round to the West, fusing sea and sky into beige steel; and in the small fields behind the port lozenges of broom flower have appeared on the green sticks, the almond blossom is out and so are the first narcissi. Yesterday afternoon an eagle hung high above me, looking for its tea. Baulked of a scuttling thing, it wailed, and floated off. Today a speckled owl cleaned its beak on the telegraph wires by the harbour-master's office. Tomorrow is my day off, lunch in Psara and a walk down the white road which leads to nowhere. The day after tomorrow, I shall start on my Turkish diaries.

Turkey: the white road 1981 – 1982

The white road
And the hot sun upon it
And the sword by my side.
Bright feather in my bonnet
And all the world;
And the world is very wide.

***Troubador's song* – Lister**

Chapter Six

Impressions of Istanbul – a boat up the Black Sea – Trabzon – Sumela
1981

Sept 23rd, Yücelt Hostel, Istanbul

Arrive by unspeakable Magic Bus, a 24-hour ride from Athens. Richard, a young Canadian, and I take a taxi to Sultan Ahmet and the Yücelt Hostel. O wonderful Darian Delu of the tara-masalata and tomatoes who recommended it. We are welcomed and our rucksacks carried. After Greece such politeness is a shock. I end up in Dorm 33 with eight bunks, four up four down, and grab Bed Four at the top next to the window. No-one told us we would change buses at the frontier and the hapless Richard left his health certificate in the book he was reading. Both have bowled back to Athens. He is also filled with gloom at the state of the loos. To cheer him up I buy him a beer in the outside courtyard, under what looks like a huge nut tree. We chat to Ronnie, a dazed little American artist, who has been adopted by the Dervishes. They are instructing and feeding her while she learns to paint Turkish miniatures. I rather like this place. Nobody seems to care much. Sleep like a log in Bed Four. 200TL, £1 per night!

Sept 24/25th, Istanbul

The Yücelt is a laugh a minute. Being on the black market route it has Nescafé. No coffee anywhere else in Turkey. I shall die. The showers are cold, the loos filthy; but the boys at the desk friendly and easy-going. On my first morning I sat in the court-yard watching angry Frenchmen wrestle with a primus stove. The notice above them said *Bringing food into this cafeteria is not allowed*. Clouds of smoke rose. All kinds of forbidden goodies waited to be heated. Serena from London had a row with Gary over loo paper:

'But it's my roll, Gary.'

'Fuck off, Serena, see you in Athens…'

A German girl who'd just escaped from Teheran exclaimed, 'I met you in the Y in Thessaloniki!' So she did. A nice girl. Another girl, languid, blonde and endlessly tall, sleeps all day and talks all night or reads with a candle pegged to the bedhead. We shall be burnt to crisps.

The sky is overcast, o wonderful clouds the first I've seen since March, and Sultan Ahmet doesn't smell of anything. Everywhere soldiers in shabby green with helmets and rifles patrol the streets. There is a curfew. First impressions are of greyness – the sky is grey, the mosques are grey, San Sophia and the Blue Mosque are grey, browsing like elephants among the dark trees and long grass. Even the quantities of Byzantine wall, though flecked with red are grey. Shabby small dark men and rectangular women in raincoats, shoes, stockings, headscarves walk quickly in the streets. They are grey too. I take a look at the notorious pudding shop which strikes me as a hash-swap joint. Down at the Galata Bridge brown eiderdowns of smoke billow from the stacks of the river steamers and a smell of frying fish floats from the restaurants under the bridge: fish with red-frilled gills look so pretty arranged on green leaves. Strolling among the rush-hour crowds, traffic, riverboats, hootings and honkings, I'm struck by a kind of resemblance to San Francisco but alas, SF is golden like Rome, so lovelier. Perhaps if those black-whiskered Selçuks had stayed in the East, Byzantium would have become the right colour. Paris and Edinburgh should be grey, *not* Constantinople. A man calls me a prostitute (I don't think he's ever met one). When accosted, this time politely by another, I lower my eyes and produce the newly-learned phrase, 'I am with my husband.'

The markets, o the markets! Everyone has their trade: silversmiths, coppersmiths, leatherworkers, shoe repairers, carpet makers – even the man with five lettuce-shakers carefully arranged on a clean cloth in front of him. A man sharpens knives using a foot treadle. One market is bright with its harvest of brooms. Slim boys load up, then shoot off, hung about with brushes. Old men sit behind weighing machines and I long for an enormously fat Turkish woman to get on and the machine to bellow her kilos. In another alley, a dark man with a deeply furrowed face wears a tawdry, golden-striped blanket over his shoulder. He looks like an African chief. The wood-panelled Turkish Maritime Office tell me that a boat goes to Trabzon on October 1st. The fares go up that day, but *tant pis*. The trip takes two and a half days and as a birthday present to me I'm going second class with a cabin.

On a milky afternoon the Tokapi seems unreal. The Emerald Room has the most vulgar gems I've ever seen; am also struck by a gold-plated cradle and enamelware embroidered with precious stones. There are several bits and pieces of the Prophet – his whiskers, a tooth, an eyelash. Outside a cool wind blows and in the overgrown gardens posses of gardeners rake and tug, but slowly, philosophically. There is an exquisite summer pavilion. Mighty planes and chestnuts tower above rose trees choked with grass and weeds. It is all very Ottoman. Oxalice, my old friend from the Dedham garden, is everywhere and it warms my heart to find a humble acquaintance in such exotic surroundings. Maybe Justinian picked oxalice? These cloudy days are a joy. To be cool is bliss, to be cold sheer depravity.

The food is beguiling. I have devoured a kind of cold macaroni in flaky pastry which sounds disgusting but isn't; gazed longingly at something soft and wobbly; and found a restaurant with a Greek waiter where I enjoyed spinach and yoghurt and *türlü* and mounds of glorious Turkish bread. An *Imam Bayildi* at 11.30am one morning made me see why the original customer fainted. Even the simplest food is beautiful.

Sept 26th, Istanbul

The waiter in my breakfast haunt is enchanted when I fluently order hot milk. Alas, we can converse no further. High drama at San Sophia when a Moslem barges in front of the reredos and salaams Allah. He is frog-marched off by boy soldiers. SS is very large and impressive but doesn't move me. The slums of Istanbul are quite dreadful. I struck a patch between the river and the university and hurried through, not in fear but ashamed in case I seemed a voyeur, past children so filthy you could hardly see their skin and rickety wooden houses. In one tiny alley, two men passed me leading bears, the men with sticks, the bears in chains. A hot, rank smell floated up my nose from the bears who very likely dance for their living. A great discovery is the secondhand book mart at the back of the Beyazit Mosque. It has all the old favourites – *Absalom, Absalom! The River Line, Whiteoaks.* I bet you'd find them in the jungles of Borneo.

Take a boat up the Bosphorus to Yeniköy. It's a brilliant day. Warships like crocodiles swish past. There the faded splendour of the Dolambahçe Palace, centre of the last Sultan's web of paranoia.

Fishing boats fish, yachts twirl and swing and catch the wind. The underside of the suspension bridge is rusting. Tufan the Turk accosts me. He stutters and holds an African marigold in one hand:

'I am very Turk. I don't like Atatürk. He was born in Thessaloniki.'

He pauses and sniffs his marigold as we chug along.

'He also hanged far too many Imams.'

I am diverted. Tufan tells me he wishes to marry a 13- or 14-year old but Mummy doesn't agree. Mummy has other ideas and another choice.

'She is 27,' says Tufan gloomily.

'Practically in the grave,' I agree.

Sept 27/28th, Istanbul

Agia lrini, pared to its brick and the Kariye Mosque. I forget the name of the original 13th century church but those mosaics and frescoes are celestial. The cisterns are noble but just cisterns. More interestingly, a second visit to San Sophia showed me its incredible beauty. From the galleries I saw the rich decorations clotting every arch, the mosaics of Jesus, Mary and John, the emperors and their spouses; above all – how could I have been so blind two days ago? – the Panagia and Child. How it stays up, I can't think. Nothing reliable seems to support this domed glory. The weedy gardens of the Tokapi lure me back, the *haremi* horrible, full of death and intrigue. The rain is pouring down and the tourists have stayed at home, leaving me the ghosts and sleepy curators. I prowl and brood and little boys make fun of me. The Hittite and Assyrian stuff in one of the Archaeological Museums is fascinating. An alarming lot, the Hittites. The kings have vast heads and tiny feet and their sphinxes sometimes wear Judges' wigs. One looks like Elizabeth Taylor. *Aslan* is the Turkish for lion and these are wondrous beasts. The art overwhelms because of the faith behind it: such wit, rage, originality. A Hittite sacrificial urn is the original bidet, a 7000 BC sculpture of a man and woman embracing makes Henry Moore a copycat. Perhaps it's true that we never learn, only remember what we have forgotten.

City of cats, Istanbul. Cats on cars, one-eyed cats with a red hole where the eye should be, tigers with torn ears. The kittens are pathetic, scraps of dirty fur asleep in a patch of sun. They are full of love and squeak and lift their tails as you approach. The dogs are big and bold and roam the city in well-fed packs, choosing to sleep in places where people fall over them. One chow-alsatian chewed my golfing jacket, so I clouted him. I see so much, forget so much. In the Nargile Garden beside the broom market sit old men in the forbidden fez; others are draped and turbaned. The porters in the markets carry their loads on special leather holders padded to one side. They're like saddles except they're for humans. Under the Yerebatan Teppich Market I give myself a treat and feast on *pasamesese*, spinach and garlic in yoghurt, brain salad, hot peppers and raki.

The two little French girls in my dorm talk in their sleep, oddly enough in English. One cries, 'Go away, go away.' The other moans, 'Leave me alone...'

Sept 29th, Istanbul, my birthday

I'm 45. Happy birthday. The day dawns crisp as a London late September, with blue sky behind the turning leaves and falling conkers. On my way through a labyrinth of streets I pause to drink delicious soup full of oregano, then enter a building which is a secret way to another alley on another level. Old men crouch over stoves and slice onions. I stop, bewildered, but smiling they wave me on. The cats watch them and me. Turks are nice to cats. Now there is an alleyway full of sewing machines and more cats – on them, under them, beside them. The harness shops are bright with beads and in a small square a man in a fez sells corn while three pigeons groom themselves on his head. I love Istanbul – the huge Cadillac taxis and pre-war Renault Dolmus, the *ayran* and fruit juice stalls, the ancient plane trees, the smells of spices and frying meats tormenting my nose, the fresh bread smell, sacks full of green henna, the plastic bucket and plate street. In the Cadena gloom of a restaurant, I sample *kazandibi* – mashed chicken breasts, sugar and milk in a chewing gum goo sprinkled with cinnamon.

Süleymaniye Camil, the little carpet and miniature museum beside the Süleiman Mosque (in the Imaret) is a haven of beauty and tranquillity. I'm just finishing *The Towers of Trebizond* for the fourth time and the handsome woman quarreling with the gardener outside the museum is exactly as I imagine Halide. It's cool again; and one pink dogrose blooms in the Yücelt courtyard. On my birthday afternoon I sit by the window on the second floor landing and drink white wine and look at San Sophia. Every so often gulls settle on the dome like so many handkerchiefs. I think about love and come to no conclusion except that it is the most important thing in life. A Beatles song is playing in the courtyard below and the end of *The Towers of Trebizond* makes me cry as it always did. From the Golden Horn steamers hoot and gulls mew. Eight years ago today I scattered my mother's ashes in the Dedham garden.

Sept 30th, Istanbul

A quiet day. I buy my ticket and stroll. My travel plan is a month to six weeks: Trabzon aka Trebizond, Erzerum, Kars, Ani, Doğubeyazit, Harran, Van, Diyarbakir (Harran should be after Diyarbakir), Adiyaman for Nemrut Dagh, Kayseri, Ürgüp... Wander over the Galata Bridge with its boats bashing in and out, the fishing boys and the frying fish and the hurrying, drab figures. The Pera Palace is a collector's piece, a gem of faded glory and dignified tristesse; its lounge looks like Cordova Cathedral. Pretending to be a resident, I take the art nouveau lift and peer into a bathroom and loo large enough for two bedsits. Atatürk had a room here. I think I am falling in love with Atatürk. Moslems are very clean. Wash, wash, wash. It is an extremely noisy religion. The faithful are called to prayer five times a day by an amplified recording from the top of the mosque. The loudest exhortation is at 6am outside my bedroom window. Apparently Dervishes sway, not whirl.

Oct 1st - 3rd, up the Black Sea to Trabzon on the Izmir

At 10.45 am on this misty morning the Izmir leaves Istanbul from the quayside near the Galata Bridge. A pale sun glimmers, but fitfully. I envy Mary Adeline Walker sailing the scented Bosphorus 160 years ago. It's still beautiful, conjured into glorious shapes by its woods and hills, palaces and villas. Not even ugly modern building has wrecked it – yet. The Izmir is a nice ship of about 50-60 metres and spotlessly clean. Twenty six years ago, aged four, she sank – but they pulled her up again! My cabin is no 41 and I am alone in it. Hot water gushes from the tap. There are two easy chairs, a big chest of drawers, a reading light and a mirror to look at myself in. There is even a bath in the passage. The third officer has already made a heavy, confident pass. 'Come to the bridge after dinner,' indeed. He does not know that there is only one bridge for me.

The Black Sea is very large and very empty. One distant shape in the afternoon towards the Russian side, otherwise nothing. A solid four-course lunch, all in with the ticket, is consumed in silence at a table with four Turks and a child Turk. The elderly couple are charming, the child ghastly. At evening little birds land on deck. One is teeny and golden-toast coloured and looks tired. Another with a dipping tail plumps into the car park. I drink beer and read and try and learn Turkish expressions and marvel that here I am, following in the footsteps of Aunt Dot and Father Chantry Pigg, on my way to their Trebizond. Children are singing a French carol on the radio and it trills out that rare Protestant joyousness. Dinner is another four courses, climaxing with *loukoumades* – those balls of dough in honey. I shall be spherical by the time we get to Trabzon.

Friday, second day: first stop is Sinop at 9.40am. My leaflet in German tells me that the Black Sea was home to the Amazons, a colony of Milesians, the Pontic Kings and the last of the Byzantines, the Commene emperors, who ruled at Trebizond. Only in 1461 did Turkey nobble it. All this in eight lines. Diogenes was born at Sinop. There are ugly modern buildings, some lovely chunks of what look like Crusaders' walls and a few old wooden houses with jutting-out balconies. I stroll the quayside with two dumpy Turkish women who fall about when I pronounce the Turkish for garlic. They pat me.

'Where were you last night?' says the third officer.

'In bed,' I reply, 'I was reading.'

Gloomily he writes me off as mad or a lesbian.

Another blissful day. Breakfast is two cups of tea, bread, butter, jam, cheese in triangles and olives. Lunch is four slices of beef with parsley, carrot and mashed potatoes, green bean salad, lettuce and radish salad, two crispy *börek* – one meat, one cheese – and grapes. My table is now talking to each other. There is a waiter whom I love to watch as he prongs the leftover bread into a basket and casts it through the porthole. He is a bear, dark and intense, and his moustache a long-handled broom without the handle. A cheerful little barman – there are four or five bars on the Izmir – is impressed that I speak bad French, German and Greek.

'What an international lady!' he exclaims.

'What is Rize like?' I ask the third officer who is looming.

'Very green.'

He eyes me balefully. I am a disappointment.

Apparently it's raining in Istanbul but here on the Black Sea, the *Karadeniz*, the sun is shining and the passengers lounge on deck in their shirtsleeves in 1930s chairs. Although built in 1951, the Izmir has a pre-war whiff – the layout, the wood, the curved bars, the mirrors which are everywhere. The Black Sea is full of jelly-fish, big white toadstools, each with seven sausage legs; a bit like chandeliers. Samsun is awful. I suspect Trabzon will be, too.

Saturday, and balmier and balmier grows the Black Sea weather. The sea itself is milky-coloured and laps, flatly, below a cirrhus sky. No-one pukes in this Euxine. At 6.30am we reach Giresun with its Byzantine castle, smallish and again spoilt by ugly build-ings. What a scourge the 20th century is: spoil, spoil, spoil. Now wooded hills, fold upon fold of ridge, ravine and gully, tumble gracefully into the sea. Giresun's quayside is covered in hazelnuts and a passer-by stoops and scoops up a handful. Someone else splits logs in a forest of felled timber. Between Giresun and Trabzon it's the Turkish Lake District. Slim minarets spear up from the villages and I sit on deck, drinking my half bottle of *Doluça*, glutted with the beauty of it and flicking through Rose Macaulay for references: 'Giresun was supposed to be the ancient Cerasus where the cherries came from, and the boys were fat-tened on boiled chestnuts, and Xenophon's army had made it from Trebizond in three days – or so Xenophon said...' (*The Towers of Trebizond*).

Oct 5th, Trebizond/Trabzon

And so, at 2pm, there before me are the tower blocks of
Trebizond; but I am not cast down. After Sinop, Samsun and
Giresun I expected Ipswich rather than Byzantium. As we enter
the harbour, the view is of the old town sprawling upwards and,
high on the left hillside, what looks like the ruin of a palace with
pointed windows. Asking a woman for a cheap hotel leads to her
asking a man, who then mistakes *me* for a man, and takes me up
a precipice of mud. I reel and totter, my rucksack as usual being
too heavy. The man hauls me up the rest of the mudface; then,
to his chagrin, realises my sex. On the right near the top of the
precipice is the Konak Hotel. The owners are dears and give me
a tiny room overlooking the harbour. The bedsprings croak and
sing and the loos are spotless.

Snooze and sally forth. Trabzon is prosperous, a Turkish Kavala:
lots of grocers, goods, fridges, hardware, hideous furniture stores,
bookshops, nuts and nuts and nuts and sublime looking dates.
Yobs yell at me but I rise above it. I suppose I shall get used to
being gawped at, mocked, occasionally insulted. Compensation
for this is the kindness and generosity of the majority of people I
meet who pat and chat and buy me tea. I don't really like tea but
in Turkey it's *de rigueur.* Late afternoon, here I am at last, in what
looks like an old palace among the plots of cabbages. A gentle
woman holding a baby unlocks the great gate. The brambles are
cleared. Whether the ghosts are glad or not I don't know.

Farther up the hill is a beer garden/teahouse, wooden latticed
cabins full of Turks eating and chatting, set among overgrown
flowerbeds and sweet-scented buddleia. Sipping my beer, tired
but content, I look out over the Black Sea and wonder if that ruin
really was the palace Rose Macaulay knew and where Laurie in
the book fell asleep. Eat in a tiny restaurant near the Konak Hotel.
Later mosquitoes bite me, so I light my Greek coils, squash two
and fall asleep.

Oct 5th, Trabzon, letter to a friend

Dearest Bel

I'm in Trebizond with the ghosts of Aunt Dot and Father Chantry Pigg and that fearful camel. Alas, it is now the towerblocks, not the towers of Trebizond – Trabzon is a container port, has a university and looks like Ipswich. There are nuts everywhere, also clock shops. Can there be a connection? I came on a wonderful ship called the Izmir from Istanbul, in luxurious second class. Lovely scenery and milky mild weather and not another ship to be seen. Rather eerie, really. There are quite a few bits and pieces of Byzantine Trebizond around and I think I found the place Laurie fell asleep after the Magician's potion, the ruined dining hall with the pointed windows. Even if it wasn't, it felt like it. My hotel, the Konak, is tiny and clean and I've just failed to find Agia Sophia for the third time. Did you get my PC from Istanbul? I picked up your letter in Athens, for which many thanks.

I'm writing this at a table in a leafy square surrounded by Turks drinking tea. Tch, tch, tch they go, great cluckers, a change from the po, po, po of the Greeks. Presiding over us is a huge black statue of Atatürk. The town is full of ravines which I've spent most of the morning walking up and down trying to find Agia Sophia, but all in vain. Lunch was a consolation: seven or eight little fish served with lemon and slices of raw onion, fresh bread and a bottle of chilled water, all for 58p. You could live a year in Turkey on £1000. All very well for us but dire for the people. Most of them have two jobs to make ends meet. My Turkish, thanks to Yusuf Mardin's book and B's list of useful phrases, is coming along. Its construction is rather fun: 'the in the middle of the table quite near the pink vase of flowers lying book.' This is hopelessly out of my reach since my Turkish is bus, hotel and restaurant Turkish plus bits of useful politeness. 'I like Turkey and the Turks' gets you a long way.

Yesterday I saw one of the wonders of the world, Sumela, a fourteenth century Byzantine monastery hooked onto a cliff. It was a hilarious day and began at 7.30am in the tourist office of the bus station, being fed tea by a group of cheerful middle-aged men. Apparently, I could get to a village called Maçka, then pick up a Dolmus for Sumela. Buses back seemed unlikely but I thought, what the Hell, if I worried about getting back from places I'd never go to them. It was a fast bus, driven by a maniac with a fine disregard for the lives and limbs of the sheep, cattle and shepherds on the road. A kind of Sunday bazaar/cattle market slowed us down a bit, the men drab, the women splashes of colour with their skirts and baggy pants and scarves.

Finally the road petered into rubble and we were in Maçka.

'Is there a Dolmus to Sumela?'

'No, not on Sundays, you must walk or take a taxi.'

So I started walking. It was now 9.30am and quite hot. Seventeen kilometres seemed a long way so I bought a loaf of bread. I can't tell you how glorious Turkish bread is. I could live on it. My road meandered along between high green foothills and hazelnut groves, horsemen trotted past and the occasional lorry full of locals covered me in dust. Then one stopped. It contained an ancient and a boy, so in I climbed. Up through ravines and gulches, beside brown rushing rivers, under pine-covered cliffs we ground and clanked. The lorry dropped me off in the mountains. I trudged on, sweating in the hot sun, until a huge car stopped. They were sweet, the people, and roared with laughter at my tomato face. Mad foreigner. At last we arrived at shady woods, a collection of small houses, a café and seats and tables beside a river. Turks are brilliant at picnic places.

These are the Zigana mountains (gypsies?) and the greater part of the monastery was built in the reign of Alexius III, Commene emperor. It's 1,300 metres above sea level, and the path up from the parking lot winds 27 bends through birch, maple, linden, chestnut, wild walnut, hornbeam, medlar trees and bushes of wild roses. It's very, very steep. I nearly had a heart attack going up it with the caretaker. The first autumn crocuses were out. The place itself is so moving. There are mosaics inside and outside, all with the vigour, wit, richness and joyfulness that I for one do not associate with organised religion. The building is extraordinary – I wonder how many workmen fell to their deaths in the chasm below? – stuck like a martin's mud nest to the perpendicular: beauty, decay, view, air. You must go and see it before mass tourism gobbles up Turkey.

Then more excitement. Sipping beer in the small wooden *bufet* and waiting for the people in the white car to take me back to Maçka, I was kidnapped by two German women called Erika and Monika, hugely rich and married to Turks. Very chic, with a long-nosed chauffeur and a Cadillac. We chatted in German and suddenly Erika, the blonde, said: 'come and have lunch with us. We're going to drive to our chauffeur's village.' Off we went, through the most extravagant scenery, a mixture of Macedonia, Austria and Switzerland, high above the tree line and carpeted with white and pink autumn crocuses. Enormous sheepdogs, the size of bears, herded flocks. It was three hours later, practically halfway to Erzerum, when we got to the village. A terrible road, serpentine, often just dirt-track, full of dust churned up by the container lorries heading for Iran and Iraq. When the snows come, it must be impassable.

Lunch was at 4pm at a roadside eating place – a kind of *khan* – with skinned beasts hanging up, dirty tables and rickety chairs. I was *ravenous*. First we toyed with fruits, figs, melon, grapes, pears, then, 40 mins later, two plates of jumbled grey meat appeared. Shoe leather but we all gnawed away at it. There's a particular corner on this road, just before a summit, where a blind beggar sits. He's a tollgate. Every car gives him a note. Erika says he is fabulously rich. I wonder if he's the one I heard about years ago who, if you didn't give him backsheesh, pushed your car over the cliff.

Am off East in two days – Kars, Ani, Doğubeyazit, Van, wrapped in scarves in order to be Kurdproof. See you all at Xmas, *inşallah*.

Much love Sara

Oct 6th, Trabzon

The weather is flaming June. I don't dare wear my dark glasses because no-one else does and it might be the mark of a foreign prostitute. A busy day. First stop is Agia Sophia miles away from where everyone said it was and ravishing. Thirteenth century, looking at the sea, ablaze inside with tawny, ochre, golden mosaics and frescoes and outside with snapdragons, geraniums, roses, chrysanthemums and dahlias. Sitting among the flowers, looking at the Black Sea and the big container ships shuffling past, I take root. Nirvana torpor. Rouse myself and investigate more of old Trabzon where sweet-faced women wave and a cow frisks wild-eyed over the cobbles. A common sight is a sheep led about on a piece of string. Early this morning, after my breakfast of hot milk and cake, I watched children going to school, flocks of them giggling and staring and dressed in a 19th century uniform of buttoned-up short black tunic with stiff rounded white collar over white trousers for the boys and a black dress with the same collar for the girls. The man in the tourist office had an *English* card on his desk.

'I'd like to know about the light industry here,' I say.

Consternation. 'There is a cement works and a milk factory.'

'Anything else?'

He gazes hopefully at his colleague. Together they shake their heads. Their English cassette has played. They are relieved when I depart.

The woman I thought was Erika turns out to be Monika. I sit in her flat drinking coffee (probably the last for a month). Her husband is a great rich bey, a lush, whose tipple is a mixture of raki and whisky. He must have a liver made of tin. She, beautiful, with a lively spirit and good mind is trapped in Turkdom. And only 39.

'I'm so bloody rich but what use is all this money? I can't go any-where, do anything.' She laughs. 'Maybe when the youngest is grown up I shall leave my husband...'

She won't. He sounds a decent man. He doesn't realise that she's been suffocating to death for twenty years.

We part with mutual affection.

'If you run into trouble on the road say you are *the sister* of my husband. That should have an effect up to the Iranian border.' He *must* be rich.

Racks of comb honey ooze beside plump cheeses. Why shops for honey and cheese? The dustmen and sweepers of Trabzon wear mustard yellow jackets and trousers and caps and sweep sadly and *very* slowly. Their melancholy is poetic. Barbara Cartland has made it into the bookshops here, naughty old thing. The Turks will love her. Rize, where I failed to go, supplies all Turkey with tea. In the evening I stroll again to the Byzantine citadel and wonder where I'll be tomorrow. Cowering in Erzerum. My dream of Trebizond – all magicians and love potions – has flown; but I have grown fond of Trabzon and, like Rose Macaulay, am sorry to leave.

Likos, 2004

The knives are out and the axes fall. A three-month old piglet, neatly jointed, lies under a paper tablecloth in the middle of the harbour taverna. Christmas is in two days' time. Festive shapes, neon-lit, have sprouted outside the shops in Miti and many a window is blocked by its furry tree and decorations. All the women are grumbling and making the seasonal cakes – koura-bies *and* melomacarona. *Thank God for a room with no kitchen. Popi tells me that we are not eating the jointed piglet for Christmas dinner but a turkey stuffed with rice, herbs and pine nuts. We shall be five: Popi and Thanassi her husband, Janni and Theo from the harbour master's office and me. Yesterday an old enemy popped out of its box. Homesickness. First cousin to loss and nostalgia, bane of the romantic disposition. Or did it start 53 years ago when – with no warning – I, like a million other war children, was dispossessed; left my home, my father, everything familiar for refugee camps in India? In my first term at boarding school I was pole-axed by it: a delayed version and all the worse for the delay, brought on by the combination of Ronald Coleman in* A Tale of Two Cities *and* Dear Lord and Father of Mankind. *I cried for a week. So what am I homesick for now? Friends, London, love, the vagabond's road – or something intangible lost long ago?*

Brooding about this I lost concentration. Then a cement mixer started up outside the door, fed by five quarrelling men. To Hell with writing. There is another Popi with another taverna just round the corner. Brunch at 11am makes a change. An open window with the blue sea half filling it, Adeste fidelis *floating from the radio, the black stray waiting patiently on the step.*

Max is a collie-cross of charm and gentle nature whom someone abandoned last year. He has a ruff and legs like twigs and, denied sheep to chase, flies at cars and motorbikes and cats. He's supposed to belong to the soldiers who have a cook who puts ground glass into the meatballs – so he's lucky to be alive. He's adopted me as another protector. So has a young tomcat with a splotch on its nose, very vocal and very affectionate. It thinks it's human which is probably why Max plays with it. This alarms my neighbours. Dogs do not play with cats. Occasionally the eccentric pair trot at my heel when I go to the baker for a cheese pie.

The wind goes round in circles, blowing from the north for four days, then swinging to the south bringing rain, then sliding west. Does everything go round in circles? We do not learn, we only remember what we have forgotten. The first mandrake is out; so is the orange blossom and the lemons are ripening on the trees. Images stamp my inside eye: a homesick Italian cooking spaghetti in Harbour Popi's kitchen, twelve brown hens and three turkeys sitting up a tree, a sow peeing in a great gush, a green sea and lilac land and Turkey, suddenly in sharp focus, luring me back...

Chapter Seven

The journey East – a flophouse in Erzerum – *Bayram* in Kars –Doğubeyazit and Isak Pasha
1981

Oct 6th, journey to Erzerum, 1981

The bus leaves at 7am playing Johann Strauss and roars off down the valley, passing several squashed dogs and others brazenly coupling in the road. My seat is behind the driver; and although normally a placid passenger, for the first half-hour I close my eyes as we avoid schoolchildren, lorries, cows, flocks of sheep, gaggles of women and other buses by a few inches. The road, sometimes tarmac, sometimes dust, is just wide enough for two lorries to pass without falling over the precipices. If a lorry is in front you can't see anything. Hard shoulders are as unthinkable as daily space travel. Scree, fallen rocks, fearsome chasms.

Soon I realise I am in the hands of a Formula One driver. Across the aisle is a family of three from Van. Beside me a young female Turk throws up into her plastic bag. More honkings and moanings float from behind. Oddly, there is no smell of sick and everyone is very neat. Having been bus- and car-sick all my childhood, I feel for them; and when the Turkish girl lays her head on my trousered lap, I hold her shoulders to steady her against the dreaded Z-bends. The day is perfect, a sharp blue sky with thunderheads throwing shadows on the mountains. I had a dreadful dream last night about my mother dying. I hadn't written to her and hadn't visited her in hospital. I woke up in tears.

Our first stop is Hamsikoy where the drivers escort me to their table in the café and feed me *paça* (*patsas*) and tea for which, o horrors, I am not allowed to pay. First the bus to Matça on Sunday wouldn't accept my fare, now bus drivers insist on buying my food and drink. It's lovely to be so protected; but worrying because I don't know how to refuse largesse without offending. Turkish loos are cleaner than Greek loos and so are Turkish villages and so are Turks. People here do not cast their litter into beautiful ravines and lakes. Gradually Alpine scenery gives way to volcanic hills and mud-hut houses with their harvest stacked on the roof. Valleys of poplars. Orchards bulge with large, munching Jersey cows. On we fly – East, East. On top of Mordor-like peaks stands a ruined fortress. We just avoid squashing three pullets and stop for lunch. I am in despair. When shall I be allowed to pay for a meal in this country? The last stage of the journey is awesome: an enormity of landscape where khaki, beige, golden, dun-coloured mountains flaunt splashes of autumnal scrub, vivid as those of the maples in Maine or Vermont. Round the edge of a monstrous plain lava hills, wrinkled and indifferent, stretch for ever; and coming over the second summit in blinding dust gives the illusion of flying not driving. Land without end is frightening.

Erzerum is full of belching industry, a dump. A quick wander round the town reveals a sheep and cattle market and acres of ugliness. The sheep are conker-brown and noble and have round, fat tails. A fortress thing sits without on a red mountain. I think I shall leave without regret, never to return. My doss-house for £1 a night is unbelievably filthy. There is a nice boy who speaks a kind of English. My fault for being lazy; but I'm too tired to look around. To judge from the women going in and out I'm in a knocking shop.

Nearby a gloomy café run by the curator of the museum. He is gentle and kind and buys me tea. Most of his clientele are small boys dressed in jackets two sizes too large. I buy a bottle of white wine and a ticket to Kars. Tomorrow is the beginning of *Bayram*, the four-day Moslem Xmas. Most of the day is spent in the mosque by the devout, then, in the evening, beasts are slaughtered and chopped up and given away to the poor and needy. It's a great family do and seems very Christian. I fret about my scarves. Are they large enough?

Oct 8th, Erzerum to Kars

Wake, dress gingerly in the filth of my room and descend the stairs – equally filthy – to find I can't get out of the front door. A Vietnamese tourist, as surprised to see me as I am to see him, is sitting in reception. The thought of missing the bus and being stuck in Erzerum for *Bayram* is horrific. I storm upstairs to where three old Kurds, draped in blankets are padding about, coughing and spitting.

'Where is the Effendi? Bus Kars! Door not open,' I shriek in Turkish.

They roar with laughter. I scream louder and we descend in a flurry of their bundles and my rucksack to attack the door. Finally one old thing gets it open and I flee to the bus office. I'd have climbed out of first floor reception and dropped to the street if necessary.

Bayram begins with a gun going off. In the bus office we solemnly shake hands. The minibus to the bus park is half an hour late. I have been bitten. Serves me right for being so mean and lazy. Maybe it's lice? The relief of being in the bus park and not incarcerated in that awful flophouse is palpable. A shy teacher with a wife and two little girls speaks halting English. The woman's and girls' hands are stained with henna. Another polite man speaks good German. So far, in this so-called wild and fearful East of Turkey, I've met with nothing but civility and kind-ness. Most of the women and girls in the bus park are bare-headed. I think about unwrapping myself, but don't.

The Kars bus arrives three hours late and decants Kurds in flat caps. Many have holes in the seat of their pants and their jackets are tattered. They remind me of Sutherland crofters at a sheep sale. Suddenly, two men fly at one another, others join in and then the people who are trying to separate the combatants are attacked from behind, just like a John Wayne movie. One old lion gets cut around his eye but not badly; the scrimmage surges backwards and forwards and I hide behind a new protector, another teacher, who is taking a hen and its chicken to Kars –

presumably to make into festive soup. The police arrive and march the flat caps off. My enjoyment of this ridiculous scene reminds me of Peter Fleming's enjoyment of the Trans-Siberian train crash – 'very dramatic and no one was hurt.' We leave at 10am. My next door neighbour is the only other female on the bus, an emancipated thing, bare-headed, high-heeled and nail-varnished. I feel like Old Mother Riley in my scarves.

Between Erzerum and Kars the landscape plays a scale of browns: dun, bay, biscuit, beige, dull gold. A hard land, Biblical, with sentry rocks, fortresses on peaks, broad brown rivers, the whole mass hillocking away to eternity. In the few villages, houses and earth merge. Some dwellings are mud, some stone and the harvests piled on top give them the air of gingerbread houses. The grand ones have corrugated iron roofs. Geese abound. The bus is small and its route local, so people scramble on and off, mostly fierce-looking men, some of them smelly. Once we stop and wait while a man goes off behind a wall where an axe is rising and falling. The fear merchants would say it was a tourist getting chopped. He returns, loaded with meat and on we go. The smart girl, a nice boy and I share our cheese, dates, nuts and bread. Because of *Bayram*, people wear their best clothes.

Felt a headache seeping in yesterday and here it is, a five-star one. Decide to stay in luxury in Kars' Temel Palas Hotel for £3.50 a night, worth every penny. The bed is double, soft and clean, there's a private bathroom and the loo doesn't smell. I must NOT get mean like the backpackers who talk only about how little they spend. As it's *Bayram* everything is shut, shops, restaurants, museums. A small *bufet* near the buses is open, otherwise I'd have to fast till Monday. Tea, bread, cheese and olives make a fine lunch and supper is tea and a deceitful *börek* with nothing inside it. A man tells me Sadat has been murdered.

Oct 9th – 12th, Kars

I sleep well and my lice have left, even if my headache hasn't. Lying in bed I brood about being here in the back of beyond where Mongols and Selçuks and Persians galloped about killing each other. The enormous power stations or cement works billowing smoke every 300 miles suit the alarming landscape. It's Friday, the second day of *Bayram*. After very good soup at the bus *bufet* (the two boys at my table insisted on paying. What *can* I do? I wish they wouldn't, they are pitifully poor) off I go to case Kars. Even with the shops shut and few people about, the town is charming; tree-lined boulevards with horse-drawn buggies, proper 19th century ones, rattling about. Turkey is doing what Greece has done and, I suppose, what all the Middle and Far East is busy doing – scarring their land with cement. Here too, towerblocks of unspeakable ugliness rise from the cobbles of Old Kars. A quote from *The Towers of Trebizond*:

'Vulgar buildings, vulgar music, vulgar pictures, vulgar newspapers, vulgar taste, all raw and brash and ugly, but underneath is the putrescence and the softness and the falling apart like rotten cheese, in which we are the greedy mites...'

Places half empty are more fun. The eye has space for detail. A woman passes me, her skirt a rich, royal purple, her blouse orange, her waistcoat and scarf adding splashes of sun-yellow and apple-green. A Hittite dog strolls by. It is pitch black, smooth-coated, with a vast head and small feet. A wrecked car lies slumped in a side street, doors swinging off hinges; front stove in, bum stove in, sides dented. Behind the wheel sits the driver, a huge tabby. Its eyes flicker with paranoia. Agatha Christie, Pollyanna, Heidi and Harold Robbins are in the bookshops. O cultured Kars. Two small boys dog me, but I shake them off, buy beer and grapes in a *bakal* and puff in the hot sun to the Armenian citadel. Inexplicably, it is open. A young soldier, Mohammed, lets me in and shows me the museum. Heartbreaking to be Armenian and Kurdish and to have lost your country. The museum has the carved doors from Kilise Kalisi, now a mosque. There's Roman stuff, Selçuk pottery, rugs, saddlebags, coins, clothes, also Selçuk writing on a piece of stone. Feel depressed and go back to bed to read up about Kars. It's at an altitude of 1750m and was an important Armenian city from the 8th to the

11th century. Endlessly besieged by the Russians during the 19th century, Kars was finally annexed by Turkey in 1920. Ani, the old Armenian capital, was founded at the beginning of the 9th century by the Bagratides royalty, whoever they were.

Turkish buses have ear-splitting horns. Saturday is a wash-out due to headache rat gnawing at my right eye. Buzzing flies, full of blood, torment me. Sunday is better. Still feel frail so loiter and sit down a lot. An extremely gloomy church called the Church of Apostles is at the base of the Armenian citadel. Pigeons stick like burrs to its roof; and between the arches running round the square tower lurk strange, Egyptian-looking figures, twelve of them. Maybe they're apostles. Near the porch, inside a stone frame, a carved lion bites his right forepaw. Armenian church architecture is not exactly jolly.

Bayram is over and the police demand papers which I don't have and say '*yok*' to Ani. The rain is pissing down so maybe just as well. Bread wagons trot about the streets, carts drawn by perky little horses. The people here are friendly and have lovely faces. A handsome policeman asks me to go fishing with him but I decline. What a *bore* it is being a woman. The exchange rate is up from 226 to 228TL to the pound sterling.

Oct 13th, to Doğubeyazit via Igdir

A most exciting day. The minibus for Igdir looks like a very, very old van. My arrival causes consternation. The driver, an Akim Tamiroff look-alike, immediately barricades me into a window seat with several stools to stop any man sitting next to me. I am the only female among a horde of young soldiers. Then a woman with a face like an apple, broad and golden-skinned, takes the place of the stools. The air is thick with smoke, the aisle crammed with crouching Kurds and soldiers. My scarves are giving me claustrophobia, Akim Tamiroff is shouting and the bus won't start. Five men leap out and try and push it backwards. It won't go. Mrs Apple giggles. Then into reverse we lurch, slide gracefully forward and – BOOM – the engine ignites and we are away. The bus sounds like a tractor; its speed is comparable as we chug cross-country on a bad road across a biscuit-coloured plateau. Ravines, precipices, mountains, cliffs, all with lion contours, a kind of dun death. We creak round a Z-bend and are dazzled by a splash of green grass, river, fruit trees, LIFE. Russia is two inches away to the left. The engine is not a well engine and when we stop for tea (a men-only treat. Mrs Apple and I are allowed a pee but nothing else) there is much muttering and tinkering under the bonnet. Akim Tamiroff's brows are furrowed. We delay for half an hour.

From here to Igdir the scenery becomes grotesque in shape and colour, scorched and tortured by billion-year-old volcanic fury, glinting with sickly greens and blues and yellows, sprouting boils of rusty damson. I fret in case I miss the Igdir connection to Doğubeyazit but Akim Tamiroff will not be hurried. 1.15pm comes and goes. Alack and woe. At long last we arrive in a small place full of drably-dressed men and urchins who goggle as if I'd come from Mars. The good Tamiroff, now flowing with sweat, places me and my *arka torbasi* (rucksack) in the care of young soldiers who are going to Doğubeyazit. The sun is hot – bloody summer again. There are pathetic cripples, barouches galloping about and frail men in suits and caps carrying enormous cabbages. In the bus office, a Moslem puts his wife and child behind a screen and beckons me to join them. They are a nice family. He buys me tea, the wife gives me a pear and I give the child chocolate. Honour is satisfied.

The Dolmus leaves at 3pm for Doğubeyazit. We speed through a desolation of mud villages melting into mudlands, only relieved by the gold of the haystacks and the odd minaret. Mount Ararat is alarming. Its foothills are Rannoch Moor crossed with the Land of Mordor, its peak is snowcapped. I wouldn't be a bit surprised if the end of the world happened here. The shepherds and their white tents are the only pockets of life, the peacock colours of the women's clothes a defiance in the face of poverty. A family sleeps among plastic bags at the side of the road. Everywhere there are conker-brown sheep. Iran is 40 kilometres away.

Exasperated by my scarves, I've swapped them for a woolly hat pulled down over the ears which conceals these sinful extremities. Collar of jerkin turned up so impossibly seductive neck also invisible. Doğubeyazit is one long street. There's a Wild West whiff to the place. An hour after my arrival shots are fired. Everyone, including me, rushes towards the action only to be chased away by a man with a machine gun. Prudently I skip into a doorway where a thin gentleman stands smoking. 'What is it?' I enquire. He makes a jabbing gesture with his hands, the right towards the left, fingers extended, then shrugs and smiles. It is a family affair.

I am in a truly dreadful hotel called the Gul. The room has two beds and the curtains are rigid with grease. Nothing else is open. The only water comes out of a barrel in one of the smelly loos. But the view from my window makes it all worthwhile – a rose red palace on a green mountain, Isak Pasha. This 17th century Kurdish wonder is only 7 km away. Immediately decide to be up there at dawn tomorrow before the sun rises. Leaving my backpack on the only clean object in the room, the bed, I prowl the town and find an ice-cream parlour with very old cakes. Its owner, an Oliver Reed lookalike, is sunk in gloom. He is only roused from his torpor by the bêtises of two apprentices making ice-cream in a monstrous vat. They stir it with long wooden poles and giggle. I sip a beer while buslag peels off me. Later I get shouted at but the shouts aren't hostile; just 'Hullo', 'are you going to Iran?' Some men call me 'Monsieur' which is good. But one old thing leers and says I am a beautiful boy and where is my wife? Help. The moon is full; the Gul, a nightmare of yobs.

Oct 14th, visit Isak Pasha

The mosque outside my bedroom window gives its wail of what sounds like 'I hate men'. It's 4.45 am. Reluctantly I get up and dress. I'm daunted by this escapade. Very likely someone will murder me on the road to the rose red palace. Outside it's dark. A few figures pad the streets. I scuttle past them, head well down in the woolly cap, a moon hanging behind me. Just out of town is a military camp with sentries patrolling the wire. They think me a Kurd and let me pass. Figures loom, driving sheep; then for a mile or so there is no-one. To my left the fat white head of Ararat gleams in the moonlight. Ahead grey creeps along the peaks. The palace above is invisible, the moon orange, the sky a nothing, pre-dawn colour. It's cold. More figures approach with horses and dogs. I'd forgotten about dogs, those bloody great bears that guard the sheep. Better ravaged than savaged. Now I am sweating with fear.

Twenty minutes later and after a steep climb, I'm there: what a marvel, over the rainbow, the land of far beyond – Isak Pasha. It's 6.20 am and the sun still isn't up. I sit on a rock and gaze at the golden-pink palace and think myself lucky to be alive. Below foothills and the folds of gullies and a huge plain slowly come into focus; and outside the palace the ruins of a once-mighty citadel, now occupied by mud huts, grazing horses and fat-tailed sheep. Near me, overhung by willows, babbles a brook. Two shepherd boys with their flock stop by my rock. I offer them biscuits, then they and their sheep swirl on. Frozen, I am determined to stay where I am until the sun rises over the peaks behind me. What a photograph. At last, at 7.15am, it appears. That first faint warmth between the shoulder blades makes you understand primitive worship; life force, God. Half an hour later a white horse with bright bags slung over its saddle ambles up to the gate. It's followed by its owner a thin, serious man with a droopy moustache. The guardian and his steed have arrived. Together, with difficulty, we get the gate of Isak Pasha open. There is no way to describe the loveliness of this place. For an hour or so I browse. Then the guardian and I drink tea while his two dogs catch fleas and sparrows bounce in the dust. He is a dear, gentle and polite, quite horrified by my unmarried state. To cheer him, I invent a fiancé who died in 1958. The horse listens and munches hay.

It's now half past nine. Light-headed from my adventure I start down the mountain, sniffing the air, taking photographs, as dauntless as Burton. Suddenly an old man and a boy appear from nowhere and join me on the road. We're approaching the military camp, awake and buzzing with activity. Behind the wire tanks churn, squaddies drill, officers shout; war with Iran looks imminent. A jeep pulls up beside us and an officer and soldier pointing a gun get out. The officer twirls his cane. He looks unfriendly and speaks Turkish:

'Where are you going?'

'To the town.'

The Turks cringe; explain how they met me on the road. The Turkish Gestapo stares at me.

'Tourist. Isak Pasha. English. Tourist.'

I go on saying this, smiling brightly, with the occasional 'I don't understand'. The Turks are frightened.

'Where have you come from?'

'Kars.' This makes matters worse. Being near the Russian border, Kars is another huge military base. I am a spy.

'What is in your bag?'

I produce a roll of green loo paper and my wallet.

'Camera?'

I extract my Kodak Instamatic from Granny's 1890 evening bag.

'Photo. Isak Pasha. *Çok güzel.*' I wave the camera at the mountains.

Gestapo looks unconvinced. Visions of Turkish jails where they are said to force broken bottles up women's vaginas pass before my eyes. Then suddenly he shakes my hand, says 'Thank you' in good English, climbs into his jeep and roars off. Bastard. A beer in Oliver Reed's ice-cream parlour revives me.

For lunch I find a small place packed with wild-looking men with holes in their trousers. The owner sits in a box by the door. One of the Turkish phrases I've just learnt is 'Is this seat free?' There's one vacant chair at a table for two, the other occupied by a fierce man. I speak my phrase. He inclines his head. Not a smile. The *türlü*, pilaf with pine kernels and fresh bread are delicious. My companion, as silent as when I arrived, departs. When I come to pay the bear in the box I find, to my horror, that the silent and fierce one has paid for my lunch. I feel shamed by such kindness. Spent the rest of the day avoiding galloping horses and carts and looking for a bottle of white wine to celebrate not being in a Turkish jail. In one booze shop three cheerful men drinking raki open a bottle of white wine for me to try. They watch attentively while I sip it. It is AWFUL.

'*Sirke*,' I say and shake my head. *Sirke* is Turkish for vinegar. Gloomily they offer me raki. I decline politely and leave.

Moslem loos don't have paper but a water spout – most hygienic. I wonder though about this bottom-washing. Every bus I've been on is full of sneezing Turks. My alarm is set for 4am. Tomorrow I go south, to Van via Agri. Syria will be just over the horizon.

Likos, 2004

A Christmas Day like April but I was sick at heart. All the beauty about me – sea, sky, flowers, orchards, terraces – might as well have been Dagenham. A fog of gloom; and not all the kindness of friends (mercifully unaware of my state), slices of turkey and parcels of cake could blow it away. That's what comes of reading old diaries – too much recherche du temps perdu *– and getting letters from home. Trying to teach Max not to chase cars didn't improve matters. Reproachful brown eyes told me I was unfeeling and unkind and that a loving companion should not be whacked with a brolly for trying to kill a motorbike. The cat was equally reproachful. What was my bed there for but to be enjoyed?*

A few Greeks look after their animals, many do not. Children torment kittens, neglect puppies. Often poison is put down on purpose. An exception is a woman in Miti with two overfed, tail-less cats. A stub is all these sofas possess. The current myth is that the original cat had its tail run over by a lorry, then miraculously bred other tail-less ones –rather in the way that ikons fly up cliffs. Likos seems a long way from the Isle of Man. Another exception is a fisherman in Psara. Every morning he mends his nets under the pine trees on the quayside, a black cat beside him. The cat sits very close, almost touching the man who works with his legs straight out in front of him, like all fishermen do. The cat is called the Arab.

What cured my gloom was a downpour. It went on all day, flooded the streets and blotted out most of the sea and sky. Likos became home, Scotland, as grey and rainswept as Mull in February. Quantities of water fell through the paneless window into my room, forcing me to wash the floor. The cat watched. It has a baleful eye. In Van in the East of Turkey there are cats with one blue eye and one yellow eye...

Chapter Eight

Van – the church on the lake – journey with Dog and Duck
1981

Oct 15th, journey to Van via Agri

Getting up at 4am is no problem. Shouts, spittings, telly and tramping feet kept me awake all night. The TAC bus office is run – as are so many things in Turkey – by two weary small boys. We leave at 5.20, going west along a straight, rubbly road. The sky is dark and full of rain. Both countryside and passengers are sunk in gloom. Outside, the brown vastness is peppered with gold stubble. Brown sheep, brown villages. If I stayed any longer in the East of Turkey, I'd never wear café-au-lait or mushroom or cream or dark brown or any of those fashionable colours EVER AGAIN. Behind the driver in my favourite position I gaze, bleary-eyed, out of the window, watching a small figure leaping across an eternity of horizon. The speck waves as it leaps but no one notices. Just in time I pull myself together and poke the driver. We stop. A man clambers in to sit beside me, clutching an object tied up in newspaper. He has brown, worried eyes, thick brown hair, a brown suit and clean finger nails. At first he seems a nudger – pressing my leg, jabbing his elbow into my eye, pumping my bosom, blowing smoke up my nose. After a bit, I realise he isn't. He's not used to buses and he's fretting about his parcel which rolls about the floor. Finally, exasperated, I wedge it between my legs.

Just outside Agri there's a roadblock. Plain-clothes bruisers, leather-jacketed and holding machine guns motion us out of the bus. It's 7am. A quick look at my passport and I'm politely waved back in. Everyone else is searched and so is the bus. I watch in horror as my brown man's parcel is ripped open and it and him taken away. Was it a bomb, a transmitter? Damn my useless Turkish and God help him. Agri bus station is full of liars. One office says there is a bus at 1pm but no bus at 8am as I had been told. The second office, a different company, sells me a ticket for a 10am bus so I decide to while away the time drinking soup. Then I see yet another office and a dreadful suspicion seizes me. As I thought. *This* is the company with a bus at 8am. I rush back to the second office who sold me the ticket for the 10am bus. Unrepentant and unsurprised they hand me back my 350TL and I fly back to the third office. It is now 7.45am. The office is full of men. I demand a ticket to Van:

'All full. No ticket. Tomorrow.'

I stand my ground, invent a flight at Van and a sick mother. I appeal to the driver. They consider me.

'OK, but no seat. Standing.'

'OK.'

For five minutes nothing happens. The men talk and the ticket dispenser carefully fills in the columns on his form. Then a man takes my arm. He has Ghengis Khan eyes.

'No good today, tomorrow.'

'No good tomorrow, today,' I reply obstinately. I am becoming very Turkish. I end up sitting on the back seat of the 8am bus to Van.

More tawny country; bluffs of rock like the heads of hippopotami sweeping down into escarpments. Farther on the land is scabbed with rock. A dun nothingness going nowhere. The towns are poor; in the villages I notice cones like peat stacks with lozenges on the outside.

Suphan Dagi towers, snow-capped. Coming into Van, we pass an ancient, Walt Disney-like castle on a bluff, massive and extending along the ridge. My nose is blocked with smoke – all Turks smoke the whole time – and I'm exhausted. Two shoe-shine boys lead me to the Bayram Hotel which is clean and pleasant. I sleep. Wake to wash, drink wine and write. Then sleep again.

Oct 16th, Van

Electricity cuts, Atatürk parks, the woo and wah of Turkish love songs, *Ullo, OK, Ingleesh, toureest, Monsieur* and *What is your name* are part of life's rich pattern in the East of Turkey. Now for Van. Van is the largest closed 'basin' in Anatolia. Van is the biggest pile of cabbages in the world, 300 or more. Van is the Solen Restaurant. Van is a thousand and one breakfast shops. They serve sesame, honey, yoghurt, herb cheese, straight cheese, olives, eggs, *ayran*, hot milk, chocolate, fresh hot bread and parsley butter. Van is snowcapped peaks behind and across the lake. Van is Scotland. Much of East Turkey looks like bits of Sutherland going towards the West. Van is white cats, but so far the ones I've seen have had eyes the same colour. Van is the Bayram Hotel. I started off in Room 214, but when I woke up and tried to shut the window the pane of glass fell off its frame. Turkish windows are made to be looked through, not opened. So I moved, without consulting anyone, into 216. I moved the carpet, the light bulb and a hat-stand. They must think me deranged. I've put up my washing line again. The central heating pipes to which one end is attached will probably fall off the wall.

Alas, Van will soon be towerblocks. Behind the town, among the shining poplars, orchards and lanes with their cool mud houses rise the dreaded concrete tenements. They are blue, rust and yellow. I hate reinforced concrete so much I may devote the rest of my life to destroying it. Van is prosperous. I like it. My leaflet from the tourist office, some sheets of typewritten blurb, tell me that I'm in one of the oldest and most important centres of civilisation with settlements dating back to 7,000 BC. The first people to set up a state were the Hurricanes in 2,000 BC, followed by Urartus in 900-600 BC, then Medes and Persians and Alexander the Great, ending up centuries later in the 11th century with the Selçuks. Then Ottomans, Armenians, Russians…The most famous

Armenian church in the world is on Aktamar Island in the middle of Lake Van. That's where I'm going tomorrow. Turkish lorries are lovely. They are hand painted with rural scenes and flaunt great eyes to keep off the Evil One. Most have *Maşallah* lettered on their bonnets. I seem to be the only foreigner in the East of Turkey.

The Van fortress, Walt Disney in mud, is four miles from town. It's a beautiful day. I sun myself in its fortifications, looking down on the lake, the green meadows and marshes, forests of poplar and silver birch. In the distance snowy peaks glitter. Sardur the First, an Urartian, built this enormity in 825 BC. A good place to spend an afternoon. The road back to town runs through a romantic study of 18th century rural life. Toddlers in brightly coloured dresses tumble on the greensward. Geese, ducks and turkeys waddle and puddle. Sheep graze, three furry dogs lie asleep. Granny is doing her washing in a stream and telling little ones a story at the same time. Despite the lack of modern amenities everything is clean including the children. Smoke curls from the mud house in its orchards. Next time I come, which I won't, there'll be housing estates with inadequate sewage systems. No orchards. Hail progress.

Oct 17th, Aktamar Adasi, the church on the island

There's a Dolmus to Aktamar at 8.15am. I get up at 5.45am so as not to hurry – I HATE hurrying – breakfast on hot milk, fresh bread and herb cheese and go to the stop. 8.15am comes and goes and five minutes later a man says no Dolmus. Very Turkish. However, the Gods are with me. There's a Van Gölü express bus for Ankara leaving at 8.30am. I rush to the *garaz*, look agitated and helpless and within minutes am ensconced on a camp stool beside the driver. He is a melancholic in a well cut suit. Off we go along the lake. It's breathtakingly lovely, as are the meadows, hills and snowcaps surrounding it. How the poplars shimmer. *Nisan* is Turkish for April and then, they say, the grass round Lake Van is knee-deep. On this October morning an Alpine sun burns; air, sky, water are clean and clear, coots dive and the wild duck fly. *Haziran* is June and *Aralik* December. *Haziran* and

Aralik: they sound like a Persian Romeo and Juliet.

We cover the 50 kilometres to Aktamar in 40 minutes. The express drops me and booms off. Silence. There is the island in the lake. A low white building up a slope from the road – a restaurant – is the only visible dwelling. The inmates are excited by my arrival. The church? The boat? Certainly. First we must drink tea. Çihan, a Kurd, is 21 and has run the restaurant for 10 years. Rashid, smiley and long-nosed, is the superintendent of the camping site – three white triangular corrugated iron huts, grass and a spotless beach. Two younger boys cook. It is now 9.15am. We drink four cups of tea, during the fourth of which I write a letter for Çihan to a Rupert in England who slept on the roof. The boat is at Gevaş, seven kilometres back down the road towards Van. Çihan, Rashid and I start walking, get a lift with a Dodge truck and arrive at Gevaş to find no boat and no captain. I am entranced to see that Turkish telephones wind up like the ones in pre-war American movies.

'Oh Kapitan,' sighs Çihan. 'Never mind, tomorrow.'

'Tomorrow,' I echo, fatalist in the hands of Allah. We start walking the seven kilometres back but get two lifts, one with a tractor and one with a car full of happy men eating walnuts. It is now 11.15am. The sun is hot. The caretaker of the church, a quiet man called Unuz, joins us in a courtyard outside the restaurant. The time, half-timeness, passes pleasantly, cracking walnuts and drinking beer and communicating in fractured Turkish. Suddenly, without warning, food arrives: a spicy vegetable and meat dish, a salad of hot peppers, onions and tomatoes, rice and bread. I am commanded to eat. Meekly I obey. To my horror, these endearing boys won't let me pay for anything – teas, beers, lunch, not a sausage. Oh you impossible Turks!

'Unuz is Turk,' says Çihan with a broad smile. 'I am Kurd. Turks no good.'

At 1pm I give up all thought of the church on the island and get

111

a lift to Gevaş with a passing tea-drinker. From there a bus or taxi will take me back to Van. Çihan and Unuz come too. As we approach the garaz where the wind-up phone is, Çihan gives a cry and we all pile out. *There* is the captain! The jaunt to the island is on again.

I don't think I've ever spent such a peripatetic day. Unuz and I wait by a broken jetty while the captain and Çihan paddle what looks like an old bath to the motor-boat. Çihan shows off and nearly capsizes the tub. 'Tarzan,' I joke.

Unuz smiles. '*Little* Tarzan.' Then he adds thoughtfully (he is a thoughtful man): 'Little Tarzan drinks an awful lot of raki.'

The motorboat coughs alongside. The captain is the most villainous-looking fellow. Off we go, the four of us, across the unruffled blue of the lake to the island.

Aktamar Adasi, set among almond trees, is the most extraordinary and moving experience. The church was built in 915-921 AD by the Armenian king Gagik and is acknowledged to be among the finest specimens of Gregorian architecture. My leaflet says it is a monastery. The contrast in mood between inside and outside is striking; the interior frescos of saints and apostles – largely washed out with only patches of blue left – are grave as bank managers, the exterior carvings quite the opposite, funny, wild, full of character. These marvellous reliefs illustrate the legends of Adam and Eve, Jonah, David and Goliath, the inevitable George pronging the Dragon. There are gargoyles, birds, animals. Armenian history, the little I know of it, is tragic. Many millions were slaughtered by the Turks in this century alone. No fun being a buffer state between the Moslems and Christian Byzantium. The captain dozes and smokes in the shade of a tree while the rest of us scramble through parched grass to the rocks at the top of the island. There's a good feeling here, peaceful, benevolent. Maybe the ghosts weren't slaughtered or tormented. I feel tearful when we leave. On the way back the captain – who is a lamb in wolf's clothing – feeds me almonds. He has also

112

picked a basket of delicious wild berries.

Now it's 3.30 pm. I seem to have been up for a week and we're back at the restaurant. At least I was allowed to pay for the boat. The smallest boy tries to make me a present of a pigeon he's caught. I drink more tea, make my thanks and descend to the road to wait for a bus or car to flag down. Is it madness to hitch-hike in the East of Turkey? Silence. Nothing. I sit on a stump and ruminate. Then I see a car and, flinging caution to the wind, flag it down. The two men inside clearly think me an oddity but take me to Gevaş. As we round the corner to the village centre, a Dolmus approaches.

'Van?' I squeak.

The men nod. We stop. They wave. The Dolmus stops. How lucky can you be?

The finale to this lovely day is pure theatre. The Dolmus is full of young Turks who speak French and think I'm a man. Thanks to my woolly hat, I don't sit in demure silence beside another woman but play Georges Sand to a backseat audience of charming young men. They chaff me: 'Monsieur, you are wearing a Kurd hat!'

Then there are more jokes about Kurds and Turks and how frightful Kurdish music is. If I bound my bosom and wore a false moustache I might get into Mecca.

The sun is aslant in the late afternoon and women are doing their washing by the lake. I buy a bottle of Buzbag and sit in my hotel room sipping it, full of happiness from the day and its charm and the adventure. This is travel. This is life. A mysterious man knocks at the door and gives me tea. He departs, only to return in half an hour with more tea. Dutifully I drink it. Has he got the wrong room number? I find out later that he's the chambermaid. I try to pay him but am rebuffed. Unable to sleep I feel angry about the fear people spread. Don't walk in New York, take a gun to Van, a woman on her own can't travel in Turkey. This fear, this suspicion is our 20th century malaise. How its poison infects. In this poverty-stricken and wild land I have met nothing but the most exquisite generosity, courtesy and kindness. As to the dirt, yes, there is the dirt of poverty, but I prefer that to the middle class filth of Athens, the smeared loo paper in the Salamis valley, Pasalimani full of raw sewage from millionaires' gin palaces.

Oct 18th, journey to Diyarbakir with Dog and Duck

I'm at last getting the hang of the different bus companies. They're in competition with one another so of course one won't tell you when another's bus goes. My bus to Diyarbakir is bright orange and very new. When I ask the bus driver if he would make a brief stop at the Aktamar Restaurant, he beams and says fine. It is some consolation to me to give Çihan and his friends *real* coffee from Athens and a thank you note in terrible Turkish. We are three women on the bus, the other two Turkish and great friends. Duck sits beside me. She has a headache, a bad heart and her feet hurt. Dog, with a labrador face, sits behind. The day is blue and brilliant, the sky full of clouds throwing shadows on the hills.

Along the lake, into the hills and down again, stopping for tea and a pee in Biltis. The colours of the turning spruce are glorious. Dog passes Duck and me a sinewy *börek* with wild greens inside, not nice but sustaining. The three of us have become friends and I, peculiar English thing, am to be protected. Across the aisle an old boy with a white beard and little brown cap smokes and chews gum at the same time. He looks like James Robertson Justice. We're leaving Scotland and the Peloponnese for drier lands. Next stop is Veysel Karani, a collection of low huts, shops, a mosque and a hygienic Tourist Hotel. It is noon, uncomfortably hot and I hate my woolly hat. Dog and Duck motion me to follow them and off we bustle across narrow streets piled with fruit and bread. The smell of frying meats and spices torment my nose. Where on earth are we going? We arrive at the mosque. Of course. The English get off a bus to drink tea, the Turks to go to

114

the mosque. There are loos in a kind of dairy where almond-eyed women are washing. I guard the bags while Dog and Duck enter. They emerge, disgusted, to say the water for washing has run out. We rush to the central fountain in the mosque courtyard where men are washing, scoop up water in a plastic container and retire behind a wall. Black cooking pots bubble nearby. My friends remove their tights, wash their feet, arms, hands and faces and enter the mosque, leaving me, trusty alsatian of the handbags, as guard. After prayers, we sit together on small stools with criss-cross leather thongs and drink tea. They are such nice women.

The countryside has become Arizona and the road is terrible. It gets hotter and hotter. Duck plunges into her crackly bag and gives Dog and me two highly-spiced, herby meat balls wrapped in limp pitta. A cake follows. I produce some cheese. On we munch. A road block delays us and the bus fills with soldiers with machine guns who examine identity cards and search luggage. This part of the country is full of flocks and shepherds and their tents. The white tents are marquee-shaped, open at the front and strung across poles, capacious and dishevelled. There are lorries full of people, children, animals, straw, fodder, quilts and faggots – all raggle taggle. Here in the south-east are the trousers with great pouches at the back, waiting to receive the second coming of the Prophet. Eternities of dark brown plough and stubble float past, reminding me of that painter who does plough and bare, twiggy elms. Mountains loom sixty miles to our right. At 4pm we approach a walled town on a hill – Diyarbakir.

Likos, 2004

The year died on a whispering sea and still night. In Miti's main square where fairy lights link the giant carob and jacaranda and acacias the dancing went on till dawn. Next morning the town was silent, the wings of the hangover angel widely spread. An odd bell rang. Then, at 11am sharp, the Town Hall cassette started up – Jingle Bells, Hark the Herald, O Du Fröhliche and Greensleeves among others. Slowly the town woke. By midday everyone was treating everyone else and I was swept off to have lunch with a friend and his wife. They are hospitable here. Kindness to the stranger is still an obligation.

Now it's the third day of 2005. Will it be as eventful and as exhausting as 2004? My Greek is improving – although misunderstandings still occur. 'Come and spend New Year's evening with Thanassi and me,' said Popi in the harbour. It was the evening before New Year's Eve. 'I can't,' I replied. 'I shall be in New Zealand.' Popi is very polite so she neither fell about nor shrieked nor asked me if I had gone off my head. I'd thought she meant in a year's time. She and her husband have been so kind to me; as has the other dark-haired Popi down the road and Polyxeni in the evening taverna. Both Popis are pretty women in their forties, Polyxeni 27. All work from morning to night and take great pride in their family and taverna; cooking, cleaning, shopping, serving, washing up and generally running the business. Harbour Popi is the best cook. Styles are very different. The harbour taverna is bigger, does a roaring trade with summer groups but is quiet in winter apart from the odd formal dinner. The other two cater for the same gang of locals, all men, Popi doing lunch and Polyxeni supper. They keep an eye on one another.

The terraces above the town are green. The other day I found some old-fashioned moss roses blooming beside a ruin – planted long ago when people brought up families on the land and had vines and made wine. My Swiss Army knife was in my pocket so I cut a few blooms for my room. I'm sure the ghosts won't mind. This is my third Swiss Army knife. The first I gave to Adonis in the Piraeus, the second to a wonderful man who took me up a Turkish mountain in the middle of the night. I shall never forget the tumbled glories of Antiochus the First, high on the summit of Nemrut Dagh...

Chapter Nine

Diyarbakir – Adiyaman – climbing Nemrut Dagh

1981

Oct 19th, Diyarbakir

In Van I froze and wore my woolly hat in bed. The washing didn't dry. Last night in Diyarbakir I sat out on the balcony at 9.45pm in my pyjamas, already bitten on the ankle by a mosquito. They should be hibernating by now. The Hotel Malkoc in a quiet alley off a busy street is excellent. I have a spotless room, my own bathroom, loo and shower with hot water and a balcony – all for 350TL per night. Downstairs is a lounge of clucking Turks watching telly. I read a bit of one man's newspaper over his shoulders: 'something Papandreou, something coalition.' I wish my Turkish was better. I wish Sadat was alive.

This is the best town yet – a truly working, bustling, labyrinthine, artisan place. All the young women are bareheaded. The market is a marvel; harness shops with pom-poms and bright beads, saddlebags, enormous copper pots, waterfalls of bootlaces, shoes sprouting and trailing like Russian vine from shack wall and ceiling. The little ways are dark and covered, their wares a jumble of spices, tobacco, jackets, caps. Diyarbakir is Middle Eastern in feel, many of its men wearing turbans or jellabahs. Syria lies 80 miles to the South. Blacksmiths hammer, little boys skip by with unleavened loaves balanced on their heads; teapots, basins, pots, pans and colossal sieves spill into the alleyways.

The meat, fruit and vegetable market is a cornucopia. Sometimes the little boys stare so much they bang into lampposts and fall off kerbs. I laughed at one who fell off a kerb. He grinned broadly which was nice of him. Turkish Persil is called *Tursil!* There are shrouded beggars. Perhaps they are lepers? I shout '*Var var*' at a little girl who begs insistently and follows me tugging my sleeve.

Then I feel awful. I could have given her some money. Having a hangover from drinking a bottle of red wine is no excuse. I am a nasty person.

The Tourist Information Office has no information that I can understand – nothing in English, one guide with the French section torn out and a leaflet in Turkish issued by the Diyarbakir Watermelon Festival. Struggling with this, I deduce that the town's basalt walls were built by that arch-builder Constantine. The information officer is distressed and rushes upstairs to return with an exquisite map of the walled town. Alas, it is a map for gnats and I don't have a magnifying glass. I adore Diyarbakir and so too, it seems, did Atatürk. He had a country retreat here, a *köskü*. The Atatürk Museum looks shut but I check with the guard, a soldier who is having his shoes cleaned: 'Yes, shut,' he says curtly. Shrugging, I turn away and chat to a woman from Van. We gaze from the Byzantine walls. 'Oh Van, beautiful Van,' she sighs. Then the guard beckons and announces that the museum is open. Presumably having clean boots changed his mind. What an incredibly attractive man Atatürk was. The photographs are terrific. Especially interesting is a Turkish Picture Post of 1936 covering Edward VIII's visit to Istanbul. The curator, another soldier, is shy and kind and lets me sit for an hour copying information about rock chapels in Göreme out of an English Guide written by Germans. One riveting detail re. rabbit meat. Apparently in olden times, rabbit was eaten to heighten sexual urges and beautify the body and skin. Pliny, that old know-all, mentions its erotic effect. And during the 7th century the church banned it!

The *Kultur Müze* is a hoot. Set back from a cobbled alley, in a shady courtyard with a splashing fountain, it has four attendants. As I enter the courtyard one approaches. The door to the museum is open.

'Is it open?'

Together we climb the steps. There is nothing inside.

119

'Next year?' I ask.

'Yes, next year.' The attendant's eyes are liquid with hope.

This town has wonderful soup. I lunch among Arabs in a spotless café on soup and a side dish of onion salad dusted with red spice. A smiling boy brings a finger bowl. In the later afternoon, head cleared by Greek aspirin and a doze, I stroll through the town walls and take the road to *Atatürk's Köskü*. It's an attractive 1930s house, set on a hill among avenues of acacias, terraces, steps and flowerbeds. The surrounding meadows are full of trees; there's a river running through the valley. Gardeners beaver. In the distance the walls of Diyarbakir jigsaw against the sky. Naturally, the house is shut. It's going to be Thessaloniki all over again. However, when I tell the caretaker and his wife that I write children's books they let me in. It seems to have its advantages, writing books for children. In Greece it turns you into the BVM crossed with the director of the LSE. In Turkey, it picks locks. Atatürk was a great dandy. His clothes are divine. So is an escritoire-type piece with a mirror where he shaved. Did he die of drink, I wonder? And how on earth did he haul Turkey hundreds of years forward in just 20 years? As I leave, top brass military with Saudi Arabians in tow arrive, all army except for a white admiral. A general with a tired face talks while the others listen. The bodyguards' jackets bulge. The chauffeurs polish their bonnets. It is exactly like a TV play.

Oct 20th, Diyarbakir to Adiyaman

After an idle morning – drinking tea among the murmuring Turks and sighing pines – I reluctantly leave this charming town. Next stop Adiyaman. It's hot again. The bus is not well. First we're held up by an accident. Then we break down which enrages the traffic which has just got past the accident. An hour's delay. A German girl, a bore, keeps talking to me but I tell her I throw up if I talk in buses. Bactrian camels are stalking about; the peaty-brown land, a monstrous expanse of Harris tweed rolls away to the edge of the world. The sun sets. Once more we break down. Harput Tur (the bus company) should be called Kaput Tur. The

German dimwit doesn't get the joke. We cross the Euphrates in the dark, exciting me with thoughts of Alexander the Great and reach Adiyaman at 8pm. My feet are boiling.

Oct 21st, Adiyaman

Adiyaman, like Van, is a building site, thick with the dust from half-constructed towerblocks and unfinished tarmac. The new building is crude, Turkish scaffolding infinitely preferable to the embryos it encases. The old town is charming. My hotel, the Ugur, has a nice young manager and no yobs. There is a pretty quilt on my bed. By noon, I'm convinced of four things: Adiyaman has the best saddler's shop in the whole of Turkey – I'm greatly tempted to buy the contents; it has the nicest people; gentle, welcoming and smiley; the food is terrible; and the tourist office grand, modern and wholly ineffectual.

A bespectacled fatling called Mechmet speaks perfect English. He is vague about transport to the summit of Nemrut Dagh (which I keep wanting to call Pandit Nehru). The director speaks perfect French and is equally vague. Neither can find an English leaflet but both invite me to tea at 3pm in this palace of non-information. Their suits are beautifully cut. Enfin. I shall stay stuffing myself with tea until these exquisites get their act together. There is no wine in Adiyaman. '*Yok*,' said a shocked grocer. I'm going to have trouble with people paying for me again. The breakfast shop treated me to hot milk, tea and a packet of cigarettes and a boy insisted on buying me grapes.

The tourist office, mortified by my morning visit, has flown into action by afternoon. There's a Dolmus on some days to the summit but it's pricey. Or I can go to Eski Kahta and take a mule. I *must* be up there at dawn. Two Aussies in Istanbul said it was an unforgettable experience. Fatling and French also tell me that Atatürk was schizophrenic and died of meningitis and present me, to my astonishment, with a rather good leaflet in English. I am becoming fond of Turks. It's a good thing I'm middle-aged and past my prime.

Nemrut Dagh is called a 'sanctuary' but really it's a monument to megalomania. Built on the summit of one of the Anti-Taurus mountains (altitude 2300m) in the first century BC by a young Commene king called Antiochus, this shrine is for both his and the Gods' glory. Not a modest fellow, Antiochus. He thought himself descended from Darius, the Persian king, on one side and Alexander on the other. The sanctuary is a tumulus 50m high which once had gigantic statues at its foot. My leaflet says Antiochus is probably lying inside this folly – 'I, Antiochus, have had this monument erected to my own glory and that of the Gods' – but so far all attempts to get into the funerary chamber have been fruitless. I fancy a night mule from Eski Kahta. Sounds mad. Later I lie on my bed during an electricity cut and ruminate. The night is full of stars, pigeons coo outside my window and the oleander still flowers. The cry of '*ayran salep, ayran salep!*' floats up from the street, accompanied by jingling of the mugs. Please God, don't let me get the curse until after the mule.

Oct 22nd, Adiyaman to Kahta and then to Eski Kahta

It's hot. Jingle, jingle, jingle go the horses in the street and the *ayran salep* sellers. Men sit about. How lazy they are.

'No-one wants to work here,' says an architect I met at breakfast. 'It drives me mad. They come for one day, then don't turn up for the next week. Even when they have no money to buy food they don't want to work.'

'Sounds like the Brits,' I said through my hot *börek*. 'They can't cook either.'

His face brightened.

'You must go to Gazientep. I come from there. It's famous for its food.'

He buys my breakfast and departs.

122

There are young boys staying at the hotel, probably at school or studying. On their day off, they play backgammon on their beds and drink tea. Shyly they scuttle past. Zealously I flush away their turds. Why don't Turkish men pull plugs? Impressions of Turkey so far:

Van – the best breakfasts and the church on the island.

Diyarbakir – the best food.

Erzerum and Doğubeyazit – the filthiest hotels and the best palace.

Adiyaman – the best saddler's shop and yoghurt. As to the mountain...?

Trabzon – the church and monastery in the mountains.

And *everywhere*, the most heart-warming kindness to the stranger; everywhere wonderful countryside of all kinds, from lush to beige wastes; and everywhere I go postcards of Atatürk. My collection is growing.

Fatling has written a letter to the keeper of the castle at Eski Kahta, requesting a mule and driver to convey me aloft to the hubris of Antiochus. In some trepidation I catch the afternoon minibus to Kahta, armed with a Greek supermarket bag containing flannel, soap, a toothbrush, bread, a bottle of water and an extra thick sweater. The bus is hot and full of flies. I don't like Kahta or the people. Their faces are squinting, twisted; they tell me many lies.

'There is no Dolmus to Eski Kahta. It has left.'

'How much is a taxi?'

'2,500 TL.' They are sneering, mannerless.

'OK. I shall return to Adiyaman.'

As I walk back to the Dolmus I think I came in, a small dark man takes me by the arm. '*Yok,*' he says. There is always a *deus ex machina* in Turkey who appears at fortuitous moments and says '*yok*'. He hails the red Dolmus crammed with people which is inching out from the back of the buspark. Miracle of miracles, it's going to Eski Kahta and I can *just* be squeezed in. The fare is 100TL for 26 kilometres. 'Taxi 200 TL!' yells a squinting oaf. Too late. Bugger off. On the back seat I find a second miracle sitting beside me – Habib, wearing a wellcut suit and speaking Oxford English.

We bounce over dust and potholes into a vast and fairytale country passing a Commene tumulus called Black Bird Hill named after the eagle on top of one column. A headless lion sits on another. Habib chats away. He's an economic planner working in Ankara and back here for a holiday with his Istanbuliot schoolgirl wife of three weeks. He hates Ankara; loves his village, Eski Kahta. A nervous man, very polite. I show him Fatling's note to the keeper of the castle.

'Demiral is a tour group man. I shouldn't go to him. (A man who spoke German on the Dolmus from Adiyaman to Kahta had said Demiral was a capitalist shit.) I'll take you to the headman of the village.'

We cross a magnificent Roman bridge, three of its four columns still standing. The land glows pink in the sunset and ahead, rearing up from gullies and foothills to its rose red cone, Nemrut Dagh catches the light. I like Habib:

'I was in Germany but I had to leave. I couldn't adapt to Western life. I got headaches…' He looks concerned. 'Do you have much trouble with Turkish men?'

Yasin beside me gets out at nowhere. 'Good morning,' he says and vanishes.

124

'He means goodbye,' says Habib quickly.

'I know. I do it all the time in Turkish.' He has a sweet smile, Habib.

It's dark when we arrive at Eski Kahta, a jumble of wooden houses under cliffs topped by a ruin. Oh God, whatever next?

The muchta's house is on stilts. Habib leads me up a thick pole ladder to a platform where the open doorway shows a room lit by oil lamps. Two men in baggy prophet trousers, jackets and caps sit smoking cross-legged on the floor. The muchta is tall and thin with a humorous face and sharp eye. Habib introduces me, then says 'Take off your shoes, goodbye, see you tomorrow,' and vanishes. The doorway is dark. It takes me ages to get my boots off. Bootless at last, I'm motioned to the divan and haltingly explain what I want.

'Why not the jeep, the minibus?'

They obviously think I'm mad.

'I like mules. Horses.' I make clopping noises with my tongue. The men consider me in silence. A heap of small children are rolling about on the carpet. The oldest boy, about 14, stares. Then he and the men whisper together.

The room glows with carpets and bright cushions heaped against one wall. Just inside the door stands a stone sink. At the other end of the room is the divan on which I'm sitting, raised, carpeted and cushioned. More carpets hang on the walls – some lovely, some awful – also embroideries. A log cabin ceiling above and the mule stamping below. Everything is spotless. After half an hour the muchta's wife, much younger than him, brings food for me and the men: three bowls of vegetable stew, three bowls of yoghurt and unleavened bread. Cross-legged on the carpet, we eat round the tray watched by the woman and the children. All those eyes. I try to eat as little as possible without offending, knowing full well that I'm probably eating someone's supper. When bowls of water are brought for handwashing I realise my gaffe on arrival. Then I dipped my fingers in the bowl I was brought. Though surprised they produced a towel. Of course. That water was to drink, not wash in.

7pm and teatime. Haziz, the oldest boy, makes the tea and I am urged to swallow five cups. Again, the tea is only for the men and me. The woman, grimacing with toothache poor thing, brings white beaded scarves to be admired – her own work – then arranges me in one. This proves an instant icebreaker. The children giggle and the men smile. Now I am a mad Turk instead of a mad tourist. Head swathed, I'm even allowed to help with the evening's work – shelling beans. We sit round the tray of dried pods, the family murmuring softly. With something to do I feel at ease. Haziz is going to take me up the mountain. We are to start at one in the morning.

I'm taken to the loo – the nicest ever – a stone cone with an earth floor and a hole fringed by three large stones. Again spotless. Then the woman helps me into some loose cotton pyjamas and tucks me up on the divan. I have a thick quilt and a bolster made of concrete. Turkish pillows are dire. The family continues to crack bean pods; lulled by this and the muchta's 'tch' noises made with a thick, juicy tongue and his 'wallas' (What *does* 'walla' mean?), I drift off to sleep. At some point I turn over and notice that the lamp has been turned down and someone is asleep on the floor. The woman wakes me at one. There has been a change of plan. The muchta, not his son, is going to take me up the mountain; hence his sleeping on the floor so as not to wake the rest of the family. We drink water, eat a biscuit and set off.

Riding a mule after nine years out of the saddle is a bad experience. The mule, a surly creature, regards our nocturnal excursion with mule-like contempt. It doesn't have much time for me either. Riding bareback on blankets, saddlebags on each side, I lurch and bounce as it negotiates the stony track. We cross a rushing river, climb a cliff. This is *not* a sure-footed mule. I swear from

126

time to time and the quiet figure leading the beast smokes and occasionally points out a landmark in unintelligible Turkish. The track gets rougher and rougher, the gradient steeper. The sky is full of stars. Much to my relief at 3am the mule breaks down. It has cast a shoe. Slipping off its back I fall flat on my face, my legs floundering bladders. I once felt the same after energetic sex when I hadn't done it for months.

We're in a minuscule village. A figure rises genie-like from a hole in a roof and it and the muchta converse. The mule, head in bag, looks sardonic. 'Muley kaput,' says the muchta in his fractured German. He picks up my plastic bag and waves it hopefully in the direction of the Eski Kahta. 'No. *Now* with feet,' I reply firmly. We leave the mule with the genie and climb into the night.

At first the terrain is easy, a smooth path up a sloping gully. I follow the slender figure with the torch and we make good time. After an hour we rest. The muchta, yawning hugely, tries to persuade me to go back to the genie's village. '*Yok*. Nemrut. *Günlish* (dawn)!' He shrugs and on we go. The next hour from 4-5am is sheer hell. At one point, falling flat on my face halfway up a precipice, heart banging, legs aching, I could have lain down among the scorpions and rocks and died. Only the thought of Dilys Powell and her ghastly trek in Crete kept me going. If a tiny, frail thing like her can, so can I. The muchta's torch lights his way but not mine. How awful if I roll down this bloody precipice and have to climb up it again. At 5.15am we reach the *yol*, the road. I have never loved a road more. '*Araba*,' says the muchta. 'Very nice *araba*.'

What he means is let's sit down and wait for the dawn at *araba* which is the first summit. Not on your nelly, muchta mine. The sky is lightening behind a sliver of moon. We climb on passing two vans parked on the road. The muchta hums to himself. I like him very much. I wish I spoke Turkish.

At 5.45 we're on the last bit, the side of Nemrut's pink cone. Foot after foot, don't look up, keep going. Then, suddenly, following a track round the cone, we're there – among the fallen heads and mad magnificence of the summit. Hundreds of people must have watched the sky lighten from this eagle's sanctuary. Now I feel their awe. And coming on foot through the starry night, I've paid the mountain the tribute it asks, perhaps demands of some. Dear muchta. We share our breakfast. 'Oh, I am so empty!' he exclaims. The dawn arrives and with it another miracle in the shape of an Englishman and a Frenchman walking down into the Gods, as surprised to see us as we are to see them. Martin works in Iraq and Jean is from Paris. One of the vans we passed on the road is theirs. They can take me back to Kahta and have clearly been sent by Apollo. The muchta has already told me that no Dolmus runs today.

Time stops on the summit of Nemrut Dagh among the fallen columns and tumbled heads of Apollo, Zeus, Tyche and the eagle. Antiochus too is there, along with some bas-reliefs of his Persian and Macedonian ancestors. Only a madman could have made this magic. After dawn the sunrise, turning pink to gold. Below, a country of dragons and ogres, daring deeds and sorrowing kings. All hopeless romantics should come here.

It's time for the muchta to return to his mule and village. We embrace and I give him 2,000TL, my Swiss Army knife and Granny's evening bag for his wife. I'm the only person I know who keeps a camera in an evening bag. What a nice man. It's a hot morning and bumpy road from Nemrut to Eski Kahta. More goodies here: a wonderful stele with a relief of the God Mithras and another of Hercules greeting a Commene king. They used to hurl unfortunates, their hands bound, off a cliff by the castle. Martin and Jean are delightful. We stop at the Roman bridge to buy grapes and eat them among sleepy old men. Am mortified that I've only got 100TL for the Dolmus from Kahta to Adiyaman so can't contribute to the minibus's petrol fund. By early afternoon I'm back at the Ugur.

Bathos this may be, but yet another miracle is in store – a shower. The shower room is tiny, the rose attachment high on the wall;

below on the floor a basin with no plug but with hot and cold taps attached. A mug waits. For what? Baling? Pouring? In one corner a grille; in another a tall tubular stove. There are four hooks for your clothes, a shelf for your false teeth and small wooden stool to keep your shoes dry. Nearly dead on my feet, I ask the young manager if it's possible to have a hot shower. Of course, he exclaims. A boy comes with an armful of wood, opens the door at the bottom of the stove, feeds the wood in and puts a match to it. Fifteen minutes later, the stove is roaring, the water blazing and I enjoy the best hot shower of my life.

Likos, 2005

On January 5th Psara, the fishing village, had a death – a very old lady – and a premature birth necessitating a mercy dash by the bread van. The flying ambulance came from Athens and practically the whole port turned out to wave the tiny patient off from the field beside the school. The baby, a girl, weighed only two pounds. Thirty years ago there was no helicopter service and she would have died. As it is she's doing fine. This drama took place in torrential rain, floods in the streets, thunder and fork lightning. Greeks become gloomy in rain. Baleful looks greeted my feeble joke that Scotland, homesick for me, had followed me here. The rains are Glasgow-style stair-rods. The animals are also gloomy. I opened the door onto the balcony to find the tomcat, sitting in a lake looking depressed. The collie also refused to take shelter. What a perverse pair.

The Panagia, the Virgin, is the protectress of the island. She must have had a word with someone in the night because the next day (a religious feast called Ta Fota*) dawned bright and blue. To the Orthodox worshipper, January 6th is when John the Baptist baptised Christ in the Jordan. The ritual is delightful. There is a short service, then the priests or sometimes bishops cast the cross attached to a ribbon into the sea three times and at the third throw, boys dive for it. The one who first holds the cross aloft is applauded by the crowd. In our case, a handsome blond boy won the cross, the grandson of a friend. The local steamer stayed to watch the fun and let off deafening wails at the crucial moment.*

Popi, a beloved friend in Psara, had asked me to eat lunch with her and her family. Leaving the crowd on the quayside I walked through the hills to the village, on the way ducking under the verandah of a half-built house to escape another deluge. To be accepted as a family friend is a great honour. It was a joyous and noisy meal, the table crammed with three different kinds of salads, a tureen of liver, juicy slices of pork and crackling, a spinach pie, pasticchio – *a kind of macaroni and mince – roast potatoes, cheeses, fruit, bread and wine. Later, helping the women and the girls to wash up, I was quizzed by one teenager about my unmarried state. 'Once I loved someone but he did not take me.' So much more dramatic than 'he didn't fancy me'. 'However,' I added, 'several Turks have wanted to take me.' I couldn't tell them about my funniest proposal for fear of shocking...*

Chapter Ten

A proposal in Konya – the glories of Bergama
1982

April 19th, Kayseri to Konya

A writer once described his character as *a stranger to the lavatory*. Constipation is the curse of the traveller. At the moment I feel like the grandfather clock in the fifties song – stopped short, never to go again. It's a dull road from Kayseri to Konya. We leave Mt Erciyes, a floating meringue behind its cloud, and after uninspired Nigde which gives off the gloomy squalor peculiar to certain Turkish towns, slip between mountain ranges and enter a plain as large as the Atlantic. Here leopard and wild bull roamed in the bad old neolithic days. It could be Africa. We shall arrive in Kenya, not Konya. A man on the bus has twelve buttons on his fly.

Despite bread and honey for breakfast I'm ravenous and wish I hadn't offered half my bread to my neighbour. A gloomy woman. The sea must have been here at some point in the millennia because sand abounds. Also quantities of tractors. Our road is so straight and goes so far into nowhere that I feel as I did once in Arizona – negligible. Honey-coloured things like voles cross the road. We miss them, but hit a pigeon which is too busy fucking to watch the traffic. Turkey is full of magpies. At the 2pm lunch stop, instead of staying in the bus and starving like a good Turkish woman, I fly shamelessly into the restaurant and order *türlü* and pilaf. Utterly delicious. By mid-afternoon we're in Konya, once the Selçuk capital and now famous for *pide*, yoghurt soup, kebab done in the oven, the saintly founder of the Dervishes, Mevlana, and spoon dances.

Konya is a surprise. Iris in Athens said it was a big city but it seems more like Colchester. The new blocks rising outside the town are poisonous but the centre is not. My taxi from the bus station has no door handles. We are four in the back seat, three of us jammed together like dried figs. The Seyhan Palas Hotel is in the old town and my hawk eye detects cleanliness as I climb the stone steps, flanked by bolts of material from the shops either side. Two elderly men are chatting in a sunny window. They look fierce.

'*Salaam aleikom.*'

'*Aleikom salaam!*' My hand is almost wrung from my wrist by the proprietor who speaks awful German. After Turkish politenesses, he shows me into a sunny room with two beds, a table, a tiny cupboard, chairs and quantities of hooks. The light is at least 100 watt and bang above the writing table. All this for £1 a night. Old Konya is full of bustle, zest and gaiety mixed with peacefulness, perhaps a legacy from Mevlana. St Paul usually had the opposite effect. Shoes everywhere; also *lokantas*, beer gardens and quiet little parks. There are two stuffed ducks wearing specs in an oculist's window and a lovely coarse-weave bag in a saddler's shop. People stare but are friendly. 'Hullo German boy!' calls a man. Male or female, I think I'll be happy here. On my way back to the hotel I'm accosted, but very politely, by a small neat man. He believes I'm a woman, speaks excellent German and suggests lunch the next day. There's an Armenian church at Sille he wants to show me.

At 7pm someone knocks on my door. An unshaven ancient in a shirt with no collar – there are at least three inches of stubble on his chin – enters, walks across to the cupboard, opens the door and extracts two crumpled newspaper parcels.

'Bread and cheese, Madam,' he says and winks. He's missing a glottis or larynx. Then he waves and closes the door softly behind him. Just as well I never looked in the cupboard. I might have eaten his supper. Or maybe it's hashish? The friendly manager has given me back my passport and refused, scandalised, a down payment; not like the cock-scratching manager of the Sur Hotel in Kayseri who kept it until he had cash in hand.

Before going to bed, I cross the hall to wash, watched silently by eight men in caps. The loo is spotless. When I emerge I find one of the men with his boot on the basin.

April 20th, Konya

For me, Selçuk art is like early Minoan, 500 BC Greek and Arab Ummayed – newborn, innocent, original, the true life force. The dominant colour is duck blue, their skill at stone and wood carving miraculous; who else would make a bellows in the shape of a tortoise? The tiles and ceramics in one museum are exquisite, the Ottoman work somehow lacking the soul which the Selçuks caught like a bird. In another museum – and both are made for lingering and meditation – a stone-carved angel seems an anomaly. I thought Islam didn't believe in angels? A blue and white enamelled cupola makes me want to cry.

Mevlana's tomb and museum is another lovely place and his message not what you might expect of the 12th century: 'Come, come again whoever or whatever you may be, come; heathen, fire-worshipper, sinful of idolatry, come. Come even if you broke your penitence a hundred times; ours is not the portal of despair and misery, come...'

What a fine man, this founder of the dervishes. His turban used to be dipped in the waters of the April bowl (for Islam, April rainwater is sacred) as a cure for palsied pilgrims. In the museum are glorious carpets, korans and tapestries which the Turks call *tissues*. *Ud* is a kind of lute. A flower embroidery glows on dusty blue silk. Soon I shall get indigestion from too much beauty. To my surprise, another exhibit is the Prophet's beard in a box.

The afternoon jaunt to Sille with German-speaking Lüfte is hilarious. First we eat *pide* in a very grand carpet shop. Its owner, an engineer Turk who speaks English, explains the Falklands War to me. The whole thing sounds mad and not a good idea. The *pide*, a pizza really, is large and boring. Butter dribbles down my chin and I feel sick. Then we bus to Sille, a sinister village among rocks. The famous Armenian church is locked – by the carvings on its tower it certainly looks Armenian; 11th century my guide says – and there is nothing else but soldiers, ruins on a crag and an overwhelming smell of dung.

'Come!' cries Lüfte and hauls me with unexpected force and efficiency up a cliff into a rock tomb. A few pitons would have helped. Arriving, covered in rock dust, in a chamber with no exit except three portholes, I find my companion down on one knee. He is proposing: 'You have beautiful eyes, a beautiful mouth and a beautiful bosom. May I touch it?' After some chaste kisses, we descend the cliff. I explain that I am madly in love with a Greek sea captain so my kisses can only be chaste and no, he may *not* caress my bosom.

'I understand. You are not angry?'

I reassure him and we continue our way downhill. His observations on sex are riveting. Touchingly, he's depressed that I won't marry him.

'Turkish women are no good. When I caress their breasts they go to sleep…A nice family, German, came last year. We became friends. One evening the wife said to me privately, "Please come to the hotel and make love to me". So I did. It was quite nice…' He shrugs and suddenly reminds me of a bank manager I once had in Chelsea. 'Then she tells her husband, "I love this man, he is a wonderful lover, his cock is enormous".'

'Gracious!' I am entranced. 'Was he furious?'

'No. Quite pleased. He is much older you see.' By this time we're on the way to the bus. 'A German woman keeps writing. We lived together for a month and now she wants to marry me. But I not. She becomes angry too quickly. No good. She wants me because I am large. I am 23 centimetres. She says she has never been with someone so large…'

135

He pauses. I'm so fascinated by the conversation I fall into a pothole. Lüfte picks me up and dusts me down.

'She sucks me off very nicely.'

'Really.'

'Yes. Sara, is it true that women like it large rather than small?'

We might be discussing my overdraft. He flicks some dust off a cuff. I feel like Alice confronting the Red Queen in one of her madder moods. Back in Konya, pleading fatigue, I buy comb honey and warm brown bread and retire to my room. This is my third Turkish proposal in a year.

April 21st/22nd, Konya

Three good things in a lazy day. Tomorrow I go southwest.

The Atatürk Museum has goodies from his wardrobe. Wow! What a natty dresser. He had broad shoulders and extremely good taste. Especially delicious are a brown leather driving coat and loud check plusfours.

A notice in the tourist office which says:

'Would you like to go to a wedding? Visit a home? See a circumcision?'

Third good thing: an old man, filthy dirty, beard matted, clothes torn, sprawls – well, reclines – on the pavement, his food spread out on a cloth. Beside him his bitch suckles ten velvet babies. Father dozes watchfully. After the babies have fed, the tramp tidies them away into a sack. He gives me one to hold. It's like a mole.

Oct 22nd, Bergama (ancient Pergamum)

This is my favourite place yet. Its delights are without number.

136

Hills and broad silvery plains stretch to distant mountains and West to the Aegean. O prescient house of Attalid to build where you built, and to leave what you left where you left it. I wonder if fine civilisations bequeath a legacy of charm and courtesy. Bursa has it, so does Istanbul. Bergama charms me the minute I get down from the Dolmus – a long, straight, cobbled street shaded by acacia and pine and in the distance ruins on a hill and white columns.

The Park Hotel is beside the bus station down a side road. Two smiling old ladies take me to a spotlessly clean room with a comfy bed and a wash-hand basin. The Park reminds me of a small English hotel, except that no small English hotel would cost £1 per night. It's green at the front and pink at the sides and has an untidy garden of Morning Glory and Busy Lizzie and some rickety chairs and tables. I lunch on hot, spicy eggs done Middle Eastern style, pilaf and bread warm from the oven. A small local place. Two doors up, in a tourist restaurant full of wine bottles, a Japanese tour munches its way through dull-looking food. Enjoy feeling superior.

There are two tea gardens: one is opposite the bus station, laid out in tiers under tall, white-socked pines. Each tier has carefully planted borders of Love Lies Bleeding, dahlias, African marigolds and abnormally high, straggly roses due to overhead blockage of sun by pines. A loudspeaker croons Turkish love songs. The occupants of the benches are mostly young and in love. The other tea garden is also pine-shaded and musical but caters for families and babies. Turks have the Greek habit of ignoring acres of empty chairs and coming to sit next to me. I am getting very reclusive.

Grocery stores spill their wares onto the pavement; sacks of Middle-Eastern spices, nuts, figs, cheeses of all sorts. Apples bought in a small courtyard taste as sweet and juicy as old-fashioned English apples. One shop with its window of nut, fudge and chocolate halva drives me out of my mind. If only I was Jewish and hyperactive and burnt up my food instead of being costive and Aryan and prone to put on half a stone in two days.

There is a Turkish lavatory cleaner called MISKOK. I wonder if Turks hold their cocks when they pee or stick them, public school fashion, through their flies. Whatever they do, this brand name implies a lack of accuracy.

The people are quiet and polite and very friendly. For one of Turkey's most famous sites the absence of *Tour* tourists is odd. Maybe they stop coming by the middle of October? No tourist tat in the shops. This is indeed civilisation. As for the local Virginia Creeper, on the turn though not yet in flames, it flops over roofs and walls and mosques and strings itself from one pine tree to the next like gypsy jewellery.

The dead hours of the afternoon pass tranquilly among the mint and brambles and shade of the Asclepeion until French tourists grumble in and a military band starts trumpeting. The nearby military base is huge; yards of tanks, acres of armoured vehicles and gloomy squaddies. Strolling the colonnades and bath chambers, I come upon a mint-edged, forgotten pool where turtles are sunbathing. They take fright and flop into the water. It's too hot. How I LOATHE heat. Wander back to town past tanks and tumbled pillars and gardening soldiers.

'German, German!' Brightly-dressed women and children playing on the steep cobbles look up and smile.

'No. I'm English.'

This confuses them. They haven't heard of the English.

What a lovely day. I like the logic of the man from whom I buy a bottle of *Lal Rosé*. 'Of course *Çankaya* is better than *Kavak*. It costs more.' Turkey is full of sycamores. My latest passion is chocolate eaten with grapes and my abiding neurosis the sound of sunflower seeds being cracked. People eat them on buses the whole time. It's the worry bead syndrome. The chef of the Park Hotel raps on my door. He wants to learn English and invites me to supper and breakfast. I decline both invitations so he asks me to supper tomorrow night instead. He seems amiable but may be the Park Hotel's only drawback.

Oct 23rd, Bergama

My plan is to do an Isak Pasha on ancient Pergamum and be up among the ghosts as the sun rises. I slip out when it's still dark and find a soup kitchen in the long cobbled street leading to the Acropolis. It's alright for a female tourist to drink soup in a male soup kitchen but not alright, in my opinion, for her to drink tea in a male tea house. Why, I don't know. Fortified by tonsil-ripping soup, I take the road to the site, only to find gates bolted and barred. There is always an old way if you look for it and five years of pathfinding have made me something of an expert. At last I find the hole in the wall. A broad flagged way, about 500 BC. Perhaps more. The dark sky begins to whiten. When the sun comes over the eastern mountains I'm above the lower *agora*, gazing down from a shrine or brothel or bronze age foot scraper.

Wonderful to be alone. That's what I liked so much about Troy: to be there by myself, standing on bits of masonry and poking about and eating Trojan blackberries. I expected grandeur and found a small friendly thing. Ancient Pergamum is *very* grand. Larks twitter as I drift through the colonnades and stoas, scramble over walls and strike again the old flagged way. How beautiful stone is when worn. It's a pleasure to walk these silky lumps over one of the world's greatest cities, now bedded down in turf and olives, a warhorse put out to grass. By 8.30 I'm on the acropolis and grumbling over the Germans' reconstruction. I do wish that people wouldn't reconstruct things. The theatre is on a precipice so a no-no for the vertiginous. Two small and furious dogs appear but don't bite. Probably belong to the keeper of the gate which isn't yet open.

There is an oddity near the palaces on the acropolis. It's a vertical shaft, circular, going down about 30 to 40 feet, with a column standing in the middle of it. What is it? I don't and never did care for the pedantry of archaeological detail, but I'd like an archaeologist to appear now and explain circular shafts with pillars in the middle of them. My trouble is, I get bored by archaeological prose – they can't write, most of them – and am more interested in how a place looks and feels and accords with time. That something un-dissected should be undeserving annoys me. There are notable exceptions like Mortimer Wheeler and Schliemann – romantic detectives both.

The Red Hall is also odd. It was once a temple dedicated to Egyptian deities, built in the 2nd century AD and faced in coloured marble. Must have looked hideous. The museum on the main street is charming. On my way there I sit outside a tea-house and watch horses and carts and the odd, nicely bred animal. I must do some riding in Egypt. One of the quainter exhibits in the museum is a calf's head nestled between the paws of a lion. The ethnographic section is full of Turkish models in shorts and tassels, several scowling in boots and britches, others with fowling pieces across their knees. Returning to the Park, I find sneezing Germans. Dodge the chef and retire to bed to brood about archaeologists. The problem with interpretation is that, like the over-zealous surgeon's knife, it can destroy rather than enhance.

Oct 24th, postscript to Bergama

At 7.30am, on the way to the bus station, I pass a bevy of roadsweepers, nine on one side of the road and five on the other, all singing.

Likos, 2005

Images of January: cormorant into a heaving, venomous sea; burst pomegranate, skin split into four sections, hanging to its branch – an art deco lampshade; rain; soap operas on Greek TV; fieldmouse prised from its hole by a pigeon; the longing for letters that don't come; black shape of the dog in the chair below the balcony; National Servicemen sidling into harbour Popi's taverna for coke or small bottles of water; the pleasure of sipping a glass of retsina after a morning's work, looking through the open door of a taverna at the blue struts for the summer awning, the white crossbars and, past them, if it's fine, the matching blue of the sea. Another gale from the south west, the third this month, has brought rainy days and a grey world. 'We haven't had weather like this for 40 years,' said the butcher.

I'm nearly halfway through my heap of diaries and coming to the end of the Turkish section. A violent urge comes over me to jump island, go to Chios, take the ferry to Asia Minor and wander down the old route, from Çanakkale through Troy and Assos to Bergama and on south. To hell with this book. Today didn't help. It's the evening of Saturday, January 15th, and everything for the last twelve hours has conspired to make me feel suicidal. First, forgetting that an island whisky is a quadruple, I gave myself a hangover. Then I went to eat curative eggs at Popi's – it was 11am and should have been peaceful – only to find two sea captains quarrelling over their ouzos. Fresh air seeming the only cure, I set off for the hills. Leaving town, I met a funeral procession of thirty or more mourners round an open coffin adorned with flowers, led by altar boys with incense and three priests. Inside the coffin was a tiny old lady. Two of the mourners were sobbing. No man is an island.

My death, the death of people I love, will happen. That evening, as another gale wailed, I thought about

141

my father's death. It was 56 years ago and I can remember every detail. Making my mother's bed upstairs I heard the phone go and my sister answer it. Her voice sounded funny. 'Daddy's dead,' I thought and went on making the bed. Then I went downstairs. My mother and sister were in tears. I'd never seen them cry before. 'Darling, you must be very brave, something awful has happened.' My mother came towards me. 'I know,' I said. 'Daddy's dead.' Dry-eyed I walked past her, out of the door and into the blue September day. I was 12 years' old.

What a mess. The first telegram said: 'Deepest regrets etc'; the second gave us the news that my father – working in Germany – had been very ill but now was on the mend. My lovely, funny father. Maybe if I'd seen him in an open coffin, if there'd been a funeral, if we'd mourned together I would have been able to say goodbye. As it was I locked him up in a precious place and went back to boarding school. Trouble was, I locked a chunk of myself up. And, looking back, that's probably when I began to erect my set of defences against life – an elaborate and careful construction, its main weapon laughter.

Now the sea is as furious as the gale.

Despite the weather I've done good pathfinding. There is nothing so much fun as following a path and not knowing where it might lead; or not taking the sensible route at a fork in the road. Security seeming prosaic, I often choose the track which trundles me over a precipice. It's this meandering nature – a friend once said crossly, 'You don't walk, you stroll' – and a desire to look under the carpet rather than walk across it which gets me into trouble...

Chapter Eleven

Cross country from Manisa to
Pamukkale – Aphrodisias – Nysa – Kusadasi
1982

Oct 25th, Manisa (ancient Magnesia) to Sarigöl

After hot milk of Magnesia for breakfast – one of the sillier reasons for coming here – I pay my bill at the Mesir Hotel, an extravagance much enjoyed, and ask the owner, a portly bear with a broom moustache, why his hotel is empty. Where are all the other guests? 'It is Monday,' he replies. The trouble with my Turkish is that it's the magpie variety. I steal phrases and use them but rarely understand the answers. Talking of magpies, the one for sorrow, two for joy game has become an obsession. My first stop is Sart for Sardis; the tourist leaflet is charming:

Sardis whose history begins 3000 years before the time we are in now is at the 87th kilometre of Izmir-Ankara highway and on the west 9 kilometres to Salihli. The city is very well-known as the richest, most powerful and functional capital of antic world during the years starting with the 7th century BC till years 546 in Aegean history. On those days to live in Sardis, was meant to live in a magnificent city in which Lydian art and architecture was shining like a star on the horizons of Greece and Asia minor. The City Sardis is important too from the point of the birth place of invitations which is director of today's civilisation.

Such as:
1 – The first Golden and Silver coins have been printed in Sardis.
2 – The first independent Bazaar has been set in Sardis.
3 – The first step has been taken in tourism Industry by setting up recreational areas, parks free to everyone and Accommod-ational centres.
4 – The first city planning and sewerage system has been carried out in Sardis...

Leaving my pack with a grocer in Sart, I start walking the two kilometres to the temple of Artemis but am picked up almost instantly by a couple in a Mercedes, he Turk and she Swiss-French. The keeper of the temple, much impressed, shakes our hands, mistakenly thinking me part of this glamorous entourage. The shrine is beside a river shaded by mulberries. The hills are curious, the olive picking in full swing, the pomegranates rosy-ripe. What a magic place. Above, on pink Cappadocian peaks, an acropolis. But to go from Hellenistic Artemis to the Roman Gymnasium is – in my opinion – to go from the glory that was Greece to the rhubarb that was Rome. It is, however, in the despised rhubarb that I make my change of plan. Surrounded by blue spiraea and munching the best brambles yet, I decide not to go to Çesme via boring Izmir but to flit cross-country via Salihli to Denizli, from there to visit Pamukkale, Aphrodisias and Nysa. Bergama and Sart have whetted my appetite. It is 2.40pm.

Salihli, reached by Dolmus from Sart, is a pleasant, horsetrading town. Two boys carry my pack to the dusty bus station.

'Denizli,' I cry. 'Izmir,' they reply. 'No!' I cry.

Consternation. Much dust. Deep interest. Finally…

'You can go to Alasehir.'

Putting on my specs, I look at the map. We all look at the map. So be it. When in doubt take a side road. The bus arrives, creating even more dust and much sneezing. Urchins clamber on board with corn on the cob and *pide* the size of boxing gloves and off we go. What a lovely way to spend an afternoon: there are curious hills to the right, English pop plays on the radio and miles of vineyards stretch away on either side. The horse and carts have a numberplate saying HORSE AND CART. We are back in the eighteenth century again – Constable landscapes, Samuel Palmers – and at one point roar through the village of Kavaklidere. The factory must be here. Countless bottles of their *Kavak*, *Çankaya* and *Lal Rosé* have flowed down my throat. *Salaam!*

144

Alasehir, and yes, there is a Dolmus to Sarigöl and from there I may go to Denizli. They gather round me three deep in the buspark and I am astonished to see a mixture of my mother and grandmother in a marvellous old lady. Despite my lack of Turkish, we instantly take to one another. 'Come and stay,' she says. I take her hand, fascinated by the familiarity of her face. Her friend is also intrigued.

'Look! Your eyes are the same..!'

It is 5.15pm. The next step is a slow, slow Dolmus to Sarigöl. Then my luck runs out. Nothing goes to Denizli, probably never did. Lies, all lies. Lorries refuse lifts. I am stranded. Old men buy me consoling tea. 'Tomorrow,' they cry. 'Look! There is a hotel here. You can stay.' Wearily I go to the Park Oteli beside a leafy parklet. My chamber is clean and made of cardboard, with pink walls and a window looking onto the parklet. The curtains are in good taste – a red, ochre, brown, grey, green stripe – and on my bedside table is a glass and an elaborate tin jug, done up to look like Tokapi silver. The bedhead is best. It has an illustrated centrepiece of a pale and dark green peacock surrounded by flames. A phoenix. A father and young son make me welcome; and after a bottle of *Doruk Rosé* and hot *patliçan*, I fall, exhausted into my quilts.

Oct 26th, Sarigöl to Denizli via Pamukkale

The tea-buying old gents of yesterday evening promised a Dolmus to Denizli at 7am. I wake at 4am and am soon out in the cold dark under a starry sky. Having disposed of my wine bottle, what to do, where to go? One teahouse is open. Shyly I enter. 'Come in! Come in!' The kind and friendly men inside tell me that there is no Dolmus at 7am. '8.30,' says one. '9,' says another. An hour later the lady sweeping leaves in the street says '10,' but she is doubtful there is one at all. Mooch about, disconsolate and starving. Tea does not fill a stomach. Am bought coffee, then another tea in another tea-house by an exquisitely-suited gentleman with Chinese features. Silent politeness is exhausting. It is now 7.30am, light. At 8am, fuck the bloody Dolmus, I leave my

145

pack in the second café and go to look for soup. Chicken soup with hot bread is worth freezing to death for.

Back in the Park Oteli for a pee, I get chased down the corridor by an elderly man. I ignore him. After my pee, there he is, still chattering. He seems to be offering a taxi to Pamukkale in terrible German. 'Too expensive,' I say but, 'No, no!' he cries, 'my wife and I are leaving now. Come along! All of us! Pamukkale!' Docile as a vole I follow. What a bit of luck. Escape, at last, from Sarigöl.

'My name is Ibrahim.' He is a fruitcake; sings and laughs as he drives at breakneck speed up an atrocious dirt road. His wife, well-dressed with a good face, hands us rotten pears to eat and talks to herself. I realise now it would have taken me a hundred years to get from Sarigöl to Denizli in a Dolmus. Occasionally we hit a new road and loose chippings over which the Renault flies with reckless disregard for its undercarriage.

'GO SLOWLY!' roars his wife.

'Frau kaput,' shouts Ibrahim happily. Then adds:

'The old shitbag's off her head!'

Suddenly he spins the wheel and we whirl up a lane to a shack. A man and shy girl come to greet us, a thin but happy puppy falling about their feet. Hens scratch and two good-looking cows chew cud. Coffee and a plate of cakes covered in flies are produced. The cakes are delicious despite flies and dust. As I devour one, a cat appears with a mouse in its mouth, looks at us and departs. Each to their cake. An hour later we set off for Ibrahim's home, passing en route flocks of black goats and nine camels. One has rickets.

'Gypsies,' says Ibrahim.

Only then do I remember the Turkish word. *Yürück* is gypsy, nomad.

'I am *Yürück,*' I say in Turkish.

We're now in this bizarre region of Turkey where hot springs spout. There's a calcified waterfall at Pamukkale. Ibrahim's and wife's relations live in Karhaït, where each house has its hot bath, Roman-style. There are several small *pensions,* each with a pool. Ibrahim shows me proudly round. I like him very much. He says he's 70 but looks 50. We refresh ourselves with coke and tomatoes stolen from a field.

'I can't see the salt,' says Ibrahim, searching in the branches of a tree. Pamukkale is just up the hill. We pile into brother-in-law's car and drive first to Hieropolis. A nightingale sits on a chunk of the ancient city but these grand ruins leave me cold. All ghosts gone. We tomb-crawl in oppressive heat, then go for lunch at Pamukkale's ritziest hotel beside the waterfall. It looks just like it does on the postcards. The owner is a friend of Ibrahim so lunch is on the house. As we munch delicacies and drink wine, I watch a couple at a nearby table.

They are sitting beside one of Nature's miracles, in one of man's more tasteful and good-looking hotels, and what are they eating? Fat, greasy escalopes. Their mouths are turned down and – in the course of an hour – they exchange not one word. Rich and wretched. Lives of quiet desperation. It spoils my appetite.

'Stay with us tonight,' begs Ibrahim. 'You can go to Denizli tomorrow.' My instinct is to press on. It's 3.45pm, I've been up for twelve hours. I need a hotel and bed.

But first I need to interpret a flood of fantasy about Dolmuses from Karhaït. Turks don't hear what they don't want to hear. On the other hand, they make up what they think you'd like them to make up; like a thousand Dolmuses storming through Karhaït every hour when there are NONE. It's a ploy of Ibrahim's to get me back there and persuade me to stay. After tearful goodbyes, I take the Dolmus from Pamukkale to Denizli. En route we billow smoke but mercifully don't blow up. Oh wonderful Gönülü

Hotel! My room is enormous; with a double bed, balcony, basin and private bathroom, all for 425TL. So much SPACE! What I really want to do is sleep. Instead – for a chance like this is not often to be had – I wash my jeans, shirt, socks, knickers, sweat-shirt; then turn my attention to my own body and hair. It is EXHAUSTING keeping clean.

By the time dark falls I'm spruce and fragrant. Stroll, buy wine and eat excellent spinach and yoghurt and *taze fasulye*. It's so warm my clothes will dry overnight; even if they don't, I've got enough plastic bags. Travel makes one a collector of plastic bags and obsessively tidy. Putting up a washing line and pegging clothes is such a pleasure.

Oct 27th, a long way round to Aphrodisias

There's a way to get by Dolmus from Nazili to Aphrodisias. Arrange to be called at 5am and catch the Izmir bus. Glowing from the Gönülü's hot shower I doze through the journey to Nazili. We arrive at 7.30; then there's an hour and a half's delay while the Dolmus for Karacasou fills up. Turks cram into Dolmuses like students into telephone boxes; this time we are 18 in the can. It's a beautiful morning and the countryside as lovely as any I've seen; lemon and orange groves, poplars, enormous willows, forests of pine and sparkling rivers. Monster pampas with the sun behind them are fit for Galahad's helmet. If it wasn't for the Turks and the olive trees we could be in Inverness-shire. Why is the grass so green? The electrician beside me smokes con-tinuously. His eyes bulge. So does his willie. Trousers that tight can't be good for you. We chat in fractured Turkish. He's deeply pessimistic about my proposed jaunt to Aphrodisias:

'Impossible! No Dolmus from Karacasou.'

'Then I shall walk.'

He's horrified. Turks are even more scandalised than Greeks at my travelling alone.

He's right. There isn't a Dolmus from Karacasou to Aphrodisias. So what? Thirteen kilometres is only ten miles. Dumping my pack in the hotel above the bus station I set off. It's 9.25am and a golden day. Wonderful to feel drunk with happiness in the middle of beautiful country. The land continues to look like Inverness-shire until a Michelin-star restaurant by a river reminds me of Stratford St Mary in Suffolk. After six kilometres a beezing behind me gets louder and louder, passes me and stops. The farmer on the tractor jerks his thumb, the kids on the trailer grin. I climb on and arrive in style at Aphrodisias.

The first settlers were Assyrians from Nineveh. It was named Aphrodisias in the third century BC. What a beautiful, peaceful place. Shady paths, fringed with ivy and brambles and blue spiraea meander in and out of ruins. At the temple of Aphrodite I pour a libation of *Doruk Rosé* to the goddess of love and find a cool pillar to eat my *simit* on. The sun burns. The birds twitter. Suddenly a German tour sweeps round the corner, circling me on my pillar as if I was an artefact. They seem nice so I follow them to the stadium. It comes as a terrific surprise – hidden below a dull-looking bank at the end of a field. Tyre's may be bigger but this is a beauty. It could seat 30,000. After a bit I lose the Germans and spend two hours poking about. The odeon is pretty and I like the theatre but the baths are TOO BIG. A fascist imposition. Pomegranates and poplars, ivy groves and little streams, grass, flowers, silence. Tiny frogs bathe in a pool.

A nicely arranged museum. The cult statue of Aphrodite is as alarming as many-breasted Artemis at Selçuk. She has dolphins carved on a layer of her petticoats. A drooping-mouthed Apollo, the head of Livia, poor poisoned Claudius, a spaghetti-haired governor of Asia called Flavius Palmatus...suddenly I realise it's afternoon and I've got to get myself to Karacasou and then to Nazili. The road is empty and the air colder; but a guardian angel sends a manure truck and I'm back in Karacasou just in time to catch the last Dolmus to Nazili. Feel extremely pleased with myself.

The Ankara Palace Hotel proves the perfect end to a perfect day.

It is a collector's piece. The staircase sweeps up to a portrait of the bey, then divides. The communal loo – squatters – is the size of a golfcourse. The basins are vast. Turn-of-the-century I should think. Alas, it has seen better days. In the wood-panelled dining room an elegant waiter serves me eggs fried in butter and a side dish of peas. My Berlitz Turkish has a pessimistic hotel section:

'The washbasin is clogged.'
'The window is jammed.'
'The blind is stuck.'
'These aren't my shoes.'

October 28th, Sultanhisar for Nysa – then to Kusadasi

They sleep late in Nazili. Disapprovingly I retrieve my passport from the pyjamaed manager and catch a Dolmus to Sultanhisar. This region overflows with figs, lemons, veg of all kinds; an almost unreal abundance. A kind grocer says he will guard my rucksack (grocers and bus stations are my favourite dumping ground), so I climb through the olive groves in the morning mist to Nysa – a slumbering site, its columns scattered among the wild cyclamen. Larks twitter. I'd have liked to be emperor here. Shepherded by a peak-capped keeper of the ruins, I marvel at the theatre, the *bouletarion*, the tunnel, the library and the baths.

'The market,' he laments, 'is under the olives.'

Cheerful workmen call to one another as they chip at bits of Roman masonry. I hope they know what they're doing.

Now it's evening in an old haunt, Kusadasi. Tomorrow is a rest day. There are 46 flies on my bedroom ceiling and I'm full of wind. Tomorrow is also Atatürk Day and every town in the land will shake and shiver with fife and drum and trumpets blown by mites in blue bandsmen's uniforms with peaked caps too big for their heads. (Others wear red and gold braid and look like doormen.) There will be scouts and cubs, small brownies and tall, crisp white-shirted sixth formers in black skirts. A guitar plays below. Children squawk. I'm very tired.

Likos, 2005

To wake at three in the morning and know you're not going to get back to sleep is horrible. This was two nights ago – full-moon time or thereabouts – and I tossed and turned and thought about old loves and childhood and offices I had known and worried about money. The blankets got heavier and the sheets colder; and outside that bloody north wind, the Tramoundana again, wailed and whistled. The jumble of rocks by the low sea wall didn't help. Over, round and through them the sea, fretted by the wind, roared and crashed and fumed. This pair are in league to give me a nervous breakdown. Good things that have happened are eight letters from friends – eight, all at once! Speechless with joy I took them from Niko, the assistant postmaster, and retired to Harbour Popi's taverna. No telephone call ever came within a hundred miles of the joy of a letter from home.

It's January 19th and ominously calm. Max, the black collie, isn't well and has either eaten filth or poison. May Saint Spiridion cure him. On the wildest and coldest night, worried about the dog and the tomcat, I opened the door of the shed under my stone steps – this is where the motor for the water lives – put some layers of the Independent *on the floor and left the door open. The next morning, a freezing wind still blowing, I looked in to see the two animals curled together like a fossil. They are becoming devoted. Popi in the nearby taverna keeps my dog food called 'Darling' in her fridge. Greek women who run tavernas as well as families never stop working. Nor do they want to. Their work is their life. I was sitting here the other morning – it was 11am – having an early lunch when Stavro, an acquaintance of many years' standing, arrived to have his first bottle of retsina; to Popi's disapproval an hour early. Stavro went to sea aged 12 and is always good company. On this occasion he told me*

151

about an arcane ritual, still observed in Likos, for blessing the foundations of a house. The owners, the workmen and the priest gather round the foundations and sacrifice a cockerel. One worker takes the bird down to the deepest point, places the head on a stone with a cross scratched on it and chops it off. The priest then sprinkles the blood of the cockerel around the foundations. The fowl is subsequently roasted and eaten by the workmen who build the house.

Tigerlilies sprout from bushy succulents. Slowly, the sun is moving round from its December setting. Now it flops into the sea at 5.15pm instead of 5pm. Despite the wind and the rain and the wild grey sea we have 10 hours of daylight. Yesterday the carpenter gave me two mandarins. Eating one, juicy and pipless, I flew in a time-machine to a market in Asia Minor where the mandarins, or maybe clementines, were so tiny and sweet you could eat the skin as well...

Chapter Twelve

Kusadasi – jaunts with a Bulgar to Priene – Miletos and Lake Bafa – Marmaris
1982

Oct 29th, Kusadasi

It's nice to be back at the Su Pension, an old house with a court-yard shaded by trees and a vine. It's homely. There's a fountain in the courtyard and an enormous blue antique jar which must have been liberated from Ephesus. Knowing a piece of a place makes you feel differently about it. Seventeen months ago I fumed about how touristy Kusadasi was; now I don't care. As in Rhodes, the cruise ships dock for a day or a night and spill out their blue-rinsed cargo. May the good Turks take much moolah. The Su is up a steep cobbled hill behind the town and I've a pink room and hot showers and a sit-on loo with an orange seat. Pigeons coo in the trees round the courtyard. I belong to the town backstage and am content.

My day off is bliss. After *iskembe çorbasi* for breakfast, I prowl the market and buy tomatoes and tiny mandarins, so fresh from the trees you can eat their skins. Seized by holiday madness and off the lead of Dolmus timetables I could buy everything. It amuses me how those in cars or tours envy the idleness of my life. If they only knew! In the bank near the quay a Turk called Nedo speaks excellent English. Everyone is strolling, bank holiday style, and the Atatürk Day procession turns out to be as enjoyable as ever. The boy drummers here wear white, German-style plastic helmets and the girls have white bows in their hair. These tiny military Turks take this event and their musical responsibilities extremely seriously. So do the watching adults. I adore the enthusiasm and optimism of Turk and Greek. They are still excited by education and processions and wonderful things like calculators. And we worn-out cynics of Northern Europe, what excites us? Violence? Sex? We used to damage our acquisitions with booze and syphilis.

153

Our cynicism is probably as dangerous.

Kusadasi has many Turks from Crete, grandchildren of those families exchanged in 1922. The yacht harbour is full of boats. Chat with a Harpers and Queen English couple in a grand yacht, eat a fiery *patlican* with yoghurt and go home to sip wine and read and scribble and doze. There is nothing so adorable as Turkish babies with long noses: carbon copies of their fathers.

Oct 30th, to Priene and Miletos

Itching and peevish at 3am, I fall asleep again and have dreams about my front teeth falling out. Am revived by tripe soup. I flag down the Söke Dolmus and arrive, coughing and spluttering from smoke expelled by tobacco-stained ancients. A giggly boy directs me down a maze of streets to where the Güllübahce Dolmus waits. It, too, is full of smoke, the driver a cross between an old lover and a girl I was at school with. He is grey-haired with bright blue eyes and wears his cap at a rakish angle. Discussing the pros and cons of Margaret Thatcher and her deflationary policies at 8.45am in my non-existent Turkish is a strain. At last we leave. The smoking ancient beside me mutters 'Allah'.

The driver, not a Turk but a Bulgar, is smitten and escorts me to the site. With us is a gentle creature who turns out to be the Keeper of the Ruins.

'After you have seen Priene I will take you to Miletos and then back here, all for 2,000.'

'Too much,' I sigh and walk off to buy my ticket from the vole-like keeper.

'1,500,' offers the Bulgar.

I click my teeth. Cast my eyes to heaven.

'1,000,' he says, resigned. We shake hands. The deal is on. (The bore of Miletos is that you have to retrace your steps to Söke to get there. Even then, there's probably only one Dolmus a day.)

Priene was founded in the 10th century BC by Carians and is the birthplace of Bias, one of the seven sages. 'Bias is binding on,' they used to grumble. Chuckling at my Kenneth Williams silliness, I climb the stony track to the site, a forgotten glory at the foot of a massive cliff. All around pines whisper and sigh. The temple to Zeus has fallen down; but the five remaining pillars of the temple of Athena, sentries to the rock face behind, are magnificent. To sit on a fallen column drinking wine at 10 o'clock on a November morning, with nothing to disturb my reverie except the twitter of birds, is a gift unparalleled. Later I wander among cyclamen and yellow crocuses, over worn flags and down peaceful paths. Priene was once one of the most prosperous cities of the Ionian League. She's left good vibrations. It is with profound humility that I salute her vanished splendour.

The Bulgar drives me across what used to be the sea – and is now a sea of cotton – to Miletos. Boats would ply between Priene and Miletos when they guarded the straits, just as they do today between Çanakkale and Kilitbahir. He sniffs the bunch of thyme he's picked with exclamations of joy. *'Ne güzel!'* (He reminds me of Giovanetti's Max.) He also keeps turning the collar of my anorak down. That's the kind of thing that makes a girl fall in love with a man. Miletos doesn't move me at all but I dutifully plod round. We take tea with a guard and workman at a wooden table, looking up at the theatre which could seat 25,000. In the tunnel behind the top tier of seats I point out the ticket office and my companion roars with laughter. What a joyous creature. As we squidge through the cracked mud of the harbour entrance, he claps me on the back and cries, 'Let us go and have lunch at Lake Bafa. Today holiday! No money. We are friends.' Gaily he abandons his day's Dolmus run between Söke and Güllübahce, as a rake a passing fancy. Not a thought for the poor Turkish housewives stranded with their shopping. Off we go to Bafa. On the way there my Bulgar declares his fondness for me, yet again gently but firmly turning down the collar of my golfing jacket. I invent a husband who died of cancer four years ago and a *friend* in London, an architect, who will come and shoot him if he trifles with me. My companion is shocked:

'But only *Turks* shoot people, not the English!'

Heracleia-under-Latmos was once a great city on the shore of Lake Bafa. The moon mountain, Latmos, is awe-inspiring. Ragged, full of crags, it rears from the lakeside. High on its flank stands one of the 56 watchtowers of the old city walls, built, I think, by Mausolus. There's a restaurant by the shore, a clean sandy cove, geese puddling in the green weed and a swimming snake. Scatterings of red-tiled houses and some higher on the mountain among monster boulders are the only sign of life. An arch frames sand, reeds and cypresses This is where the Moon Goddess Selene fell in love with the shepherd boy Endymion. Even the Bulgar is meditative. Sitting by the lake we eat eggs and salad, shaded from vicious sun by an olive tree. Despite my protests he insists on paying the bill.

There is a slight wrangle about going back to Kusadasi. My companion wants cuddles on the beach but I have other ideas.

'You can work in the evening,' he wails.

Hardhearted I am and not to be budged; nor will I give him a kiss. His labrador smile fades and we drive off in silence. Happily he finds treasure trove on the road in the shape of an iron bar and cheers up. There are fruits growing in the undergrowth, like strawberries but on a woody shrub. He gathers a handful for me. They are delicious, the inside flesh soft and yellow. What a sweet man. He loves the English but doesn't care for the French. Our conversations – all in Turkish – range across the Liberal and Social Democrat pact, the greatness of Tito, the incumbent Junta ('Not democratic,' he sighs and looks sad again), Prince Charles and Princess Di, JR, Sue Ellen and Bobby. As we approach Söke where the river Meanders wriggles like an eel through cottonfields, he waves a paw at a Spanish-type villa and cries 'Dallas!' Why he isn't

156

married I can't think. I press 1,500TL and my photo into his hand and take the Dolmus back to Kusadasi.

Oh for soft pillows! This one is like a rock. Trying to pound affection out of stone bolsters is the fate of the traveller in Turkey.

Oct 31st, Kusadasi

An Indian summer of unreal, milky weather. Kusadasi is full of ravens. There's a castle on the little island across the causeway with gardens full of tutting Turks and a bar serving coffee, beer and soft drinks. Turks tut as severely as Morningside aunts. An extraordinary thing happens on my way there. A gull dives at a fish just hooked by a boy and gets hooked too. This morning the gardens are empty except for the boy at the bar and a middle-aged couple in love. He's about 60, she 40 and he's singing *Love is a many splendoured thing*. Turks are terribly romantic. When they sing their eyes fill with tears. Now *Volare* soars Caruso-like from the table by the palm and a woman's laughter after. Ah, love.

Nedo in the bank is delightful. He worked for years in big hotels in England and before that was a professional footballer. He reminds me of Prince Rainier. We are to have dinner together this evening. First, however, I've promised myself a treat at Diba, a restaurant by the sea where the locals go. Sitting by the fishing boats watching urchins with bare feet bounce about in them, I feast on fried mussels, brains on a bed of some fresh young greenstuff, *pasamesese* and *esme,* washed down by a jug of raki. Today the sea is crystal; the sky has turned from milky into a window someone's washed. It's a marvellous month, October.

In honour of going out to dinner, I change from light blue jeans to dark blue jeans, comb my curls and apply fresh lipstick. Nedo arrives in a state; firstly because he's seven minutes late and secondly because he's grieving for his brother-in-law who fell off a building site in Germany and died from his injuries.

'We're going to eat at a friend's restaurant. He used to be a

157

barber. You will have to forgive him. He was a good barber but has only been a chef a short time.'

The barber's place is down a flight of steps in a basement. He has a dolphin smile and greets us with a bow. Immediately I love him. The room is small, with a blue ceiling so low my head touches it. The walls are decorated with nudes in seductive poses and the atmosphere that of a 1930s French film about low life in Marseilles. It's really a club for the barber's friends. Two are here tonight: Ates, a seller of tea who used to work on the buses; and Mechmet, a 60 year-old pussycat, who guards a hotel. They both love Nedo.

'When he was a footballer,' the old guard says, 'he was like fire.' Ates refills his glass with raki. 'He starts on it first thing,' whispers Nedo. Most Turks, like Greeks, drink for sociability or when they get *kaif* (*kefi* in Greek). This is almost untranslatable but roughly means joy of being. They hardly ever drink from despair or boredom.

The time has come to order food. Sabri, with that mixture of deference and dignity I so admire about the Turk, stands with his pad at the ready. It is a serious matter. With our raki, we nibble brown bread, *esme,* a salad and a dish of piping hot liver. Whatever else he can't cook Sabri is a dab hand at liver. Not for years have I enjoyed an evening so much. We talk, Nedo translating backwards and forwards, we philosophise, we dance, we sing. Ates sings old Turkish songs with that Eastern quaver so similar to the music of Northern Greece but Sabri wants love music. He is Caruso, Madam Butterfly, Orpheus deprived of Eurydice. When he eats he stands at a narrow shelf in the corner of the room. It is eleven, midnight, one o'clock in the morning.

'Tell Sabri,' I say to Nedo, 'that if he was as good a barber as he is a chef, then his previous customers must be in despair.'

The barber beams, roars with laughter and directs a stream of Turkish at us.

'He says he drank too much raki to be a good barber.'

All four men are such gentlemen, so full of humour and generous with their friendship. At 1.30am a sulky boy lets me into the Su. What I shall feel like tomorrow morning after three quarters of a bottle of raki and two beers, God knows!

Nov 1st, Kusadasi

Awake feeling parched but astonishingly well. Am halfway through my tripe soup in a nearby kaf when Nedo walks in. I've grown fond of Kusadasi. In the evening, when sunset colours the cruise ships, it turns them into dreamboats, anachronisms with sweeping staircases and Fred Astaire dancing down them. Merle is an Australian girl in love with Turkey and she and Nedo and I lunch at the barber's. More delicious liver. I explain to N that I am in love with a Greek sea captain so can't sleep with him. He laughs.

'I didn't ask you out to dinner to take you to bed.'

He has a passion for gambling. Our second night out is with Uncle Bas, an elderly man who works with Nedo in the bank; and a slant-eyed, burly man from the Taurus whose name I've forgotten. First it's cards in the back room, a green baize table and an air of conspiracy. We climbed in through a kind of window. If the police catch you gambling with cards that aren't marked, you go to jail and lose your job. Then we move to the restaurant. Though becoming more used to the ways of Islam, I still find it disconcerting to be the only woman – apart from the belly dancer and two in the band – in a place full of dark men with dark eyes who stare. The band is good: two drums (a *dümbelek* and *daval*) a clarinet (*klernet*), and a *cümbüs,* a banjo-type thing played by a most respectable elderly woman. The only other female, young and sulky, beats up the *dümbelek.*

We eat *mezzeler* and chicken and drink quarts of raki. I shall probably get brain damage. Many 500TLs are tucked into the belly dancer's corsage. She's not good. Do all the dark eyes watching want to fuck her? Tchiss, tchiss, tchiss…the flange of fat above her hips wobbles to the tambourine's hiss. The evening ends in gloom because the bill, when it arrives, is enormous. I can't think why they are so dumbfounded. Bands and bellyfloppers must add 500% to any bill. At least, this time, I'm allowed to pay my share.

Nov 2nd, Marmaris

Sitting on my fast bus to Marmaris via Aydin and Mugla, I think about something both Nedo and the Bulgar said:

'It's alright for tourists with their exchange rate. But for most Turks living in Turkey it's very difficult.' Turkish salaries are so small that everyone, even teachers, has to have another job to make ends meet. Yet their kindness and generosity is beyond belief. We arrive at 3pm in a tropical Marmaris. Shit. I'm fed up with summer. The tree-furred hills round the bay are as lovely as ever. A Danish woman in the Tourist Information Office who speaks perfect English recommends the Pina Hotel – 'He's a very religious old man and cleanliness seems to keep close to godliness' – so there I go. It's pleasant and as spotless as she says. To my surprise the boy who shows me to my room kisses me on both cheeks; so, later does the Hadji, the garlic-smelling owner. In the night I am embraced by mosquitoes. Only Antisan applied at 2.30am stops me waking up like Quasimodo, lips all inside out and swollen.

Nov 3rd, Marmaris

In the six months since I was here there are more supermarkets and more pine-panelled coffee bars; any minute now Fast Food will hit Turkey. The woman in Tourist Information, a delightful person, tells me how the dubbing of foreign programmes for TV is changing the Turkish language: now, instead of '*tessekur ederim*' for thank you, many people are saying '*saou*'. The mouth makes the same shape for '*saou*' as it does for 'thanks'. Another slow change is '*salim*' instead of '*merhaba*' because '*salim's*' shape corresponds to 'hallo'. We also touch on politics. She is a liberal, an Eçevit follower, but thinks he should stick to poetry. He sounds a bit like Adlai Stevenson. He was apparently incapable of using people he disliked, even though their particular talents fitted a job.

'Who was the most dangerous before the Junta took control – the right or the left?'

'The right. *Much* more dangerous than the left who basically stuck to tracts and printing presses. The right were well-organised, ruthless and cold. Not human at all. All of us were longing for the army to take control.'

I digest this. This is a Roy Jenkins/David Steel woman talking.

'When my son got into university, I didn't know whether to be pleased or whether to sit down and cry.'

'Why?'

'When you first went onto a campus, you were taken aside and asked if you were left or right. You had to make your choice then. If you chose right, you were likely to be shot by the left and vice versa.'

She sighs.

'I sent him to a battlefield.'

There is a valley behind Marmaris of lemon and orange groves, pine, poplar and cypresses. Rivers flow down from the bumping hills. They do bump. There is no other way to describe them. I buy wine and sit in my room. The building is old so the room lovely and cool. Twitter of sparrow and rumble of male voices waft up from the street. Later, drinking tea, I watch the rocking of blue caiques on green water, the primness of four little tea glasses on a table-top. Music drifts across the bay. Atatürk's statue gallops out to sea. And all around are the curious hills and the smell of dust and spices. Occasionally the peace is shattered by a pleasure craft with its radio on full blast. A bent old man clutching a stand of postcards drags past on crutches; and a small boy on a bike, with an even smaller boy on the crossbar leans forward to kiss his brother, seeming to mimic the angle of the cripple.

At last the sun sinks behind the white domes of the Customs House. I love the twilight walk of the Mediterranean, the stroll of the family, the swagger of the slim-hipped boys. Turks are a beautiful race. Children are playing football round the base of Atatürk's statue. I don't suppose he had time to have any.

Turkey, *how* I shall miss you.

Likos, 2005

So there it is. Greece and Turkey, for 20 years confined in grey covers – a time past, forgotten and unread – are now present fact in my laptop's memory. Ah, the joys of technology. Being ex-advertising, I lack the editorial tricks you learn in publishing; although seven years in government information and a man called Nicholas who sat opposite and disapproved of my charm, taught me copy editing skills. 'I'm halfway through the book,' I said this morning to Harbour Popi who was sweeping her floor; then confided my worries about the tomcat. Last night he was very ill. I'd given him water, then lifted him into the shed under the stairs where he curled up on Independents, *eyes dull, fur dull, hardly alive. Poor little man. It's awful to see a confident, healthy thing turn into a wreck. 'At least he's eaten that bit of fish you gave me,' I said to Popi. She clucked over her broom. 'Don't worry, Sara, cats are like that.' I intercepted the bread van from Psara, the Miti bakery having collapsed in a mass of pipes, and hurried back to check on the invalid. How am I supposed to write with a dependent dog and a cat dying of flu?*

Likos bread is awful. So are the cheese pies. Worst of all are the rolls which would be better used for lagging boilers or put in bedroom slippers. In 1982, the year I went to the Middle East, I spent the summer in Psara. Then the abysmal quality of the bread could be laid at the door of the baker's marital difficulties. A whisky-drinking philanderer is not the bake oven's best friend. But 23 years later, the bread is still awful. Deliverance may be at hand in the shape of Giorgos the schoolmaster's cousin who is taking over the broken-down bakery in Miti. He has a diploma. We shall see.

Along with the eight letters came two bundles of newspapers. Lying under my blankets one rainy afternoon, I read of an Israeli 'execution' and felt the habitual upsurge of sympathy for the Palestinians – not the fundamentalists or suicide bombers, but the ordinary decent people who don't want to blow anyone to bits but yearn for that luxury which we who have it take so much for granted: an ordinary, unobserved life. The Israeli invasion of Lebanon in 1982 had enraged me. Reading my Middle East diaries I wondered how I'd managed to get into Lebanon in the sixth year of a bloody civil war. Perhaps it was the blizzards in London that January which addled the embassy staff. Outside, Holland Park glittered like a Christmas card. Inside the embassy all was gloom, no lights on and two young staff hunched over their desks. Their depression was tangible, urn-shaped. Politely I asked the girl if I could have a visa for Lebanon – going there first, then to Jordan, then to Syria and back to Greece through Turkey. Sadly she shook her head:

'I'm sorry but I cannot give you a visa. There is a war in my country.'

'And who would look after you?' added her colleague.

'Look after me?' The faint outrage in my voice caught their attention. 'I'm not a tourist, I'm a traveller. I've just been in the East of Turkey, in Doğubeyazit and Van, near the border. The people were most kind and hospitable. I can look after myself.'

There was a moment's silence. Outside it had started to snow again. The man and girl looked at each other.

'Alright.' The man smiled at me.

Freya Stark, genius of travel writing, illustrates with her usual rigour the tourist-traveller difference:

'A good traveller does not, I think, much mind the uninteresting places. He is there to be inside them, as a thread is inside the necklace it strings. The world, with unknown and unexpected variety, is a part of his own leisure; and this living participation is, I think, what separates the traveller and the tourist, who remains separate, as if he were at a theatre, and not himself a part of whatever the show may be.' (Alexander's Path)

On the 26th of February, 1982, I flew from blue weather in Athens to dark skies and turbulence over Beirut. My knowledge of the political situation in Lebanon was hazy. All I knew was that Beirut used to be known as the Paris of the Middle East and that I had to see, whatever the difficulties, Tyre and Sidon, Baalbeck and Byblos and Lady Hester Stanhope's grave...

The Middle East and Egypt: cardamom lands 1982

The hunchèd camels of the night
Trouble the bright
And silver waters of the moon.
The Maiden of the Moon will soon
Through Heaven stray and sing,
Star gathering.

Now while the dark about our loves is strewn,
Light of my dark, blood of my heart, O come!
And night will catch her breath up, and be dumb.

Leave thy father, leave thy mother
And thy brother;
Leave the black tents of thy tribe apart!
Am not I thy father and thy brother
And thy mother?
And thou – what needest with thy tribe's black tents
Who hast the red pavilions of my heart?

Arab Love Song
Francis Thompson

Chapter Thirteen

Beirut, the sad city – Tyre – Sidon – Tripoli – Byblos – Baalbek

1982

Feb 26th, to Beirut from Athens

It's hot in Athens. Waiting for my flight to be called I wonder, not for the first time, what on earth I'm doing. As always at the beginning of an adventure, I don't want to go – least of all to where I'm going. We arrive at Beirut in the dark. Only six of us leave the tarmac bus for the city. The rest, including a distinguished-looking Englishman travelling with a Greek girl continue in transit. Cravenly, I long to go with them. The airport is small and dark and full of men in uniform. Signs made out of cardboard hang from the ceiling – one says *No tipping*, another *Money Change*, another *Tourist Information*. The *Money Change* says 'No' to my English fiver. Enraged, I fly to *Tourist Information* – a big burly, uniformed man sporting a Cretan moustache. He marches me back to Money Change, shouts, and waits while the clerk reluctantly changes my fiver into 400 Lebanese pounds. I'm solvent.

Tourist Information speaks English. He knits his brows over me and two Greek students with backpacks. 'Hotel?' I ask hopefully. The Greeks are surly, she a Cretan, he from Agrinion. Our protector bustles us over to a taxi, a beat-up 1960s vehicle. Off we bump into the dark, God knows where. It's an extraordinary feeling to come through a 1940s war film airport, then, in a taxi, falling into potholes, drive towards a mysterious destination. A city at war. We have a puncture. Beirut looks dilapidated and doesn't smell. I always feel safe with men with moustaches.

Our destination turns out to be The Club House in West Beirut near the top of Hamra. It's run by a handful of young Lebanese who arrange cultural outings. It's cheap, the loos are clean and the showers hot. I share a room with Marie, a pretty New Zealand girl, and George and Michael, Californian bums, full of hash and bonhomie. They're photographers. Their untidiness is impressive. A friend in England gave me the name and address of a friend in East Beirut. By glorious fluke one of the Californians knows his phone number. The bad news is the Club House is shutting in a couple of days for redecoration; and the flophouses and Y cost a fiver a night, way over my budget. Marie briefs me over Nescafé in the kitchen. There are no buses in Beirut but there might be one to Byblos. Otherwise transport is by Servis taxi, the Middle East equivalent of the Dolmus. No museums either. *No nothing*. The city is divided into two by the *green line*. Also staying here is a creepy Syrian. He once wanked in the bunk above Marie. George has stolen a pair of his shoes.

Feb 27th, Beirut

Saturday morning is soft and muggy-grey. There are no telephone directories in Beirut and sometimes you have to wait hours, if not days, for a line. After Nescafé I try my luck in the Club House office. A fuzzy-haired man is muttering over mimeographed copies of next week's cultural jaunt. A sweet-faced woman smiles encouragingly. To everyone's astonishment I get through to Peter Heyman.

'Oh good. A new face. Come to lunch. The Gilbertsons will pick you up at 1pm.'

Someone is practising Chopin on the piano in the Syrian's room. A low-pressure headache has driven me into the garden. I doze there until a Mercedes appears with the Gilbertsons, a professor from the American University and David Hirst, the Guardian correspondent and author or co-author of a book on Sadat which is currently causing an uproar.

Beirut is the saddest place; the souks gone, gun-pitted shells of buildings, refuse piled on what used to be chic promenades, a vast area destroyed. I am aghast and depressed. The port is bombed out. Two big hotels, the George and the Phoenicia, stand empty, pitted in an acne of bullet holes. Likewise the Holiday Inn. Road checks are mostly Syrian in their battledress of patchy pink. Or perhaps it's the Lebanese Army? Alec Gilbertson is an engineer working here and manoeuvres his Mercedes with the chutzpah of a Rome taxi driver. He and his wife Betty, an extremely pretty woman who used to be an actress, have lived in Beirut for years. They have no intention of leaving.

'The other day,' he remarks, negotiating a crater in the port area, 'the Syrians were having target practice and their shells ricocheted. All the pedestrians fell flat on their faces.' Betty laughs. I like them both immensely. Lunch is on the other side of the green line. Peter Heyman is a Maths professor at the Lebanese University, with a bird head on top of a corpulent body in a grey-blue jellabah. His wife, Jo, is a journalist. The lunch is delicious and the conversation fascinating.

'If ever re-built, Beirut, including the whole Lebanese coast, will be monstrous,' says David Hirst. He is a gloomy man. The Heymans have been here for years. When the Syrian peace-keepers moved into their house, they lost all their possessions. The President of the Republic intervened, but in vain. I'm amazed they stay. Later in the afternoon, before Alec and Betty drive me back to the Club House, I borrow Hirst's book, *The gun and the olive branch*, about the Arab-Israeli conflict. I'm ashamed I know so little.

In the evening, Marie and Michael and I gossip over a bottle of wine. Marie is the youngest of a family of nine from New Zealand, whose grandfathers emigrated from South Ouist. Her nose is crooked. Her mother called Sara died before she knew her. She's been travelling for eleven years. I fall asleep, my head buzzing with Druze, Falangists, Maronite Christians, Shia and Sunni, Uncle Tom Cobbley and all.

Guide to who I think is who and the warring parties:

Maronite Christians, Shia Moslems, Sunni Moslems, Druze, Palestinians (Beirut is ringed with Palestinian refugee camps), Syrians, Lebanese Army, United Nations. These splinter into 82 or so further groups.

Religious parties are:

CHRISTIAN
1) *Catholic* – Chaldeans – offshoot of Nestorians, Greek Catholic, Maronite, Roman Catholic.
2) *Orthodox Greek*
3) *Protestant* – some fringe sects. (Armenians can be Protestant, Gregorian (Orthodox) or Catholic. Many are leaving because of harassment from the right who are irritated by their neutral stand.)

MUSLIM
1) *Sunni* – old Moslem families of Beirut and Tripoli.
2) *Shia* – Southern Lebanon, and Northern Bekaa.

THE DRUSE
Their stronghold is in the Mountains of Lebanon. They call themselves Muwahiddin, Unitarians, or Bani Ma'aruf; the Sons of Knowledge. The first Druse were converts from Islam and their deity is the indivisible source of light, both spiritual and physical. The word Druse comes from one of the founders of their faith, a Persian called Darizi. Since they practise *takiyah* – concealment of their faith – little is known of it. Jumblatt, a Druse, was shot a few years ago.

How did it happen and what's going on now?

The war began in 1975 when a bus carrying Palestinians from a comrade's funeral passed near a Maronite church. A Maronite politician was addressing a meeting. The bus was attacked and its passengers massacred. Hirst in *The gun and the olive branch* says: 'All the peace-seeking Arab regimes shared the same strategic purpose: they all wanted to cut the Palestinians down to size.' Someone else – Tahjim? I can't read my notes – writes: 'In the first half of the war, when the Egyptians were encouraging the right-wing Christians (Maronites), Assad threw most of his weight, albeit cautiously, behind the Palestinians and their local Moslem-leftist allies. In the second half, when the Christians were getting the worst of it, he contracted an alliance with them that was even more flagrantly unnatural than the one with King Hussein. The Christians' other ally was Israel...' The Christians, however, didn't want the Syrian peace keeping force in East Beirut and flung both them and the Palestinians out.

A year ago one Christian faction murdered another on a beach in East Beirut. They say the next war will be between the Syrians and the Palestinians. A consensus of opinion from all 82 or so factions agrees the Syrians MUST go. What Israel is up to I don't know. I should have asked David Hirst. According to George the photographer, the Israelis hope the Maronite Christians will move South and catch the Palestinians in a pincer movement. He says the Pink Panthers are the Syrians' dirty-business men.

Feb 28th, Beirut

Storm and thunder rage without. After breakfast go back to bed. Chink of glass and voices from the kitchen finally rouse me. By dint of looking pathetic and expelling vast quantities of charm I think I may be allowed to stay on during the redecoration. George and I go for a walk. I like George. We wander through a Shia Moslem area by way of his office in Jeanne d'Arc Street, along the Avenue de Paris where I buy crescent-shaped bread, salted and sprinkled with *rigani* and into the American University campus. Here soft calm reigns and trees and flowers scent the air. One strange tree has roots growing from its branches. The market garden and shady walks hold a whiff of the old Beirut. I didn't know Israel wouldn't let either the Red Cross or Amnesty into the country. Reading Hirst's book I'm not surprised. Nor did I know that the Israelis invaded the no-man's land between the Golan

172

Heights and their border, were condemned by the United Nations but stayed to build kibbutzim. A notice near the university buildings says 'Two hours parking for tennis.'

Walk all day, getting more and more depressed. Beirut's new building is ghastly. Like the Athenians they've pulled down most of the pretty French Colonial and Turkish houses. I'm also depressed by how quickly I've got used to the scarred city and the crack of rifle fire at night. Torrential rain continues to fall and my sneakers squelch. Soon penicillin will fur the soles of my feet. Have found a tolerable wine called Ksara which costs just under £1. The Greeks are driving us mad. They get pissed and smoke too much hash. Now they're going to the PLO, now to Damascus. It would be a relief if they went somewhere *soon*.

March 1st, Beirut

I splash down Hamra in the pouring rain. It's difficult to believe this mess was once the Champs Élysées of Beirut. Its potholes are full of water. Beirut is the wettest city on the planet.

'You are the first person who has ever asked for information,' says Gladys in Tourist Information. She looks at me as if I've arrived from Mars and has no idea how I can get to Baalbek. There are police lounging outside. One, dark and swart, says he will take me. Not a good idea. Beirut is more dangerous than New York, not because of villains but the really dreadful driving. The pavements are full of parked wrecks. If you jaywalk you risk life and limb. Even I, prone to skip merrily under the wheels of cars, feel vulnerable. I managed to find Marie's supermarket and buy Scots Porridge Oats. She leaves for Syria tomorrow. Fucking Greeks. I wish they'd go away. They eat everyone's food, sit in everyone's chairs.

Dear Majid. Of the boys who run the Club House, I like him best. He has doe eyes and a long-suffering look. He suggests I share with the Syrian. I refuse and look pathetic. I end up in what I think is his office – a tiny loft up a ladder. There is a small, barred window, outside a bit of untidy garden and the Syrian

Intelligence Headquarters. A comfy bed, good reading light and a shelf for my books, sponge bag, diary, Bible and wine. Daddy would be amused at me carting his battered schoolboy edition round the Middle East. Somehow it seems appropriate.

'You are a drunk,' says Marie affectionately before leaving. Michael laughs.

'You just hang around till you get what you want, don't you Sara?'

He and George are moving out too, to share a flat with a witless bimbo. She is blonde with almond eyes and will have them for breakfast!

'I'm the most interesting thing you'll meet in Beirut.' What an idiot.

A tired-looking man, Lebanon's answer to Cary Grant – even down to the prowl – is talking to Majid. 'The Palestinians' confrontation with the Syrians will be the crunch one,' he says. Apparently, big fighting is coming soon. On Saturday evening a car bomb went off and killed eight people.

March 2nd/3rd, Beirut

I've seen rain before but this is ridiculous. Spend the day in bed, drinking red wine and reading the Bible, fortified by Dairylea and porridge. Outside the hail clatters. Peter and Joan Heyman appear at 6pm. After nearly destroying a palm tree in the Club House parking area, we drive to Mr Pickwick, a facsimile city pub for ex-pats. Joan is delightful and has a touch of Madame Arkati. The bartender is a retired MEA pilot. It rains and rains. Go to bed depressed by my writing which is dreary and stilted *and* by myself. Wake with a splitting head which depresses me even more. Angrily I shop, only to discover back in the loft that I've confused yoghurt with milk. I HATE milk. What a strange interlude this is. There's a cat in the baby palm tree outside and a bulldozer roaring about. Downstairs a floor cleaner spreads what looks like mud. I could die up here and no-one would know. A tin of condensed milk cures my headache. Refreshed, I finish Genesis and begin Exodus. Chapter 9, Verse 28 is my sentiment exactly: 'Intreat the Lord (for it is enough) that there be no more mighty thunderings and hail.'

March 4th, to Tyre and Sidon

The day – O miracle of miracles – dawns bright and clear. The Servis taxi leaves at 7am. I change at Kola and Sidon and three hours later reach Tyre. Three checkpoints yet no one checks my identity. The Lebanese drive horrendously fast. Sidon to Tyre in one hour flat. If bombs don't kill me the taxis will. My companions are friendly and kind; only one a trial because he eats and smokes at the same time. At last countryside is visible – it was raining so much before I couldn't see beyond the next puddle. Not far away are snow-capped mountains. The asphodel blooms and so do broad beans. Lorries which pass us wear feather dusters on their noses; as we bounce through orange, grapefruit and banana plantations the radio plays Johann Strauss. At Sidon a man with a cake gets in. Squashed between me and a fat mother, he looks anxious. The cake is worry to him.

Hiram's Tyre is impressive. There are sarcophagi everywhere but I don't know which one is his. King David's Glue abounds. A sea breeze blows in through the columned ways. We are very near the Israeli border. I like Roman Tyre. The hippodrome is vast. I sit in it and ruminate. The presumably once lovely coastline is now wrecked with shell holes, litter, an old refinery and horrible new buildings. Alas, Lebanese Modern makes Athens look like Bauhaus. Present day Tyre is provincial and smells of curry, its souk suitably dark and twisty with an open drain down the middle. Carcasses the size of camels hang overhead. It is now 12.15. I drink an orange juice and go back to Sidon, sitting beside yet another fat woman feeding a baby.

Sidon is the capital of the South and behaves like it. There is a covered and vaulted souk by the harbour where you could get lost for a fortnight. The *khan* in the souk is now a school. I investigate the harbour and look at what seem to be piles of those crushed things – murex – from which they made dye for the royal purple. The sweetmeats in the souk are a severe temptation: slabs, flanges, mounds of oozing goody, green and pink choco-late, *kadeifi*, pancakes. The falafel looks terrific. I must return one day for an orgy. Apart from a couple of yobs, everyone is friendly. Near Beirut we pass a lorry so laden with green bananas it looks like a cactus. The return trip costs £3.40 (27 Lebanese pounds).

That evening in Beirut I walk by Rouaches where the pigeon rocks lie in the sea. Every car seems parked in a puddle of blood. A distraught-looking woman reverses away from a fresh smear. The food and drink shacks are shut. The rich ghetto horror is so awful, the patches of blood so disturbing I go home.

March 5th, Beirut

Getting God's tabernacle right – and anointing both it and Aaron – is like a Proctor and Gamble critical path analysis. What a fusspot (Exodus chaps 26-31) Moses was. There's an excellent Scandinavian exhibition on. Afterwards I go to a reception at the Danish Embassy with Peter and Joan. The gin and tonics are watered and the food tasteless. Most of the guests are well-groomed, rich and boring; some, especially the nouveaux riches Lebanese, as tasteless as the food. Peter and Joan are so greedy. My getup is Turkish – a black dress over blue jeans; my toes so clean they squeak. Why are ex-pats frightful? One woman said that if you took a Servis taxi you would be robbed, raped or both. Another so-called old hand declared the fare to Tripoli to be 400 Lebanese pounds. I'm going there tomorrow and the fare is 20. Dorothea is the only person I like. Her father practically founded Beirut.

March 6th, jaunt to Tripoli in the north

An uneasy night of bad dreams and farting; chick peas the culprit. At 6.15am my Servis taxi leaves Beirut mudguard-deep in water, the driver, true to previous form, a Jehu. At well over

176

100mph we career up a beautiful coast. One of the men speaks English. My Arabic has now got to 30 words, including counting from one to ten, please, thank you, lovely, may I, Allah be with you etc.

'Don't you know it's dangerous to go alone to Tripoli? This lady is worried about you. Why have you no companion? Tripoli is full of soldiers.'

I make soothing noises. We pass an accident, the car upside down in glass and blood, its occupants either squashed or dead. Our driver reduces his speed. He's very good looking.

We arrive in Tripoli. The concerned woman takes me to her house below Saint Giles. She is pregnant, with nine children all of whom cluster round. The eldest daughter speaks French. The woman's brother, roused from his quilts, explains in fractured German that his brother-in-law works in Germany. His salary must have provided the green plush horror of the front parlour. If I were the brother-in-law, I'd stay away otherwise he'll find himself with 30 to provide for. We drink scented coffee – this Lebanese coffee is the best I've ever drunk – and my friend presses biscuits, a brooch, a bikini and a pair of knickers on me. I flee before she fills my bag with the contents of her house. These people are so kind – my hostess with her sweet face, her tired brother, the funny drunk friend who wandered in. When I compare them with those idiots at the embassy party, it's the latter I pity.

The eldest boy escorts me to the Taynal Mosque. He backs away in horror when I try to give him money. Doze in the sun until the curator lets me in. It's a very pretty mosque, chunky, vaulted, serene. The Syrian guard outside waves his machine gun so I retreat to the mesh of the medieval souk below. The thunder-heads are grumbling above Saint Giles; shopping fever rages in the *khans, hammams* and *madressehs*. Dodging carts, nuns, old boys in flowerpots, shoppers, I loaf. There are spices and sweet perfumes, rotting balls of black cheese, tripe, savoury morsels on spits – my nose is maddened. One *khan* is full of old men working at sewing machines. The goldsmiths, coppersmiths and silversmiths live in an Aladdin's cave. By midday it's time to look for a taxi back to Beirut.

Into my life comes rip-off Greek-speaking Abdullah; a fearful scoundrel but worth being ripped off by because of his charm, his philosophy of life – in a nutshell, all comes to him who lies his head off – and his Oddjob mien. First I am to share the taxi with a client going to Beirut airport. The client cancels. Abdullah is outraged. Then, if I pay him 40 Lebanese pounds he will take me to Byblos and show me the ruins. Another scheme for another ten pounds is to show me Santa Maria and the big castle at Batroun. This I wisely resist. What he actually does is to swap me into another taxi at a checkpoint, thus making a tidy profit. My fellow traveller is a man in a huge grey cardy with a knitted hat. The hat has an uncontrollable bobble. Arabs are as eccentric as Greeks. I can't get over the tasteless building, especially the Christs and show-off churches in the hills outside Beirut.

March 7th, to Anjar

The ruins at Anjar, rosy and grave, stand in a plain under snowy mountains off the road to Damascus. Peter and Joan pick me up at the Club House and we drive over the pass to Syria, 4,000 feet above sea level. The day is blue and flawless, the countryside lush and beautiful, full of orchards, cornfields and vegetables. Chtaura is a shanty town surrounded by vineyards. We doze in the sun and gossip. Some extraordinarily rude teenage girls appear and pester Joan and I with questions. One with big tits demands to be told how beautiful she is, then asks me where my husband is! Giggle, giggle. Eyes like knives. 'He died,' I reply coldly. Silence. Big tits turns crimson and the others slink off. 'I didn't know you were married,' says Joan. I tell her I've invented and killed off more husbands than Zsa Zsa Gabor. Bare poplars rattle in the wind. Finally we rouse ourselves and bounce down shady lanes, past copses and glittering trout streams. Our lunch in a small restaurant, delicious fresh trout, comes out of these streams. Fish, salad and wine in the warm sun. What bliss. Peter and Joan steal the leftovers from the nextdoor table. They are incorrigible.

The Golan Heights are white with snow. We get caught in a late afternoon Sunday traffic jam. Is Sunday the same everywhere? Mist cloaks the pass and soldiers checking cars only increase the confusion. I now know what scents the coffee so deliciously – cardamom. In the car beside us sits a man with a foot-long moustache – six inches of rigid black brush on either side of his nose. That evening, wandering near the green line, I dive into lettuces when a car backfires (or a rifle goes off). The greengrocer, a nice man, dusts me down. So much for the bold adventurer. Later, reading *Bitter Lemons* in bed, I hear screams. Grunts, screams, silence. Then AH AH AH like an orgasm. It's coming from the headquarters of Syrian Intelligence opposite. Someone is being tortured.

March 8th – 13th, Beirut & Byblos

A bomb goes off on the morning of the 8th shaking my loft. I'm reading the end of *The gun and the olive branch, Flight into Camden* and *The Colossus of Marousi* by Henry Miller. Very pleased with himself, Miller is. Hirst's book fills me with increasing disbelief, horror and fascination. The massacre of Deir Yassin in 1948 is particularly shocking, a lodestar in the spiral of violence and hatred between Zionist and Arab. What a monster Ben Gurion was. Start *Beer in the snooker club* by an Egyptian writer, Waguih Ghali. Albeit a book about despair it's hilarious and whets my appetite for Egypt. Walk and read and brood. How comic that, in 1976 when the war started, Rip-off Abdullah was making *hummus* in Athens. No wonder his Greek consists of 'my darling' and 'my little doll.'

I have a new recipe. Salted porridge, mixed with spring onions, white beans and hard-boiled eggs. It is quite delicious. I eat it in my loft, watching the sparrows bounce about the garden. What irrepressible birds they are. Feel reclusive. Read. Sleep. On the

179

evening of the 9th emerge from my nest to go and listen to an old love, Humphrey Lyttleton, blowing his horn in the American University. Ageless, just as good as when I first heard him in 1954. *Like someone in love, Beale Street Blues, Body and Soul:* the arabic-fretted vaulting – Gothic – of the hall quivers to his horn. A stodgy audience ends up cat-calling and yelling. Go home in a trance of pleasure and fall on Iraq dates and cream cheese.

March 10th, Byblos

A delightful jaunt to Byblos with Alec and Betty Gilbertson. It's cold again. Temples and tombs browse in the thick green grass. Sea stocks bloom in the crannies of the Crusader Castle. The place is wonderful, full of damp spring smells and ghosts, placid on its promontory facing the sea. The weather is Scottish – fitful sunlight then wild rains brought in by a west wind. Alec and Betty propose another jaunt to Baalbek and I accept with delight. We picnic, drink wine and gossip. What nice people they are. The stone at Byblos is a soft gold, almost strokeable. That night I lie in my loft and listen to the rain. Feel ill for the next two days. The wind now blows from the North and my loft is freezing until the morning sun strikes it. I stay in bed wearing two sweaters, only venturing out once to change money for Jordan and Syria. Am confused by their currencies. Counting and re-counting my Lebanese change, I find I only have enough for dates and cheese. No wine. O gloom. I really can't stand Henry Miller.

March 13th, jaunt to Echmoun and Lady Hester Stanhope's grave

We meet at the Madhaf near the green line: Peter, Jo, a man called Peter Francks and his friend Samira, a Druse. Jo is gloomy and predicts rain as we crawl through the squalour of the suburbs. Happily she is wrong. Echmoun I find unimpressive but I'm spoilt by Greece and Turkey. Lady Hester's grave is a delight. There's a *Café Stand Hop.* The grave lies high on a hill beside a ruined monastery. Nearby in the orange groves bloom red anemones, cyclamen, daisies – the spring flowers of the

Mediterranean. I pick a bunch to honour her indomitable spirit. It is, alas, no thanks to the British Embassy that the grave is well-kept. They didn't lift a finger. The Canadian Ambassador did the honours when the re-consecration ceremony took place last year.

March 14th, Baalbek

If the Greeks had built Baalbek in 600 BC it would have accorded with its surroundings, blended in, achieved a kind of unity – something the Romans never understood. Their buildings are impositions on the landscape so nearly always FAR TOO BIG. Baalbek is colossal – certainly conceived as a public relations exercise. This has been a lovely day of sun, fun, jokes and foolishness. It's cold, the sky a bitter blue. Alec and Betty have just become grandparents so all day long we drink the health of Thomas Gilbertson. In the Nekad wine cellars they bring out champagne. Heino and Ilsa make up our party of five. He works for UNRA and plays the buffoon to perfection. She is a glamorous lion.

The Bekaa plain is impressive, a patchwork of fertility. Zachlé is dreadful – ugly, dirty and war-scarred. Apparently, Baalbek is the centre of the stolen car industry. About fifteen cars a day go up the road and none come back. Driving through this glorious Lebanese countryside the irreverent thought strikes me that it's not so much war that has fucked up its beauty but money. Two nice details: a bedouin tent with a TV aerial on top of it; and a soldier in a Druse procession with a water bottle stuffed in the end of his rocket launcher. Like Humpf with his sink plunger mute!

I'm sad to leave the Club House, arched under eucalyptus. I've even grown fond of battered Beirut – familiarity and friendships breed unexpected feelings. I shall remember rain and bananas and porridge, Ksara red wine and *Nakad Rosé*, the crump of grenades, hooting taxis, falafel sandwiches and the spit of rifle fire at night. I shall remember the dreadful architectural ugliness and the rain; the smell of gum trees, coffee with cardamom, rain; war and despair and rain – and more litter than I have seen in 45 years.

Likos, 2005

The cat nearly died but is now being nursed back to health on a diet of Corned Beef and milk. Its hospital is the box full of newspapers in the shed under the steps. This morning it tottered out, eyes looking alright for the first time in a week. One of its lives is gone. Max, the collie, comes and goes on his ballet dancer's legs and gives the invalid an occasional sniff. Sometimes they sit side by side looking pensive. Animals know all about emotional blackmail. The women cleaning their fish on the low sea wall outside my room are surrounded by a parliament of cats, each rigid with longing. Greeks are not sentimental. The convalescent wandered towards a burly party gutting fish. 'He's been very ill,' I said. She smiled and went on gutting. When the cat got too near she gave him a whack. Result? Back to its box with its eyes crossed. You've got to be resilient to survive as a Greek moggie.

 Fish and fishing are the island addiction. Everyone catches them – with rod, line, nets, probably their bare hands. Everyone eats them: blue tunny, small sole, whitebait and others I know only by their Greek names – lithrini, melanouri, sargos, kefalos. *No food is as good as fish from the sea, strewn with herbs and grilled over charcoal, served with oil and a chunk of lemon. Fish should be eaten with the hands. Harbour Popi's husband goes fishing for small tuna with Nearby Popi's husband. Often the kitchen in the harbour taverna is knee-deep in fish. Thanassi works like a surgeon, cleaning, filleting, slicing. He stores the rich meat in salt, layer upon layer in olive oil containers, the tins to be put away for a year. The priest in Psara is keen on fishing. So was the one back in 1982. The only souls he caught had fins.*

 The first lupins have flowered and soon the terraces will be blue. Asphodel have burst from their spear-like sheaths. The jagged-stemmed euphorbia, possessed of extraordinary elasticity, wags its bracts. The council is busy pollarding. Spring must be on the way. Today is Saturday, the 29th of January. Ilias the tailor found me having an early lunch at Nearby Popi's taverna. We talked of this and that. 'Oh for April and broad beans!' I cried. My passion for certain foods is a source of amusement to my Greek friends. Greeks serve baby beans in their pods in dill sauce. Arabs mash the beans in a green pepper, lemony sauce. That was the supper at the YWCA in Amman on my first night there...

Chapter Fourteen

Calm Amman – Madaba and Mount Nebo – Petra – Kerak – Jerash
1982

March 15th, to Amman

Wake at 4am and luckily stay awake. As in Greece, nothing goes the time it says. Our taxi to Damascus leaves its scruffy office at 6:30am not 7am. As we climb the road from the airport I look back at Beirut and wonder what will become of it. We're four including the driver: an elegant woman in the front seat and in the back a fat Syrian boy with green eyes, and me. It's freezing. We stop at Chtaura for coffee and the Lebanese woman and I talk. She looks 30 but has a 25 year old son, speaks perfect English and tells me about her family who came from Italy to Lebanon 500 years ago. Her husband is in intensive care in Damascus with a heart attack, his second. 'He was told not to smoke and drink. He takes no notice. He is a criminal.' As we drive on, she waves a despairing hand at the driver and the Syrian, both chain-smoking.

Syrian Customs are unbelievable. They take two and a half hours to let us through. We are searched twice. One examines the contents of my wallet.

'What is this?'

'Money,' I reply coldly.

The oaf has the grace to look abashed. As we approach Damascus every illusion of a beautiful oasis crumbles. It is the ugliest thing yet, a mess of building sites. After a pee in a filthy loo, I leave in the Servis for Amman. It's noon but still cold. There must be an old part of Damascus somewhere. Just as well I'm coming back to see it before it vanishes. I might loathe Syria but I MUST see Palmyra, Aleppo and Krak des Chevaliers.

The road from Damascus to Amman goes straight as a skewer, traversing bare gloomy country. Our grey-haired driver drives fast, overtaking nervously. This is a container truck highway so everything's going at 100mph. I'm scared. A girl and her Circassian mother are in the front seat; in the back me, a square woman in a gown and cardy and a man with a little boy. Suddenly Nemesis strikes. One of our tyres blows and from side to side we career and screech, missing by a hair's breadth the oncoming lorries and buses. It seems an eternity, is probably a minute. We land in the dust just off the wrong side of the road. Silence. No one says a word. We are white as sheets including the driver. If this is the road Saul of Tarsus was struck blind on, it's living up to its reputation. As the driver changes the tyre we slowly recover. The girl in front speaks English and is at Damascus University reading electricity. She is called Sahar. The little boy is quietly sick.

Leaving Syria is worse than entering. The Customs' officials are thugs. I'm taunted, mocked, humiliated and the contents of my rucksack pulled apart and thrown on the ground three times. Talk about a lesson in self-control. There is only one answer: I smile politely and say thank you, even when my passport is flung in the dust at my feet. The more offensive they are the more polite I become. The final search nearly undoes my good work. In a pouch in my rucksack is a mink's foot, gifted to me by a friend who shares my fur fetishism. The tall Syrian with straight black eyebrows and straight black moustache opens the pouch. His brows knit as he fishes out the foot.

'*What* is this?'

Giggles rise inside me but to laugh would mean no Jordan.

'Fur,' I coo.

He examines it minutely while I look at my feet. Then he puts the foot back in its pouch – a voodoo foot! By the time we get to Jordanian Customs, I'm exhausted. What a contrast. The soldiers are polite and look like the RAF, trees have been planted and litter is minimal. With some difficulty I get a month's stay. No one asks about currency. The taxi, all Jordanians, is now cheerful. They're horrified by my treatment at the hands of the Syrians. The driver laments as we drive along.

'No foreigners will come to Arab countries if they are treated like this.'

'Pigs,' says Sahar. Her mother is beautiful. I seem to remember Circassian women are renowned for their beauty.

North Jordan is enchanting with its green rolling hills and mountains of Gilead, olives, crops, wild flowers and below – winding broadly south and glinting in the sunlight – the river Jordan. We pass Jerash. At 5.15pm, after nearly eleven hours of dust and disillusion, near death and torment by Syrian thugs, we arrive in a city of building blocks worming in and out of ravines – Amman. No one in the taxi park knows anything about a YWCA or hostel. I stand mute, helpless and exhausted while Arabic *wachs* and *bachs* around me; one group appeals to another, a man says he thinks he knows, more discussion involves another group…

'If he's right, it's on my way home. I will take you there.' An angel with a car who speaks English. What a good kind man. He likes the English. After what they've done to the Middle East I can't think why. We ferret round and round the streets and then find it – a baby Buckingham Palace built in the thirties – the Young Women's Christian Association. The residents look over-dressed and glam, giving the place a wicked whiff. Bed and breakfast and sharing a room with two others is a fiver. My room mates are Ayesha and Kholud. Once over their initial alarm, they feed me coffee, green loquats and tea. Supper is broad beans – *foul*.

March 16th/17th, Amman

At my first Y breakfast everyone stares and eats in silence. There are fried eggs, tea and bread and *zatar*, grass seeds that are good for you. Mixed with olive oil, this *zatar* is delicious. The Y is in

186

the Kolonaki of Amman beside the embassies. Roads descend into ravines of daunting complexity. The city has an oddly Scottish 1930s feel, half familiar and yet quite foreign. Hills are steep. No tourist office exists but there's a Ministry of Tourism on the Third Circle, whatever that might be. Also, somewhere near, are the British Council and ubiquitous Goethe Institute. The stone is mushroom-pink, calm and mellow. Amman strikes me as a calm place. Forsythia blooms. There's not a backpacker in sight. Prices are too high for them in Jordan.

Downtown in a ravine I find the souks and beside them the Cliff Hotel, old-fashioned and not very clean. The boy in reception speaks English. It's about £3 something a night so could be a fall-back from the Y if funds dwindle. The souks are a delight, full of spices and little shops and stalls selling envelopes of meat and cheese and everything under the sun. After hummus in a kaf, I track down the Servis taxis to Madaba, look at the Roman theatre and puff back up the hills to the Y. In the evening Ayesha takes me for a walk, she swinging her hips and stopping every man in his tracks, I feeling like an aunt. Ayesha's dramatic sexuality and Medea looks conceal a kind heart. She is a dear. So is Kholud. I could listen to their Arabic hiss and whoosh and whah and purr for hours. 'We hope you will stay a long time. We are very lucky in you.' Kholud has an angelic face and large thighs. She's in love with Alain Delon.

The Jett Bus Co do trips to Petra. Find the stop. Tick. Done that. Spend most of my second day in Amman in the Folklore Museum, looking at Bedouin art. The materials, the weave, the patterns, the workings of the simplest kind are full of natural taste. There are delicate embroideries; rugs, bags, saddlebags – my head swims with the colours. As to the jewellery – amber in edible chunks, the silver, black enamel and agate bangles, rings and necklaces – what glory. The Circassians were great makers of jewellery. Shapes of cooking utensils, carved, beaten, cast, are so satisfying. When the Bedouin move, they carry their coffee beans and other comestibles in gourds like droopy bagpipes. They grind their beans in a *Mabash*; as one thumps away, the others sing. Begin to learn some names for dress: *Dishdash* is a man's robe, *Hatah* his headress; *Foustan* is a woman's dress (the Greek for skirt is *foustani*) and an old woman's dress is a *Thob*.

The *Rabada* enthralls me. It's a musical instrument for home use only and consists of a skin stretched over two rough pieces of wood, one string running from its base to the centre of a crude wooden handle. The bow is a bent stick strung with gut. Like playing a toboggan. Of all the exhibits, the most superb are the Bedu masks. Clambering back up the hill in the late afternoon, I compare the taste and beauty I've admired with our post-war barbarism.

March 18th, to Madaba and Mount Nebo

Breakfast early on grass seed, cheese and three cups of tea; then go by way of the 253 bus to the Servis taxi station. One is waiting, its contents three old gents in *hatahs* and *dishdashes*, fierce and unsmiling. My nervous *Salaam aleikom* is rewarded by cries of *Aleikom salaam* and handshakes. They're not fierce at all. We drive off in drizzle through calm, rolling country. The Salisbury Plain appears on our right and I wonder whether Glubb Pasha helped Hussein shape Jordan geographically as well as politically. The wheat is green. The desert lies to the East.

Madaba's a friendly place. In the 6th century Byzantine church – almost a ruin – there's an extraordinary mosaic map of Palestine. I particularly like the fat fish going down into the Dead Sea and coming up again – clearly didn't care for the salt. Suddenly bag-pipes skirl. I investigate and find a procession at the bottom of the hill – Cubs, Brownies, Sea Scouts and a band. Cheerful boys in *hatahs* play small bagpipes and fifes while girls beat drums and shake castanets. They wait so patiently in the rain; the priest shivering, the young schoolmistress blue with cold. The wind plays havoc with the banners, wrapping them round their bearers. No-one gets cross and everyone's happy. Local urchins skip about. Policemen confer. Expectancy hangs heavy...

At last the event. A motorbicycle escort followed by a cavalcade of grand limos engage the hill only to become enmeshed with the leader of the procession, dancing like a flea and screaming at his followers. Pipes wailing, drums banging, they advance. The limos slip and slide on the steep gradient. One forced to brake rolls backwards and nearly squashes the motor bicycle escort behind. No-one taught *him* how to ease off a handbrake. Cars, procession and band finally make it to the top. To cheers and clapping a pink bishop gets out of the last car. Banners flying, the children lead him proudly to church. He has come to confirm them.

The museum has quantities of relics – Stone Age, Ammonite, Moabite, Greek, Roman, Abbasid, Omayadd. A large black tablet (the original is in the Louvre) proclaims the victories of Mish-Mash, son of Shibboleth the Moabite, over King Imri of Israel in the 9th century BC. Very Monty Python. The English-speaking guide says it's Aramaic. Two Germans and I make up the guided tour. We peer respectfully at mosaics, all 6th century, then take tea with the museum director. The guide, who tries to kiss me and smells, says I can go to Mount Nebo with the Germans. 'There is room in the car.' Presuming him to be the organiser, I climb in. The Germans look surprised. Later I discover that it's *their* car and *their* driver. He's a baron of industry who fishes in Ireland and has a farm in Australia.

Mount Nebo is beautiful, the sky black and blue and the wind like a knife. You can see Jerusalem and Jericho across the Dead Sea, the green snake of the River Jordan. Here Moses stood. It is all quite extraordinary; probably the more so because I thought these places were make-believe. An American is excavating for Moses but hasn't found him yet. More churches and more mosaics, again 6th century AD. A fine woman with sad eyes gives us Bedouin bread, wafer-thin and salty. I can't tear myself away from the view. When I do, I fall into a hole, only to be rescued by the evil-smelling one. Actually he's a nice man and entertains us in his home to coffee, glasses of yoghurt and sweet tea. There are strange plants here. The stalks of one – it looks like dead asphodel – they roast.

Poor Germans. I stick like a burr. They can't very well dump me so take me back to Amman. From the 7th circle I catch a bus to base and the welcoming smiles of Ayesha and Kholud. They have become maternal; say I must put more cream on my face.

March 19th, Amman

To reach Amman's citadel you climb stone ladders between houses. It reminds me of the Hill of Lycabettos and I feel a frisson of nostalgia for Athens. Ruins litter the mount. Among the sighing pines all is tranquillity. Burnt broad beans with salt and parsley bought off a stall taste good. Amman is coming into focus and I like it more and more – the mushroom-pink stone, Baly's Laundry, the Thinner Factory (where is the Fatter?), the baby Fortnum's grocery owned by Elias B Hoshe under the Baghdad Grand Hotel, old men with desert faces; I linger by stalls selling brains and pilaf, sample mysterious mixtures of green sauce and chickpeas, notice what good business my old client Rowntrees does here. Smarties and Kit Kat rub shoulders with Mars and Marathon. Amman has a touch of Cheltenham and Bath, a kind of pre-war solidity. In the afternoon, I lie on my bed and read the Bible. No wonder the Zionists follow Old Testament God; He defines boundaries so precisely.

Ayesha and Kholud arrive, exhausted, from their hair-dos. Sahar, fellow-sufferer in the taxi from Damascus, rings. She and her pop star brother Riad collect me and we drive to their home. All the brothers look like filmstars. Mum is one of three wives – with a smile to melt a monster. The men eat first, then girls and women settle down to what's left of the dishes of eggs, hummus, *zatar*, yoghurt, cheese and stuffed peppers. What a nice family. They revere the King and say I'll probably see him driving about. Am getting more adept at using bread like a spoon. It stops you eating too fast.

Drama back at the Y. Two girls have quarrelled over which TV channel to watch. One hit the other and she's been unconscious for an hour. The hitter is bonkers. Every morning at 6.30am she

lies in wait for Ayesha and asks her for a match. What a funny Y.
Some girls are friendly, others rich and rude. Miriam whose nose
is like the claw bit on a bulldozer sleeps in the oddest places.
Yesterday I saw her emerging from the lounge with her blanket.
She's told me about her family, old and respected in Syria, and
her uncle the colonel-general. 'I say to them, come to Jerusalem,
we shall together be.' She is *very* boring. At breakfast, I munch
my bread and jam and *zatar* under the pensive gaze of Christ. It's
the usual picture – Margaret Tarrant's blue period – of Him in the
moonlit garden of Gethsemane. This Y is grander than the
Thessaloniki one but the girls still scream. Tomorrow I'm off to
the Cliff.

March 20th, Amman

The sky is blue, the air crisp. The Cliff is one of those places
neither clean nor dirty. They are kind and polite and have given
me a room as far away as possible from reception and the gossiping, smoking men. How I *wish* I was a man; then I could go
into the cavernous, stove-piped coffee room halfway up the
stairs. My room has two beds, a table, chair, wardrobe with no
coat hangers, a bedside cupboard and a basin with a dripping
tap. You have to be King Kong to open and shut the door. To my
amazement, there is a clean sit-upon loo as well as a squatter and
PINK LOO PAPER! I lie on my bed and ruminate, pleased to be
downtown and away from middle-class girls. Outside the sun
shines. Taxis hoot.

There's a fine archaeological museum on the citadel. Trying to find
it, I mislay the steps and climb purposefully onto someone's roof.
They are astonished. Today, for the first time, I've seen tourists.
Poor Jordan, longing to get into the tourist game, unaware of the
horrors in store. The museum is empty; a cool silence disturbed
only by the squeak of my sneakers. Am unnerved by remains of
rhino, wild horses and wild boar from Azraq, 600,000-200,000 BC.
(Lower Palaeolithic, 100,000-400,000 BC, is called the Achaulian
Age.) These wastes of time are intimidating. Am comforted by a
goddess from Petra and a burnt brick from Jericho, dated a mere

6,000 BC. Trumpets, Joshua and all-consuming fire. The earliest-recorded statue came from there. I squeak on. From a side room float voices – the director and his friends. Decide that a skull with holes in it, again from Jericho, is Sisera. The label says the man was operated on. I prefer my Sisera theory. A tragic exhibit: the skeleton of a tiny child curled in a jar. Dead infants were buried in jars and often put under the living room floor so that they could stay part of the family and not be lonely. Tyche is the Goddess of Amman. They found her on the citadel. Drifting into the relative mundanity of Hellenistic and Byzantine, I investigate a side room and discover astonishing anthropoid coffins from the Iron Age, made of rusty red pottery. Spooky.

I shall never be rude about the British Council again. Amman's is a gem, housed in a grand, Edinburgh-like building with a library, garden and nice class of loo. Now for an orgy of Freya Stark starting with *Alexander's Path*. Opposite the Cliff is a cupboard where a cheerful creature makes coffee. He likes the English and will take no payment.

'Good morning, sister,' says an old man in the hotel. He calls me 'sister' to reassure me. It is the custom.

March 21st, to Petra

Sleep fitfully due to the alarm clock in my head. A friend pinched a lover of mine years ago and in the dream there they are, gazing hungrily at one another. Fancy feeling jealous after 20 years. We are five in one of Jett's small vans – Serena, a tall blond doctor; Aurelia, a nanny; Passy from Finland and Terry from Lincoln. The men are on business. Down the desert highway, crash and bounce, going at the usual improbable speed; a scrub desert flecked with green. Bedouins with their flocks. Tents are few, dwellings mainly scatters of square brick or mud. Pylons and telegraph posts stalk the wastes; a railway goes somewhere. There is no real sand. Serena is sociable, Aurelia suspicious. She looks like Richard III. She also hates fresh air (a nanny trait?) and glowers at the window which, due to our speed, keeps popping off its latch and flying open.

At 11am we arrive at the hotel, pick up our guide, climb onto horses – thin and knackered – and ride down the Siq into Petra. Rose red city half as old as time. The Siq like Ariadne's thread, is labyrinthine. No wonder Petra was impregnable. The Nabataeans came out of Arabia in 600 BC. By 300 BC they had expelled the Edomites – chucking several off a cliff, the rock of Sela of the Bible. The Romans knew they could never take the fortress so they cut off the water supply. Petra fell in 106 AD. Clever buggers, the Romans.

Hanni, our guide, is a serious man. The Bedouin have long faces, furrowed by sun and emotion. They look wrong in suits. We scramble after him into cave dwellings, tombs and a great hall where Nabataeans chose beautiful girls to be human sacrifices. Petra is magnificent but I don't like it. The vibrations upset me. Perhaps it's the screams of the beautiful girls or the terror of the first born. Eight Bedouin tribes still live here. Next year they leave to be re-settled by the government. 'They have become greedy,' says Hanni gloomily as we puff up and down pink slabs of rock. He shows us the cave on a nearby hillside where he was born. There is no time for the High Place of the Monastery. Lunch is indifferent. The loos are jammed with loo paper. When I pull the plug, urine and tissue rise in wrath and pour over my Kickers. There is nothing in the museum.

The trip back is more crash and bounce. My prickly-eyed feelings have turned to sick headache. Bulldozers are constructing another lane to this one-lane road, doubtless to transform it into a Super Tourist Motorway.

The verges are littered with wrecks – on their backs, stove in, minus wheels. *Inṣallah* we shall not join them. Terry tells a good story about the Syrian secret police. They have ordered special white Peugeots, a model not available in Syria, thus making themselves the most un-secret police in the Middle East! Back at base, head banging like a drum, I'm told I will have to leave the

Cliff. May its carpets ignite! The police have ordered it to be closed for a week for re-painting and cleaning of quilt and curtain. I plead with the boy while painters crash about. He relents.

March 23rd, to Kerak

Spent all day yesterday in the British Council. What nice civilised people. Not only do they provide me with a cup of tea, Freya Stark and a loo, they also let me put my bottle of *Latroun Rosé* in their fridge. I've caught a fever from drinking Amman tap water.

Today, Kerak. Arrive at 9:15am. My Bedouin driver from Amman, bad tempered and full of cold, says there are no taxis back to Amman and he will give me a special price. Lies, all lies. One goes back at noon. O foolish Bedouin. Rumpled be thy dwellings, ring-wormed thy flocks! Kerak is very fine. In its heyday, with 5,000 souls in the massive keep, it must have seemed unassailable. The museum director explains how they signalled across the Dead Sea to Jerusalem: one extra stone on the walls meant 'I'm alright'; two stones 'Are you alright?'; three stones 'HELP'! Morse code in building blocks – very smart. They also had communications shafts, kind of 13th century telephones, linking the levels and sophisticated water systems. Happily scramble about the keep, a mixture of Crusader, Suleiman and Mameluk, plunging into sunken chambers and tunnels. There are spatters of rain and hot sun, perfect for ghosts and castles. Later the director, a charm-pot who speaks perfect English, takes me down one level to the best-preserved pieces of the Crusader period – superb galleries, probably council chambers or reception rooms. 'I do not do this for everyone,' he says (liar) then escorts me to a chunk of keep to drink tea with his archaeological colleagues. While the wind moans without I rail within against the horrors of mass tourism. They listen courteously but don't believe a word. Why should they? Everyone else is doing it.

In Amman, downtown is fresh after the rain. I rejoice in the almond blossom, the glow of honey-pink stone and a thunder-head, genie-like behind the Citadel. Tonight my falafel man is nearly friendly. Eight of his hot, melting morsels devoured with cheese and washed down with a bottle of *Latroun Rosé* make a banquet. After a week's abstinence, this humble wine tastes like Veuve Clicquot. Outside the traffic complains and growls. Voices mumble. I sit in my room with its grimy silk curtains in complete content.

March 24th – 27th, Amman

My nose runs and my head aches and reading *Beyond Euphrates* by Stark I realise for the first time that Mesopotamia means between the rivers. Have I learned Greek for nothing? Snooze and sneeze and feel dreadful. The African painters crash and giggle outside my room. Who would know if I died – or care? An animal has bitten me on the leg, taking up residence in my sleeping bag, enjoying the generated heat. Soon I am covered in bites. There is nothing for it, despite flu, but to get up, get dressed and go outside. It's freezing. The sky is Parker-blue and camels sail past, one with a honey-white baby. Giving birth to a camel must be dreadful. Totter around, then buy what must be the oldest hard-boiled egg in Jordan; when peeled it is brown. Parsimoniously I mash it with a triangle of Ramek cheese.

Things improve. Rab Butler has died. March is going out like a lion. It's so cold I'm wearing gloves and every time it rains my Kickers fill with water. Shades of Beirut. I've learnt much in a month, now read Middle Eastern news with attention, wonder how I could have been so ignorant so long. The West Bank situation looks serious. Will the Israelis blow us up? The British Council has huge forsythia trees guarding its front door, waterfalls of yellow. The cherry blossom is out. Best of all, the biter has stopped biting. Probably killed by the egg. There's a marvellous bit in Samuel about the Philistines – Palestinians – capturing the Ark of God. God is not pleased: '…and he smote the men in the city, both small and great, and they had emerods in their secret parts…' (Chap 5, verse 9). He gave them piles.

Elias, a Palestinian guide, says the weather is too wet for the desert forts. He fought with the Scots and Irish in the war. My orgy of Freya Stark continues – finish *Beyond Euphrates* and start on *Dust in the lion's paw*. Decide to stay in Amman for one more Stark and a trip to Jerash. To sit in comfort and read, breaking the day with a walk or snack, is such pleasure; one day beer and hummus, prepared with slivers of spicy meat and pine kernels with a side dish of spring onions, olives and radishes; another day a take-away *Musakhan* to share with Ayesha at the Y. We sit on her bed, demolishing it with our fingers. The bread is baked to a crisp succulence of onion, pine kernels and chicken juices. Savoury chunks of chook lie jointed on top. Another memorable meal is Friday lunch (Friday is Sunday here) with Sahar and her family. We eat *Mensaf*, a Jordanian speciality, chunks of lamb on a pilaf thick with pine kernels. A tangy, hot yoghurt soup is poured over it. Arabs eat so beautifully with one hand, scooping out the rice and deftly rolling it into a ball. To the amusement of the family, I end up with a pawful of rice and no ball. It rains and rains and rains. Sahar's mum has insisted on her leaving Damascus for the time being because of political unrest. Maybe I should call my trip to Syria '*Head in the lion's mouth*'?

Last night I heard the wail of 'It's going to be a LONG, LON-EL-Y summer' floating from reception TV, reminding me of the summer of 1962 and lying with flu in a flat in Cornwall Gardens. Today I have consumed 20 falafel and two Mars bars. It's so bloody cold my bottle of *Latroun Rosé* is chilled from being in the wardrobe. The coffee man took me up to see his birds this evening – budgies and tiny ones like finches. One female budgie had just given birth. Her babies squirmed round her, naked and horrid. I have discovered *Zachlab*, a hot vanilla drink dusted with coconut and cinnamon.

March 28th, to Jerash and Adjlun

My taxi leaves Ad Abdaly at 7.15am. It's full of workmen. One of them – his hands are huge – taps my shoulder and offers me a sandwich. To share your food in the Middle East is basic courtesy. From the ravines of downtown we climb to the heights, then down past the Palestinian refugee camp. The road north becomes beautiful, the land carpeted with red anemones, yellow and white asphodel, blue flowers, pink flowers and mimosa. The day is chilly – glove weather. Shadows smudge the hills. We pass *The Holy Land Hotel*. At 8.15, the taxi drops me at Jerash. Through an arch beckons a vista of sweeping, curving columns.

Having been so rude about Baalbeck, I have to admit that Jerash is spectacular. Originally a prehistoric site, then Hellenistic, then Jewish for a time until Pompey overran the Middle East, it is a wonderful example of a provincial Roman city. A well-written guide book encapsulates its charm:

'In a remote quiet valley among the mountains of Gilead lie the ruins of Jerash, at one time a city of the Decapolis, and the only one of that powerful league through whose streets and monuments we can wander and see them as they were in its heyday, untouched except for the hand of time. Greater cities, such as Gadara and Philadelphia, have vanished almost without trace, but the remoteness of Jerash has saved it from being used as a stone quarry for nearby towns and villages. The setting adds greatly to the charm of the place, lying as it does in a valley running roughly north and south and with a perennial stream running through the centre of it. The banks of the stream are covered with walnut and popular (poplar?) trees, which look green and cool even in the heat of summer, when the surface of the surrounding hills is reduced to a harsh brown aridity...'

The setting of the city reminds me of Apollo's temple at Bassae behind Adritsena in the Peloponnese. There is such space, such beauty in the hills. Workmen are building a new museum. The Visitors' Centre is empty and as I pad around it, brooding on Jordanian good taste as compared to Greek love of tat, a man approaches. His English is near perfect, his smile delightful and his manners are impeccable. Over breakfast in the hilltop café – I got up before the sesame bread and hard-boiled egg and cheese men so am famished – we talk of Jerash and Jordan and politics. The shadow of a broken arch, the lines of columns, the smell of

197

the cypress fir – this is going to be a good day. Achmed breaks into my reverie. 'I'm free till the afternoon. Come. I will show you the city.' It's a fascinating guided tour of two hours or so, a vivid picture painted. Here the marks of the chariot wheels, there the 'moving' column – it's wobbled since the earthquake of 1927. Sitting by the temple of Artemis, he tells me something of himself. He is a lonely man. His American fiancée was killed in a car crash eleven years ago.

Borrowing a policeman's car, we drive to a 12th century Arab fort on a hill outside Adjlun. It was built by one of Saladin's commanders. On a clear day you can see the two seas – Galilee to the north and Dead to the south. The countryside is a fairytale, olive-dotted hillsides folding into one another, carob, cypress, eucalyptus, poplar, oak; red earth; a gentle land misted in heat haze – George Seferis would have liked Gilead.

'I shall now take you to lunch at my Aunty's. She loves me very much.'

Aunty is a darling. The house is small and simple. Sitting cross-legged in the dim light we are served hot bread, *lebneh*, tart peppers, olives and tea. Beside us in rumpled bedclothes lies Uncle. He has flu. The deaf son beams and blows the dust off an apple. How I respect these people with their beautiful manners and deep-rooted hospitality. In honour of my visit a box of Dairy Milk – quite the biggest I've ever seen – is produced. There are seven chocolates left in their frills at the bottom, so cherished they've turned white.

March 29th - April 3rd, last days in Amman,

Someone has carved 'I love your Vagena' on a table in the British Council Library – doesn't say much for Jordanian 6th form spelling. Read *Riding to the Tigris* and Xan Fielding's book on Crete. Suddenly one morning it's spring, the sun is warm; slow-motion fig buds burst and blossom fluffs in foaming mass. The city seems asleep, a golden labrador grey about the nose. Elegiac melancholy has me in thrall. Back at the Y for a few nights of luxury I study the small pink tree outside the bedroom window. Surprised by the sudden warmth it has burst into blossom and a finch sits there singing an anthem. The bird is so fat it has no feet. Kerryman, a teacher and friend of Ayesha's, is just back from the West Bank where her mother is ill. Her stories bear out the reports of thuggish Israeli behaviour; boys of nine and ten kicked and slapped. Some women, one with a two-day old baby are forced to stand for hours in the heat.

'My baby will die!' The woman is distraught. The soldiers laugh.

'Let him die. He is an Arab. Just another terrorist.'

How dare the world, including me until recently, not know what is going on?

Impressions click on the mind's eye: the nylon fur above the facia of a taxi; three square shapes crossing an empty road – nuns; a man droops, half asleep, over his barrow of loquats, his sweater a brilliant orange; Mars Bars in the sun. Read as if I am never going to read a book again, the last two being Ann Twose's *The Lion of Athens* and *In the steps of St Paul* by HV Morton. Jordan grows small, crisp cucumbers. Sliced lengthways in the Greek fashion they taste better than cut our English way. I doze and drink coffee with Ayesha; it's sometimes so strong I feel drunk. Tomorrow I go to Syria.

Likos, 2005

No sooner is the cat alright – as I suspected, it already has an owner – than the dog is not. Someone's turkeys have been savaged by dogs, one black and said to be Max. In a small community with livestock, once a dog is under suspicion, it's curtains. The hippy poet with his black ruff and feathery tail may not be long for this world. It makes me very unhappy. I could take him to the animal welfare people in Athens but they would put him down. Even if someone wanted him, what kind of life would it be tied up or in a flat for a dog who's been free as air? After much agonising, I've decided to do nothing. Who knows? He might enjoy another summer with the tourists before Nemesis falls. The fatalism of the Mediterranean is in my bones.

Hunting in my 1981 Greek diaries for a story I'd promised the tailor – of which more later – I came on a double page spread headed MOSTLY ABOUT SPIRO. There I am, besotted, burbling on about this funny gentle man. Like the Bulgar at Lake Bafa he was always turning the collar of my jacket down. 'Your hair is all upside down always.' After lovemaking he preferred to sleep alone... 'Once we leave Skopelos you sleep in the little room next door and I'll sleep in here. Like vegetables in a garden. I mean, you don't mix up aubergines and carrots and tomatoes in a muddle, do you?' Thinking how like my adored father he was led me to the theme of anticipated loss. It makes sense. If love and loss collide early on, then perhaps fear of the next loss is a constant? And, alas, a wrecker of love.

I found the story for Elias: about 10 years ago, Michael, an Englishman working in Athens, was knocked down by a taxi in Syntagma. Lying stunned, M was aware of the driver getting out of the cab, clearly concerned. But no. A kick in the kidneys, a boot in the ribs. 'You fucking idiot!' Then he drove off. That's Athens for you.

It's February 5th. Despite the cold, the verges of the roads are thick with lupins. The mountain lavender, the first I've seen since that winter in Salamis so long ago, is in flower; and in a sunny corner near the harbour poppies flutter. Mild islanditis infects me, that affliction which turns sensible people into stealers of boats or swimmers out to sea. It will pass; but what wouldn't I give for Sunday roast and claret with a friend, a wander around the Tate and good television. Greek television, especially a station called Mega, is dire. Nothing but basketball played by pituitary dysfunctionals, quiz and game shows hosted by Greek Terry Wogans and soaps. Worst of all is the off-loaded American tat. The only decent things I've seen have been two old black and white films – both Greek.

Visits to Militiadis and Angelica are always a delight. If only my Greek were better and I could understand their stories and legends. Before he retired, Militiadis was the fisher king of the island. As a young man, he often climbed up and down the mountain at night between Psara and the top village – there were no roads then – to deliver his catch. He tells a tale of one wild night when a blizzard raged and drifts had covered the track. Fearing he might lose the path and fall over a precipice, he decided to spend the night in a cave. He found it, crept inside and then – o terror! – heard strange heavy breathing and saw two huge glowing eyes. He addressed the monster: 'If you are human, speak to me!' Whereupon the thing roared and rushed past him into the snow. It was a bull belonging to a friend. Angelica is a poet. Her stories are full of myth and blood. This evening I shall tell her the one about John the Baptist's head, once upon a time in Damascus...

Chapter Fifteen

Damascus – Happy Homs – Krak des Chevaliers – Palmyra and the Zenobia Hotel – Aleppo – journey to Az Az and the Turkish border

1982

April 4th, to Damascus

The muezzin calls to the faithful. The dawn smells fresh. Waiting in Amman's Petra Travel, peaceful among the dust and the cake-crumbs, I doze. We leave at 6am. The hills are lovely in the morning light, the verges thick with campanula. We pass men, each waving a single fish. Who stops to buy a single fish? For some reason I have boundless faith in Petra Travel. It turns out to be justified. At the iniquitous Syrian Customs and Excise we storm through. Not a sneer, not an insult. One official even wishes me a pleasant stay! We approach Damascus over a parched *steppenland*, its monotony broken by rocks and plastic bags. The day is hot and sticky, the time 12.30pm. Our entry to the city is through the car repair district, smelling of tar. The place is a bomb site. Everything is halfway down or halfway up. There are phalanxes of flats on the nearby hills.

What a dump. I wander about looking for the youth hostel. One boy offers me a sip from his teacup; another yells 'Can I push my penis up your vagina.' Ignored, he becomes pettish. 'Don't you hear me!' he cries. The Chtaura Hotel turns out to be a better idea than the youth hostel; clean and cosy and £2 a night. I've got my own loo and basin and temperamental shower and there are touching signs that the place has seen better days. Snooze in clean sheets till the cool of evening, then stroll, depressed that I've come from a gracious Bath to an inferior Athens.

First impressions

Does everyone feel apologetic in strange cities? I do – I don't know why – and am easily cast down. Thou shalt not tell the sausage by its skin. London isn't Ilford; and the middle of Damascus is pleasant, the French in some intangible way having left their mark. The railway station is fine and the souk souk-like and fun – tall and vaulted, surrounded by Roman wall. It's mostly full of rubbish. Tumbledown Turkish has a soporific effect; that and a mix of dust, scent, horseshit and wood shavings. Dust storms and rain make me cross – also grappling with yet another currency and getting lost. The yobs and soldiers are as rude as Athenians, the tea so strong you could trot a mouse on it.

The Umayyad Mosque has the joyfulness of early Minoan or 500 BC Greece. Cowled in black, I walk its courtyards. It was built on top of John the Baptist's tomb; when the Turks tried to get the head out of its resting place, the mosque ran red with blood. The great Saladin lies here. What an honourable man. I didn't know he was a Kurd. My bad temper is soothed by its loveliness. The street of the cabinet makers is horrific by comparison; they're busy concocting 18th and 19th century copies for the middle classes. Walk and walk, much stared at. I have removed my headscarf because everyone thinks I'm a man when I wear it. The museum is badly laid out and labelled; you have little idea what is what, and from when, or where. An attendant tells me I'm so beautiful he can't understand why I am not married. Perversely, instead of being flattered, I'm exasperated.

The street called STRAIT *is* straight, full of dust and buses. An old man rubs his eyes and when he removes his fists from them reveals the stare of a mixamatosis rabbit. A crone refuses to open the house where Paul took refuge; may her headscarf fill with ants. Instead the skies open, the thunder snarls and it hails – here we go again. But there are good things too. An English old-timer, a Philby in a bush hat carrying a silver-topped walking stick, marches across the road followed by his plump wife, also bush-hatted. I feel like saluting. The parks are full of marigolds and snapdragons, the grass is so green it looks dyed. Five falafel and two glasses of yoghurt cheer me; also the taxis, enormous 1930s things from America and the haberdasheries with their wooden cabinets full of cotton reels and Scottish solidarity. Swallows fly over the minarets. Extravagance in Jordan means I must live on £4 a day including the hotel.

April 5th, Damascus

Today Damascus grows on me. Slept for 12 hours and ate no food for 14 hours. A milk shake and six falafel gave me legs. I don't feel apologetic anymore. If you go down the street of the cabinet makers, left under an arch before the painted wall, on until Bab Touma and turn right – there it is, just before the church, the best cup of coffee in Damascus. Sipping the sweet, cardamom delight I watch schoolchildren in their blue or khaki uniforms and frail old men in white caps. There is a signpost beside a traffic light advertising the skills of five medical specialists: urologist, neurologist, gastroenterologist, cardiologist and internist.

No longer blinded by hunger and headache, getting lost is fun. The souk's lingerie section is a fairyland of sequinned bras with tassels, shiny slips and knickers, naughty suspender belts. Sacks of almonds big as sacks of coal; crystallised fruits and chocolates fan out; slippers swing like bananas. In a forgotten corner reptilian hubble-bubbles brood. A souk is Christmas all year round. What we miss in the West with our drearily logical precincts. I'm sure they dye the cage birds. They certainly splash paint on the doves' tails near the prison side of the souk.

A bakery gives me quarter of an hour of pure pleasure. Beside the round clay bread oven, its entrance roaring and glowing, is a stool. On the stool is a cushion. Using the cushion as a glove, the baker flings the thin circle of dough onto the inside walls of the oven, leaving the dough and removing the cushion. All done at top speed otherwise he'd lose his hand to the flames. But, at the same time as he's 'cushioning' the raw circles of dough into the oven, he's whisking the brown cooked circles out by hand. What skill. I could watch for hours. There is innate sensitivity to colour, shape and display in the Arab world. An old man with a barrow of broad beans will decorate his merchandise with tomatoes, an orange or two, a lemon, even a Coca-Cola bottle. The shape of a minaret against the sun. Dust and more dust. In the pelt and fur street is a pitch dark hole in the wall. Inside two old men chatter in a nest of skins.

Kasr el Aazem is a 17th century Turkish palace whose owners live abroad and own four cinemas. In the courtyard, two cypress trees stand guard over bolsters of oxalis. A fountain splashes and pigeons make love with crashes and flurries in the windows of the palace. Oh, those pleasure-loving Turks. The tiny chapel below, presumably the house of Ananias, is very touching. As Stark says, thank goodness for the indolence of the Turks because they never pulled anything down. My beloved Greeks, devoured by restlessness, wreck their inheritance and move onto the next destruction without a thought. Stark also suggests that the design of the mosque must have occurred to someone looking at the two cypresses on either side of a hill. Wandering on, I examine slices of tumbledown Turkish and marvel at the ingenuity of the builders – straw, mud, delicate pole-framing, balanced and unified. Soon, I suppose, they will all be demolished. No more cool alleys. No more balconies rubbing noses across the street; some, embracing, have melted into a bridge, Venetian-style.

Salam picks me up in just such a street; and with what gusto. He's Kurdish, 28 and studying English Literature at the university. In next to no time he sweeps me off to lunch, tells me about his syllabus, quotes Byron and says that he must go to his doctor to find out why he doesn't like oriental girls. Him, not the doctor. He's charming and very good-looking; also astonished and slightly shocked that I am 45. Munching hummus, I explain between mouthfuls that I have only one boyfriend, a Greek sea captain, who is insanely jealous.

'You are very oriental,' he murmurs.

I promise to visit him and his family next year. He's off to Beirut for four days to get his Arabic-Kurdish-English dictionary printed.

The camouflage battledress of Syrian soldiers is gaudy; how can a green and pink splotch melt into Syrian countryside? There is also egg-yolk and green. Perhaps it's the white Peugeot syndrome? The evening is cool, promenade time. Turning left off the top of the Via Recta, I stroll through an arch into a forgotten Damascus. Sun slants through gum trees onto a quiet road. No flats here. Just children playing an old Syrian game, a tethered horse, cats asleep on the stones and two men wrestling with a python coil of cable. I wander home, stopping to buy a flap of bread, hard boiled eggs and half a kilo of yoghurt.

April 6th, Damascus

Wherever you go small patterns of life are the same: a crying child, an old man with a broken bootlace, someone flinging a packet of cigarettes up to his wife and children on a balcony – and missing. The shopkeepers, like the cats, doze outside their shops. The chemists mix potions from bottles brought down from tall wooden cabinets. Scents are blended, love and hate mixtures concocted. It looks like alchemy. There is a strong smell of menthol in certain streets. Cars are not yet in the ascendancy; reluctantly give way to donkeys, carts, horses and traps, bikes and pedestrians. Abandoned Buicks slump in side streets. The oil drums for the central heating stoves come round on a cart drawn by a richly-adorned horse. I have maligned the street called Strait; it is full of goodies.

The glass blowers behind the Suleimaniya Mosque are marvellous to watch. They twirl their batons – cheerleaders – blowing, twisting, manipulating the glowing blob which swells or shrinks at a touch, flying about on the end of its baton, a hot lozenge. Buy a ticket to Homs tomorrow, just over £1 with Karnak. As usual I'm constipated. Even after years in the Eastern Mediterranean, hooting cars make me dance with rage.

April 7th, to Homs

Very grand, Kamak buses. We leave at 10.30am and roll north past shatteringly awful blocks on hills. I ponder Easter and wonder why Catholic, Orthodox and Protestant can't arrange it on the same weekend. Our route is through bare brown hills, rock and dust, scrub and here and there in a fertile fold, almond trees in blossom. An arid, merciless land. My neighbour is an exquisitely-groomed, gloomy man called Bassam; his dark blue jacket would shame Savile Row. He, too, has a dead fiancée killed in a car crash which accounts for his gloom. I'm surprised anyone reaches breeding age in this land of manic drivers. Boiled sweets and glasses of water appear. My companion sighs. He's studying engineering at Damascus University and his finals project is translating a treatise of English sewage systems into Arabic. His family sound well-to-do and own a house in the hills behind Beirut. He knows Paris, speaks French and English and LOVES Homs.

'Good people, nice people. Damascus isn't like that.'

His face breaks into the first and only smile of the journey.

Homs is a merry place, full of bustle and food. Damascenes were a dour lot (my Kurd Salam excepted).

'Where are you going?'

A woman stops me as I look for a hotel. My Arabic is so minimal it's difficult to explain. There are hostelries hanging above, suitably small and flophouse-like. I wave at these and she points at the Al Khayam: 'My friend sleeps there.' Now so do I. Its entrance is by the taxi office, full of smoke and drivers yelling 'Beirut, Beirut, Tartous, Tartous!' As I seem to be the only foreigner in Homs and very likely the whole of Syria, the proprietor is startled. He has a funny eyelid. We agree on £6 for three nights. It's a nice little hotel; the two squatters are spotless and the basins have cakes of soap. Those lazy Turks could learn a thing or two from the Syrians. I shall cleanse myself in the communal basin before the workers get up. One drawback is the light bulb – 20-watt and inches from the ceiling. The proprietor soon gets over his shock and becomes cordial.

Food, food, food! Spitted chickens twirl on every corner. Men with huge knives bend over boards – de de de de de – fine chopping chunks of flesh as if meat will cease tomorrow. Everyone is eating and taking pleasure in it – soups, roasted meats, kebabs, falafel, hummus and savoury pannikins of vegetables Turkish-style. My plate of aubergines and mince in hot sauce is delicious. Most magnificent of all are the cake shops, jammed with all manner of sweetmeats, their displays irresistible: four-foot high cones of pink and white sugary stuff; a three-foot marzipan tree; flanges of honey-soaked cinnamon cake; trays of gooey triangles, tottering mounds of cream-filled fancies, chocolate fudge barricades. The rice puddings are topped with hundreds and thousands. Slavering, I fly past rockfaces of halva and nougat... Ice cream shops abound. Also restaurants with napery; also, at last, small clean cafés suitable for single ladies where you can eat cakes and drink espresso coffee. To my astonishment, there are self-service Nescafé machines in the street. It's chilly. Homs is higher than Damascus.

Prowl all afternoon and find out about buses to Palmyra. This must be a Catholic or Orthodox part of Syria. There are Easter eggs in shops and ikons of the Virgin in buses. In the vaulted souk, much sewing of quilt and beating of brass. The owner of the café beside the Karnak office refuses to let me pay for my coffee and asks me to stay in his house. I bet he's 28. Every handsome Syrian I meet is 28.

'You have a wife?' I politely enquire.

'A mother. I would you to eat like come.'

April 8th, to Krak des Chevaliers

Freeze to death in damp sheets, under a quilt as heavy as stone. Transfer to my sleeping bag at 3am. At 5am the Servis drivers start yelling their destinations and the streets are busy. After breakfast, I spend two hours in a stationary microbus (Syrian Dolmus) which says it's going to Housen – Krak des Chevaliers. The buspark is a theatre of colour and activity, the buses so decorated they have a fairground air. They roar and reverse and swerve and clash round men hugging lambs and girls feeding babies. One man with two boisterous lambs resorts to 'the cloth flung over the cage' method of control and tucks his charges under his skirts. Heads covered, they become docile. Our problem is the clutch. Driver and mate, brows knitted, lift a hub thing off and fiddle with a bent wire. The woman in the next seat sighs. A man leaves two gas cylinders in the bus, only to return an hour later and remove them. There is a Greek supermarket bag on the driver's seat. I long to ask him if he speaks Greek but am struck with shyness.

At last we are mobile. From a cupboard above the Virgin ikon, our driver extracts a box of tissues and a pair of neatly-pressed green trousers. Syrians have thick hair and straight black moustaches and eyebrows running parallel. Not a baldy to be seen. After a tour of the shrieking, hooting park to pick up last-minute passengers, we leave Homs and the oil works and drive into rolling country. On our left is a lake formed by the Orontes on its way through to Turkey. You could be in Northern Greece on this plain of broad beans and corn, the earth the colour of chocolate cake. The country becomes more rolling, even more familiar: olive, cypress, fir and bare poplars; the grass vivid green and dotted with asphodel, lupins and poppies; white horses and cattle grazing the lush pastures. Very romantic. Finally terraced hills. On one stands the daddy of all crusader castles – Krak des Chevaliers.

It's a tiring two hours. My guide never stops talking and neither do a group of student architects from Aleppo. I wish I was alone. I prefer ruminating in ruins, not being force-fed. The guide, built like a bull, speaks a patois of French, German and Arabic. He takes me into dark holes, down crumbling, dank steps, into recesses where I doubt even the knights penetrated. Occasionally he pats my back and my bottom. Wild mint, King David's Glue and marjoram sprout from Krak's bulwarks. It is *enormous*. The knights had well-designed loos; and the jars where they stored the oil are still *in situ*. From the battlements you see for miles, the snowcaps of Lebanon seeming near enough to touch. The student architects – we all met at 6am in Homs looking for coffee – are lovely kids. One girl's mother is one of seven wives! Four wives is legal. '*No other* wives for us,' say the girls. A morose ex-professor of English at Damascus gives me a lift back to Homs. He asks for £10 but I give him £4. A Turk wouldn't have taken money.

Back at the hotel all is bedlam. A girls' hiking trip, a kind of Syrian St Trinian's, has blown in. They have a drum which they beat when they're not playing football against my bedroom door. My hotel man who changes the pillowcases every day and makes me cups of tea says 'No!' when I mention Hama and the water wheels. He makes the gesture plus sound effect of a machine gun. I get the message.

April 9th, Homs

It's Good Friday and my rest day. Didn't get a wink of sleep due to St Trinian's. The little pigs leave their shit round the loos and even smeared on the basin. I complain to the proprietor and go forth in a rage to find coffee and pancakes. Bulldozers are busy knocking down old Homs. It abounds in stomatologists and dentists – probably as a consequence of all the cake shops. Stroll about the empty souk, then out north of the town where patches of green survive, trees in blossom and market gardens. Going, going, soon gone. This idyll is ringed by scabby blocks, their litter smeared on grass and flowers. Children jeer. I turn round just before one shies a rock. Cheer up over lunch in a farmer's restaurant – french beans with meat, couscous, a dish of hot peppers and two flaps of bread the size of dinner plates. Meet X and agree to talk to him and his friend over coffee in the evening. Both are 30, dark and bear-like. They want me to know the truth about Assad.

St Trinian's have left, thank God, so my hotel is peaceful. Even the taxi drivers have stopped yelling. Lie and read my traveller's guide to the Middle East. It pokes fun at a famous Egyptian singer called Um Kulthum, some of whose songs last two hours: 'There is the feeling that people can no longer afford the time to sit listening for hours to the heartrending masterpieces of Um Kulthum…'

Over coffee – and conspiratorially – the two Xs and I talk politics. One is a university graduate; many of his friends are in prison. He says he'll probably never see them alive again. Main points of information are: 1) Everyone hates Assad. 2) Syria publicly refers to America as 'the imperialist pigs' but America is secretly ploughing money into the country. 3) The rising in Hama against the Government was *not* inspired by the Muslim Brotherhood – that's the Government line – but by a collaboration of Christian and Muslim. The Government brought tanks and troops in, killed 15,000 people and knocked most of Hama flat. The two Xs say there were terrible atrocities: houses bulldozed with people still alive in them and women's hands cut off for their bracelets. 4) The pollution will soon be dangerous. Czechs run the oil refinery and standards are not good. One X says that looking at the water through a microscope is alarming. I wish them luck and we say goodbye. Good, intelligent people. Very brave.

April 10th, to Palmyra

Actually *inside* the ruins of Palmyra is a small, old-fashioned hotel – that's where I'm headed. Karnak's office is a maelstrom of panic and shrieking passengers. By dint of treading on feet and shoving and using my elbows, I get to a window and buy tickets for Palmyra – and on Monday, Aleppo. It's two hours to Palmyra. A doddery gent accosts me on the way to my bus: 'I have a car. Will you come to Palmyra?' No, I won't. What a wicked old thing. He probably lurks every morning looking for a victim to ravage on the sand.

Our road follows the line of the desert wells, betrayed every so often by patches of shattering green, passing mud-baked villages

– some mini-fortresses – and a huge military base. There are tanks, lorries, aircraft and what looks like an underground weapons installation. If there are rockets under the scrub, I wonder which way they're pointing? At noon we approach the city of Queen Zenobia – Palmyra.

This is the most magical sight I've seen in the Levant – sweeps of columns, honey-gold in the haze, backed by date palm and desert and stretching as far as the eye can see. An army waiting for its general; or maybe for the queen who lost it to the Romans in the first century AD. An Arab castle frowns on a hill. In the hot afternoon I investigate but it smells of shit. Also investigate alarming tombs, one of which looks Nabataean. But for me, Palmrya is not to be walked *through*, but looked at from a distance; tranquilly, on a broken capitol outside the Zenobia Hotel – a long, low, ochre-yellow deliciousness from the beginning of the century; inside the ruins so somehow part of them.

'You want a room?' The proprietor stares in disbelief. It's probably my sneakers which have fallen to bits or my rucksack. He's the spit image of Mr Mace in Dedham Post Office. Muttering he puts me in Room One which has an unmade bed, no hot water (so much for the blurb) and nests of fluff on the carpet. To his credit, he gets the bed made and the water hot. I couldn't care less. My room is bliss and the ruins are outside the window. Leaving most of my clothes soaking in the bath, I eat pancakes, cheese, spring onions and a Mars Bar and investigate the premises. From the cool reception hall four doorways, one arched and open, lead to bedrooms, kitchen and divan-lined TV room. Floor-to-ceiling pink pillars act as room separator between reception with its wooden easy chairs covered in faded brocade and the long wooden dining tables. The walls are bathroom green, the floors marble with rusty-pink splotches. A fan whirrs. In the dim light the desk looks Jacobean and behind it hangs Assad – for once not wearing that maddening smile. Two glass-fronted cupboards contain brass and copper. The Zenobia's front door is guarded by pillars and a stubby palm. Broken capitols, casually plonked in the shade of olive, palm and cypress, make tables and stools. There I sit until evening falls and a breeze blows in from the desert. Then, dismay. My hard-boiled eggs bought in Homs are raw. The kitchen cook me an omelette. '*What* is this?' snaps the proprietor as I and the omelette pass him en route to my room. His brow darkens. I am bad news.

April 11th, Palmyra

Morning mist blurs cornice and capitol, blotting out the castle. The temple is superb and for an hour I have it to myself. Then tours appear; also, to my horror, St Trinian's with their bloody drum who fall on me with shrieks of delight. If I find them at the Zenobia I shall cut my throat. The 'Meridien' is the 'tour' hotel outside the ruins; it looks like a factory and behind its wall to keep the natives out I find cheerful women washing fleeces and urchins bathing in the basins. Modern Palmyra is pleasant with date palms, Karnak's office deep in sand from last night's dust storm. The men are disinclined to give me a ticket for Homs but I sit, Arab-like, and finally they relent. Along with the ticket I get a cup of cold tea.

Write up my diary among the jumble of capitols. The proprietor appears, oof! his eyes pop and he vanishes, reappearing with a cup of coffee. Suddenly he is charm and affability. I deduce that I am now a famous journalist and he wants a good write-up for the Zenobia. Two more coffees appear before I leave. O wonderful hotel. Please God don't let it close.

April 12th, Homs to Aleppo

Spring is bursting over Syria, leaves green as lettuce thrust out of dead bark; apple and cherry are in blossom, wisteria waterfalls. I eat a farewell rice pudding in Homs, buy a Mars Bar and board my bus. For some reason Mars Bars taste marvellous in Jordan and Syria. We pass Hama, the bus strangely silent. The north of the town is almost entirely destroyed, burnt-out apartment blocks, rubbled houses. The water wheels are beautiful but don't turn anymore. I am too late for Hama. Sleep until we reach

Aleppo at 12.15pm. The Hotel Baron looks Edwardian and bliss. I decide to spend my last night in Aleppo in its arms – even if I starve in the process. To fund this extravagance – £5 B&B – I book myself into the Wadi el Nil. The proprietor speaks French, and looks entirely untrustworthy. I rather like him. There are women here so it's probably a brothel. The bottom of my bed is jammed against the wardrobe and the outside area full of smut. On the plus side, the sheets are clean, I have a minuscule basin and the loo is round the corner.

Aleppo is fascinating; the souk the most fairytale I've seen, a medieval city in its own right, sprawled over an area of God knows how many square miles. Figures from the Arabian Nights do business on flying carpets, doze over fleeces, eat their lunch reclining among bolts of silks and brocades. Aleppo's souk is the real thing, so old and full of smells it makes Damascus look like Butlin's. My Aleppo boyfriend, met on a dark corner, is called Abdullah and speaks excellent English. He, too, is 28. Later, eating hummus in a grubby café, I discover I've left my money in the hotel. The kitchen boy shrugs. I thrust my passport into his wet hands and rush into the night.

'*Meskin,*' I say when I return with money. It means 'poor thing' in Arabic. He agrees.

April 13th/14th, Aleppo

Am struck down by a headache and can't sleep. In despair, dopey with aspirin I leave the hotel at 6.30am, causing alarm and consternation. A lot of whispering which probably means 'Has she got her luggage with her?' The proprietor appears as I linger reassuringly on the doorstep.

'Madame! Where are you going?'

'Me promener,' I reply. He is aghast. He reminds me of the bus driver in Likos.

The souk is mysterious at this hour, dark and empty. A tureen of *Zachlab* steams in a dimly-lit recess and I drink a glass. It's most comforting. Later in the morning all is colour and bustle and business. Combs of honey ooze on counters; there are nose-tickling pyramids of brown spice decorated with coconut and something red; the rope and loofah section doesn't belong to the 20th century. I doze in the courts of the Omayyad Mosque, watching little boys whip fleeces. The citadel is shut so I take my headache to a park which must have been laid out by the French – big and airy, full of white iris, stocks, lilac and masses of trees under which men stroll, delicately holding hands with one another. At last a country where everyone walks like me: very slowly. Aleppo's fretworked houses are gorgeous; not so gorgeous is the open sewer running through my park. There is something Irish about the Arab.

In the evening rain, thunder and lightning. The proprietor bustles in to shut my window. Life is not good. I am hermetically sealed, nauseous from headache and deafened by a row between other residents which starts at 9pm and goes on till 2am. Screams and roars and the sound of breaking furniture. The row breaks out again at 5am.

The faded splendour of the Hotel Baron makes up for everything. My private bathroom is pink and the room smells Scottish. Wash all my clothes, lie in a hot bath and think about sparrows, such cheerful birds, like mice with wings. They bounce about Arabia from Amman to Aleppo. For some insane reason both the citadel and the museum are shut but I manage to track down the taxi point for Az Az and the Turkish border. Snooze for the rest of the day. Outside rain and the chirping of the mice. I shall miss the juice stalls and their bulgy canopies of fruit.

April 15th, to Az Az and Turkey

Breakfast at the Baron is magnificent. The head waiter is French-trained so predictably rude. A 'cultural' American tour absorbs him. Finally, I lose patience and he flutters off to brief a minion.

Muffins, olives, cheese, jam, tea and a bowl of cracked wheat cooked with sugar and cream, a kind of Syrian porridge. Could it be *asure*? Farewell Hotel Baron. One day I might come back. The Servis taxi point, a sea of mud, is full of old men on tiny stools surrounded by tea-making, falafel and hard-boiled egg shacks. Back to the sun, scarfed, suitably Eastern in a dress over trousers, I perch on my stool and read Edward Thomas. The old men think I am reading my *Qûran*. They murmur approvingly. Two with crinkly eyes buy me tea. I love old men. I was always picking them up as a child which worried my mother. Taxis splosh in and out. At 10 o'clock one stops by the tea shack. 'Az Az,' say my old men.

I get in. No one comes. It's like Adlestrop. An angry-looking man talks to the driver. They argue. The man glares at me.

'Alright, go away,' they say to him and he goes. I doze. It's nearly eleven. Then everything happens at once. The angry man returns with a fat, black-veiled wife and child. More muttering and staring. Then I pay the man who makes the tea 20 Syrian pounds and we're off. 'Off' is an optimistic way of putting it because we have to be pushed before the taxi coughs into life. 'It's OK really,' says the driver. To be on the way to the border is a triumph, the state of his taxi an irrelevance.

The north of Syria – plains of spring wheat dotted with poppies. Asphodel and olive-planted hills. Pat Boone should come round the corner singing *April Love* except that it's too Balkan. Rain batters the ancient wipers. At Az Az, a muddy village, we swap our driver for a lad. The road is deep in mud and potholes. Finally we arrive at a *Fiddler on the roof* border post – three or four shacks and more mud. It rains and rains. The lad takes our papers. The Turks get theirs back but I am commanded out of the taxi and into the shack. Four fierce men are scrutinising my passport. Oh *no*, whatever now? First tea appears. Then one official gestures at my occupation – 'copywriter' – and asks what it is. I tell them it's a kind of typist and they stamp me out of Syria.

Half a mile on a barber's pole and a guard box: the Syrian border.

216

The taxi leaves, the pole rises and the family and I, the man carrying the child, walk under it. Ahead of us a dusty road leads to what looks like a village. On either side are fields of brilliant green; this is what crossing frontiers must have been like before the last war when Paddy Leigh Fermor travelled Europe and Transylvania still existed. It's a mile's walk to the Turkish barber's pole. The family and I have grown fond of each other. The child is much too quiet. They're taking her to Istanbul to see a doctor. Back into Turkey and world news. The Israelis have invaded Lebanon and my country is at war with Argentina...

Shepherds with lambs still walk down Baron Street in Aleppo. My last seven weeks in the cardamom lands feel like seven years.

Likos, 2005

It's Saturday afternoon, mild and overcast. Valentine's Day is nearly upon us. With luck I should finish the book in another six weeks. A death has shocked the community – a man well-liked and respected, only 38 years old. A heart attack. On the day of his funeral every house and shop in all three villages was bolted and barred, the corporate grief of the island deeply moving. Here so many people are inter-related that the web of cause and effect, initiative and reaction binds everyone. 'He was our lion, our plane tree,' wept an old lady. The children became sad and silent, suddenly aware of the unthinkable: their own parents' deaths. Slowly the island is coming to terms with his loss.

Out in the countryside Nature, impervious, goes her way, breeding litters of piglets and toylike calves and kids. The way pigs eat their dinner – with their front two feet in the dish to hold it steady – is endearing. Most are well cared for. Why are pigs' eyes tiny when their head and ears are so huge? Talking of heads: Angelica much enjoyed the story about John the Baptist and told me one in return; about a girl who, crossed in love fifty years ago, killed herself with a knife on one of the old tracks over the mountain. 'You can sometimes smell the blood,' said my friend, rolling her eyes. Angelica was married at 16.

Talking to a beautiful teenager one day I thought how proscribed her life was. No running away to Paris or studying dance or reading law. Married by 18 and four kids by 24. How lucky I was with my unorthodox parents who, meeting in Edinburgh, scooped two strangers off the street and got married in a nearby registry office. Disgraceful behaviour for 1928. My sister and I were brought up in deep country, free to vanish for most of the day if we wanted to, taught to be independent of mind and untroubled by 'what the neighbours thought'. Nor did it occur to Susan and I to defer

218

*to men. Both my parents were passionate about educa-
tion. The proposition that men might be intellectually
superior would have been greeted by us with hoots of
laughter.*

*After the Middle East and Turkey, I spent the
summer in Likos. I arrived in a May of hollyhocks, corn
marigolds, scabious, lavatera, sea poppies and lilies –
all growing wild – and took a room in the house of
Popi, my friend in Psara. During that long hot summer
the fishing village under its hills became more and
more dreamlike and I more detached from reality. A
black and white rabbit nibbled lupin leaves. Pigs swam.
Sheep arrived for their summer pasture. The heat grew
intense. In spite of the lazy days, I still felt tired. Ahead
lay Egypt.*

*It's in the Egyptian diaries where the fatigue begins
to show; the writing disjointed, sometimes muddled; the
mood increasingly querulous. I detect a kind of unrav-
elling. Reading the warning signals now I'm amazed I
didn't pick them up then. But then was a million years
ago. Another part of the wood. So. Here we go. Cairo...*

Chapter Sixteen

Arriving in Cairo – the train to Luxor and first impressions
1982

Nov 26th, to Cairo from Alexandria

Egyptian railways are smooth and comfortable. Images from the National Geographic sail by: weeping willow, moley oxen creaking round wells, *fellahin*, donkeys, camels, pampas and slow, primitive ploughing. All is green and the earth chocolate. Not so picturesque are the sewage, litter and squalor of the villages and towns. Everywhere people pissing and shitting – mostly pissing. My first glimpse of the Nile is a great excitement. Tea and soft drinks are served.

Cairo station at 1.30pm. Outside the extraordinary Ramses Square, a dementia of overpasses chock-full of cars and pedestrian ways mirroring the chaos below. A good fairy with a beard and backpack presses his town map into my hands. Then I meet George. George is a bore aged 24, newly graduated in Italian and French and over-sexed. With toothy flourishes he promises a cheap and clean hotel and leads me off, holding my hand to cross the road and tickling it. The man is an idiot and Egypt exhausting. Severely I invent a husband and point out that *I'm* older than his mother. His completely unnecessary guided tour of Cairo is quite fun – it feels familiar and has interesting smells. Tahrir Square, a drab spaghetti junction, the Nile; after an hour we discover that the Hotel Ashbilia in Adly Pasha has vanished and the Hotel Select is full. Puffing up its eight flights of stairs (Cairene lifts are workaphobic), I lose patience with palm-tickling George and dump him. The Pensione Roma is full, the Golden and the Tulip, both indescribably filthy, also full; slowly it dawns on me that the world and his wife are in Cairo.

It is now 3.30pm. *Never* ask Egyptians where a street is; it stimulates their creative juices. They will send you to right and to left, would include up and down if they could. At one point on a crowded pavement, exasperated beyond endurance, I throw my pack to the ground, roar, and dance up and down. This impromptu act so convulses two men that one has to sit down. Just in time a girl shaped like a box of tissues points out the Felfela Restaurant in Hodi Sharawi Street. A sandwich saves my sanity. 'Try the Plaza,' suggests an Aussie at the counter. I do. They're full. So is The National. Finally I give up and take a dingy suite at the Hotel Suisse for 485PT. Cairo, O Cairo! City of crumbled splendour, Athenian, neurotic, cheerful, squalid, anarchic. City of marbled staircases – all filthy – wrapped round defunct lifts. Mercifully it's cool, about 68 degrees.

The new shoes for winter are in the shops. Groups of fashion-conscious women window-shop, blocking everyone's view. Cairo is full of women at night so I stroll unmolested except for the usual hisses and invitations. The only decent light is in my marble-floored bathroom; after a delicious supper of garlic *foul, baba ghanoug*, bread and tea at Felfela I shift the armchair and table in there and read. My face is like a melon and I don't pee. It's the dreaded water-retention.

Nov 27th, Cairo

Freeze all night like I did in Alexandria. A breakfast of tea, rolls, cheese, butter and jam arrive but no eggs. Due to lack of sleep am disproportionally put out by lack of eggs. By 10am I've walked another three miles; but at least have found a room within my budget – back in Ramses Square outside the railway station. The Everest Hotel is neither clean nor dirty. Even 15 floors up you can hear the honking chaos in the street. My small room has a wardrobe, basin, table, chair, bedside cupboard and a broken bed. Only the side of the bed is broken. We shall see. My friend Ann Cacoullos in Athens gave me the name of a friend of hers, a Doctor Hochmann at the American University. That twit George said the university was on the other side of town. The information desk at the Nile Hilton (which knocks spots off the

London one) tells me it's three minutes' walk away. I meet Hynn who's a darling. We are to lunch on Monday.

The museum is a marvel, deserving hours of admiration. I am entranced by the Old, Middle and New Kingdoms; Anubis the greyhound with bat's ears who turns out to be the God of Mummies, the shimmering beauty of the Tutenkamen treasure, the four sphinxes, the pharaohs and more and more mummies. The figures carved from wood (sycamore?) of the Old Kingdom are so natural and lifelike you can't believe the scribe, the overseer and the young man lived 5,000 years ago. Minoan seems almost frivolous. *Let's Go*, my trusty guide, says 'the Middle Kingdom works show a greater harmony of form and subtle control over detail.' I don't agree. They're just more stylised. Am fascinated by Akhnaton, as loose-lipped and ugly as Nefertiti is exquisite.

No one in Cairo has change so the tourist comes off worst. The Felfela is all that *Let's Go* said it was, serving exactly the kind of food I love. Lunch at 5pm *foul* with tahini and *tamayia* with egg. My waiter has a Greek mother and tries to date me. I politely decline, go home and wrap myself in my sleeping bag. My toes are blistered. What a baptism of fire, what a lava of frustration! I shall doubtless emerge a new and wiser person.

Nov 28th, Cairo

What filth! Cairene dustcarts – full of garbage, excreta and dead cabbage stalks – are pulled by trios of donkeys. The dust is swept mournfully from place to place, frequently all over me. Sweepers of roads, pavements and front door steps have a fine disregard for the passer-by. The pavements are blocked by parked cars. Cairo is a jaywalker's paradise, a car-dodging anarchist's dream. Suits me. The authorities try and stop jaywalking with railings but – like the Egyptians – I hop over them.

An ancient Copt called Muhammad Aziz – I met him yesterday by the Nile – is going to show me Old Cairo and its Coptic churches. First I endure an hour's nervous breakdown at the station trying

222

to book a seat for Luxor on Wednesday. Muhammed is a dear, deaf as a post and about 180. For three or four hours we do the tour of Coptic churches, some falling down, some standing over open sewers. They are gloomy and architecturally hideous. Oddly, the frescos and ikons inside glow with life as if painted yesterday. In the church of St George devout Greek tourists wrap up in his chains. Poor George. He survived the wheel, the rack, thrashings, bashings, spokes – only to be taken to Palestine and cut into pieces.

I have peered into the crypt of the Church of Abu Serga where the Holy Family are supposed to have stayed. I have seen Al Malaka, the Hanging Church. I *think* I have seen St Bidabas. The synagogue is shut for repairs. By this time I'm exhausted and extricate myself from Muhammed's clutches. Oh dear. He has a room prepared for me in his house. Beside the Cairo tower is a cenotaph-shaped thing. 'How old?' I enquire. 'Oh, about 5,000 years.' I wish I'd seen the Nile in the 1930s when only villas flanked it. Sadat's, white and elegant, is one of the prettiest.

The food find of today is *kosheri* – lentils, rice and macaroni stirred together with a basin of hot sauce on the side. A large brown bottle contains an even hotter sauce. Aargh! The place is a working man's eatery in an alley behind 26 July Street, nice and clean with marble tables, big plastic jugs of water and crinkly tin mugs. It reminds me of Syria and Happy Homs. Other goodies are the Brazilian Coffee House on the corner of Orabi Square – excellent Espresso for 22PT – and a promising-looking, old-fashioned restaurant in Alfi Street. Meet Mike, a Dane with no money, and watch the moon sail over the Nile. I feel better. Never has a country exasperated me so much. *Inṣallah* I do not end up in a psychiatric ward.

The manager of the Everest dislikes the English – he thinks I'm French since that's the language we converse in. Some Empire leftover once told him his English was terrible.

'So I told *him*: "At least, Sir, I have taken the trouble to learn

223

YOUR language!'"

I apologise for my countryman.

'But you are *English*!'

He is flatteringly astonished.

I'm unnerved by the Egyptian virus of never finding anything. When the lift stopped last night at the 15th floor I emerged to find myself in a strange passage with no reception desk. The Everest had vanished in a puff of smoke. It was the back lift. I found the hotel again at the front. The early morning tuning-up of traffic below is quite pleasant. It reminds me of Amman and the Cliff.

Nov 29th, Cairo

Cairo is a treasure house of twenties and thirties buildings. The two lions either end of Tahrir Bridge are British. At 7.30am I heard CRUNCH! A lorry below had run into and over the bonnet of a small car. No blood when I pass later. It's a crisp morning. Smilingly barred from the citadel in Islamic Cairo, doused by hoses, splashed by bucket-swinging mothers, spattered with mud from passing carts, I find refuge in a seat-less park beside the enormous Sultan Hassan Mosque. Fancy a park with no seats. I grumble to myself in a Raj-like way and hear the ghostly chuck-ling of a thousand dead colonial administrators.

Breakfast is an egg roll bathed in something potent. I consume it in a dark alley off Adly Pasha. *Assam* is delicious – a green, foaming concoction made from sugar canes squashed in a wooden mangle. I wander up from the Sultan Hassan Mosque through local markets and alleys and – not to my surprise – fail to find the fabled tourist bazaar, Khan el Khalili. An old man passes, a cauliflower held like a club over his shoulder. A child gives me 'Welcome in Cairo'. I walk and walk. Sandalwood is sold in lumps. Everywhere women and children carry *foul* in basins, all they can afford to eat. The mothers make vain attempts

224

to keep their urchins clean – a splashing of water from a tin can. On the way to lunch with Hynn at the American University I see Michael Arlen's *Green Hat* on a second-hand bookstall in Opera Square and pounce on it.

'How do you feel about Cairo?' asks Hynn. She is delightful. We are lunching beside Coca Cola crates outside the university restaurant.

'With increasing affection and exasperation.'

We discuss the political situation and Egyptians' attitudes to their previous colonial masters. Hynn is very funny:

'The Egyptians love the French but admire the British. When the French were here they wanted everyone to share their art, literature, laws, food. The first thing the British did was build a club into which no Egyptian was allowed.'

Cairo is Damascus-coloured but even dustier. Strolling down July 26th Street, I meet sheep with crimson patches in the middle of the road, impervious to the ravenous traffic and followed by a robed shepherd. There is a clean and pleasant fruit juice stall near the Everest. My latest passion is a banana and milk shake. A Banana Daquiri would be better.

Nov 30th, to Giza and the Pyramids

A feather duster anoints me with the day's new dust. A dustman empties his garbage bucket over my boots. A bicycle and a motor bicycle collide with me. All this en route to coffee and croissants with Mike the Dane. By the time we get to Giza, mist envelops all; not a sausage – pyramid rather – to be seen. It's surreal. Suddenly a triangle snouts from the fog – the Cheops. Slowly the mist clears – and there, at last, they stand, the wonders of the world, the Pyramids. A confusion of camels and horseflesh mill about, tails held high like plumes. Scarab sellers tug at the sleeve. Old things in turbans proffer lumps of alabaster with dreadful scowls. Of the touts and scallywags, I like young Nasser Ah Al best. When I come back from Aswan I'll ride with him to Sakkara.

8.30am and still chilly. Climbing pyramids is exhausting. Up and down outside, down and up inside the Cheops, the Chevron, the Mycenerinus; then up the outside of a little one and – finally, alarmingly – right to the centre of another with Halibut. That's not his name but something like it. Halibut guards the small pyramids past the Mycenerinus and for baksheesh produces tombs and hieroglyphics galore. We crawl into the heart of a rock tomb, snake-like on our bellies, Halibut holding a flare. Now I know what the living dead must feel like. The flare goes out; the two reserve candles are guttering stumps:

'We will be quiet and pray,' says my guide.

My main worry is not so much claustrophobia but whether the previous inhabitant of this tomb approves of visitors. Outside again, the desert air smells sweet. At last REAL sand, Lawrence of Arabia stuff. The Sphinx is a mild disappointment, smaller than I thought. A Turkish actress and I gaze at it. It is extremely sphinx-like. Round and round in my head go those lines:

'…which accounts for the hump on the camel and the Sphinx's inscrutable smile.'

The people on the buses are very kind – smiling, applauding my pathetic Arabic, jumping up to give us seats. The Dane is a bum, his plan for a free lunch at the Felfela doomed. What a dotty restaurant. And what *folie de décor*. It could best described as rustic *Schuhplattler* crossed with Abergavenny dresser. Ditching the Dane I move from the *foul* section on the menu to the egg. Wheat-stuffed pigeon sounds wonderful. Checking out food stores is an old copywriting habit; all kinds of familiars are on the Cairene shelves – Imperial Leather, Mars Bars, Smarties, Quaker Oats, Heinz Strained Baby Foods.

Cairo traffic – a short dissertation: I cannot work out the logic of

Ramses Street's eastbound carriageway. Secure in the knowledge that the traffic is going one way, you meet a ferocious cream and red bus going the other way. Buses bulge, outside and in, youths clinging to their doors and others running to fling themselves onto a foothold. The skill of this catch-and-leap is superb. If you take to the road you can't get back onto the pavement because it's jammed with cars. There is only one solution: to stay in the middle of the road. Another good reason for staying in the road is that Cairenes are maddening on pavements. They pass you, then slow down and block you. Or they lollop towards you, changing to a collision course at the last moment. They bang into you, circle in your path chatting to a friend or coast abreast of you, muttering.

Bus and car horns are ear-splitting. I was deaf for three hours yesterday. How do those garbage donkeys manage?

I enjoy Cairo at night – strolling through cheerful, noisy thorough-fares, squinting into stores and bars and cafés, idling over books, collecting grand buildings and dodging cars. The pyramids have traumatised my thighs. Hot shower vital. After it, the desk clerk gives me a piece of chocolate and the tea-girl chats. It's nice to be known.

Dec 1st/2nd, Cairo and train to Luxor – first impressions

A London September morning. Coptic Muhammed will have to find another lady. Love El Azhar Street with its snakes' nests of sausages, falafel stalls, bread shops, markets, bolts of cloth and the inevitable sweepers sweeping dust into my face. The El Azhar Mosque is a marvel. I peer from its doorway into the courtyard where two classes chant in two corners; decline to climb the minaret to the astonishment of the attendant and retire to a shop to eat *fatirah* or *fatayia* – an enormous pancake with jam and icing sugar. Spend the rest of the day reading a child's book on Egypt and Abu Simbel at the Everest and *The Green Hat* in the reception of the Nile Hilton. Discover a Greek grocer. What a pleasure to speak the language again. Buy a bottle of beer and go to the station.

All is chaos; mobs of robed figures flying about with suitcases and sacks and cardboard boxes. When the train arrives, it's only by looking distraught that I'm helped to carriage 7, seat 41. The information man said it was seat 7, carriage 41. The beer tastes wonderful. Next to me is Mamdu, a young lawyer from Luxor. As we whizz through the night to Upper Egypt he plays Um Kulthum and *La Vie en Rose*, then falls asleep, bumping into me from time to time like a muscly dog. I wake to find myself next door to a kid from Kilburn covered in mosquito bites to whom Mamdu has heroically given his seat.

6.20am and dawn in Upper Egypt – the world outside the train wreathed in mist, the Nile broad and beautiful. Green seas of sugar cane, palms, irrigated crops, kindly oxen and the twinkle-toed donkeys of the *fellahin* whizz past. We arrive in Luxor at 8am. The Cleopatra hotel, 'very clean', is recommended by Mamdu's friend. Soggy with cold, my sleeves a nesting box of tissues, I shower and fall on the train food I never ate. Drink fuchsia tea (disgusting) and mint tea (delicious) and go out to look at Luxor.

First impressions: its location is lovely, looking across the Nile at gold pink cliffs and the Valley of the Kings. *Feluccas* skim the river. By its banks, like so many chocolate boxes, the tourist boats are moored. The old Winter Palace is Edwardian dignity, the new Winter Palace an abomination. The garry drivers and boatmen are a pest. One loon in particular haunted me all morning, whipping his poor bony horse; he looked like Jerry Lewis, and when I answered him in fluent Greek, his eyes crossed in the same way. Equally bemused were three lounging youths with bicycles and their 'Hello Madame, do you speak English?' The answer is NO, I DON'T.

Luxor is being bulldozed from stylish turn-of-the-century to package tour hell. Dust everywhere; but at least the markets are good. Drinking coffee on a blue bench, watching the robed shapes flit past or sit over their pipes – a figure bent to a brazier, a head, hawklike, turned to talk to a friend – I could fancy myself

228

in a different time a hundred years gone by. Um Kulthum sings into my left ear. 'When she died, millions wept in the streets of Cairo,' said Mamdu reverently. Arabs are nice to children. A small boy wobbles by on a bike and crashes into some boxes. No shouts. No abuse. The owner of the boxes smiles at him.

The tourist man in Luxor says the boat from Aswan to Abu Simbel takes a day and a half. Decide on a change of plan and buy a ticket for Aswan tomorrow. I'll pick up the boat the day after. If there is a boat. My faith in reality is dwindling. The two colossal temples, Luxor and Karnak, will keep till I come back; also a bike ride to the Valley of the Kings. Eat Beecham's pills and *kosheri* and go to bed, depressed that such a lovely place is being wrecked.

Likos, 2005

My closest friend in Psara is Popi, a pretty woman with a mass of black hair. She has three daughters – Evgenia married in Australia, Artemis and Nicoletta. Dionysis, the father, comes from Kalymnos the sponge fishers' island. He skippers a tourist boat. Popi's mother, Kyria Evgenia, is a handsome old lady. She's either in tears or roaring with laughter or both at once. On Saturday afternoon I walked to Psara. In Popi's kitchen beside the wood fire we reminisced about old times and those long, hot summers of 1981 and 1982. 'Do you remember the time I got stuck in the loo?' I said. My friend dissolved into peals of laughter.

It was September and very hot. In the night a banging door woke me. It's probably that bloody loo door, I thought and got up, draped in a sheet, to have a pee and fix it. The door was stiff to shut. When I tried to open it, it wouldn't budge. 2am in the morning is no time to shout for help. The loo window was high up and tiny, about two by one and a half feet, but I knew there was a balcony outside which bordered the other guest rooms; one occupied by a poet and his wife and the other by two Germans. Standing on the loo, I snaked through head first and fell into someone's washing. It was a tight fit; at one point I thought I'd stick, like Pooh in Rabbit's front door. One of the doors to the balcony was open. Could I sneak through unnoticed? Deciding that I couldn't, I tapped. There was a cry of 'Scheisse!' and the two Germans shot up in bed. Stifling giggles and garbling an explanation I rushed past.

Today has the feel of early summer in England – the sky milky, the sea placid and the air full of herby scents – thyme, sage, oregano and rosemary. Max the collie is visiting the soldiers more often; being fed by them as well as by me. His coat is glossy; well-fed he's friskier. Nemesis hasn't fallen so perhaps he'll survive. The cat is a pain. It looks like a rabbit, is short-sighted and refuses to give up its hopeless passion for me. I hope it isn't a dead aunt. If it were an Egyptian tom, it would be dead meat. Those in Aswan are cheetah-sized. They fight to the death...

Chapter Seventeen

The great lake trip from Aswan to Abu Simbel and back – the charms of Aswan

1982

Dec 4th, Aswan to the High Dam – we embark

I've been bitten during the night; a plague on the biter. What puzzles me are the squashed mosquitos on the ceiling. Was someone so tormented they levitated? These cold dawns have a soft edge. By 8.15am, I've bought my boat ticket and am provisioned with falafel, Dairylea, bread and water. Five days to Abu Simbel and back. At the High Dam we are 30 foreigners drinking tea and waiting to embark. Bomber and Goldie (who looks 14) are from California. Bomber has a strain of Blackfoot Indian and a homespun yarning style. He tells tales of pirates in the Red Sea (200 miles to our left) and the Philippines. A cassette player, the information purrs out of him: cheap plane from LA via Alaska to Hong Kong. Japan good for hitchhiking. The cheap *dhow* from Kenya to India…

12.30pm. We are summoned to our boat. Love at first sight. She is a double-decker ark – a structure of wood, hardboard and iron superimposed on a flat which was once a tender. Our engine is a separate vessel, a small tug-like thing bound to us, not by bonds of steel but rusty rope on the starboard side. The ark is 120 foot long. A cardboard roof full of holes covers the top deck. The railings are polo-ed with lifebelts. This is the foreigners' deck; also home to two soldiers who have bagged the best section, forrard in the shelter of the only cabin. The cabin belongs to a grizzled Nubian in a woolly hat, robe and long brown scarf. Below are two other cabins – one for Fatty in the White Sheet who is in charge and the other for two Nubians. The other Nubians going to Abu Simbel – this is the weekly boat – are ensconced aft beside the galley with the shelter of the ark's three walls around them. Their animals, a glossy cow, two white donkeys, a flock of lambs and a few goats are stalled forrard by the loos. There are four squatters and four basins, all spotlessly clean.

Midships, sacks of flour and potatoes stack high; also fodder for the beasts. There is a lovely grainy smell. The galley is commanded by Abdul the cook and Bilharzia Harry the teamaker. The tourist office in Cairo spoke with forked tongue. Fatty tells us tea, soup and bread will be provided. As provisions are loaded, we sit on our chosen sections of deck eyeing one another; time-honoured routine of fellow travellers at the start of a journey. It's going to be chilly up here.

At 4.30pm we cast off and chug down the first stretch of lake: colossal, man-made, lunar. Tender Tug's engine makes a terrible racket. We bucket into a sunset of technicolour cirrus. By 5.45pm it's almost dark, getting cold. Amid much shouting and pulling of warps the Ark parks by a chunk of rock. Freeport Maine sleeping bag is my pride and joy – sheetsack gets demoted to groundsheet to protect it. It's now very cold. Flaps of bread stuffed with falafel and Dairylea make a sustaining supper. Then commotion. A bongo-beating, singing, chanting vessel, comes alongside to dock. It's the Sudan boat, going to Wadi Haifa.

This feels like the beginning of *real* Africa. To our left, the Nubian desert, one of the most terrible in the world. The ancient Egyptians called gold *nub* and believed Nubia to be full of it. The chanting, laughing and beating of bongos continues. We lie bagged up like so many seals – French, Swiss, American, German, English. To escape the wind I snuggle down my bag, thankful for its drawstring which pulls tight around the neck. The light on the upper deck goes out. Tender Tug's generator coughs into silence. Lap...lap...lap...sleep. I wake briefly to see the moon bob out of its cirrus blanket, then sleep again. Hard on the hips, this deck.

Dec 5th, second day on the Ark

Settling-in day. The tug woke its crew with loud shouts at

233

5.30am. Go below for a cold wash followed by a hot, sweet tea. It tastes marvellous. Up comes a pale sun into the bitter day. We roost like fowls along the starboard side to catch its warmth. The tug's captain tries to stop us but unsuccessfully. He's worried we'll fall overboard. Soup smells waft from the galley. The animals stamp. Khaki-green water and the sandcastle contours of the Nubian Desert melt together. It's a dream landscape we travel, a drowned world.

The upper deck has split into two: aft, the lost souls, the flotsam and jetsam of the travelling world, among them two Frenchmen with tubercular coughs. Midships and forrard gather the businesslike travellers – us. Beside me are a couple of Americans, Fox and Bun; on *their* other side an Aussie and his Lolita girlfriend who shuffles about in woolly socks and flip-flops. They giggle and cuddle. I christen them the Half-Humpers because they *just* don't. Michele of the brilliant blue eyes must be a vet since she's deep in a book on animal husbandry. Her companion is a fair girl from a kibbutz. Beside them are two Bold Boys, English. I like them. John is well-organised and serious. Moose wears a Pangbourne hockey shirt which gives him the look of a troubadour. Next along, three solitary men; they read, sleep and keep themselves to themselves. Forrard behind the Nubian's cabin and on the other side of the soldiers, the Solid Germans. They sleep and knit. The man only wakes to hold his girlfriend's wool. She has a dog's face and will look exactly the same when she's 70. Two menaces: a Swiss who jangles because keys and a Swiss – of course – Army knife hang from his belt; and Harold.

How Bomber *loves* to talk. He's a fantasist but in no way does this lessen my enjoyment of his tales. He was a pro baseball player, earning millions. He has been a pirate. He has been a hobo. He has smuggled cobras' gallbladders from Burma through the Golden Triangle into China where decrepit Chinese will pay the earth for them. (It seems a cobra's gallbladder equals 100 Vitamin B shots, the ultimate get-it-up. Bomber says they taste like figs.) He has watched a fakir in India making magic with little snakes. First the fakir swallows water till his stomach is tight as a

234

drum. Then – o horrors – he swallows the snakes. You can see them, says B, wriggling inside him. They come out down his nose. I DON'T believe it.

Read *Zadig* and Moorhouse's *White Nile*. A lemon meringue sunset. Night falls and the wind gets up. I climb down the rickety ladder to the lower deck and find a Nativity lacking only Joseph, Mary and the Babe. A lantern at the stable end picks out the soft noses of the lambs, the bulk of the calm cow, the fronds of fodder. Forrard another lantern lights the galley; a chiaroscuro image of faces and flashing teeth – the women and children among their boxes. Shyly we smile at one another; a few words of Arabic and grave beauty breaks into a giggle. There is shelter here from the night above. The Nubian men smoke and talk and hot, sweet tea flows like the Nile from Harry's pot. Abdul the cook is playing cards with Fox, both sitting cross-legged on Harry's tea table. The cook cheats. Fox is a nice man.

A night of stars. They are sprinkled like hundreds and thousands on the waste of darkness. Leaning against stacks of flour, smelling forgotten childhood smells, looking at the tug with her thin, worried captain, I'm so happy I could sing, dance, make love, turn cartwheels – all at once. Later the moon peers down through a hole in the cardboard. It's FREEZING.

Dec 6th, third day, we arrive at Abu Simbel

The lake's so enormous it's a sea. One stretch of its coast looks West Highland, a croft adding authenticity to the delusion. The knife-edged purity of sand – why don't architects look at sand? Now sand castles have given way to meringues; black ones not white. This terrible desert gets its grip on your mind; always the same yet never the same; listless, scabbed, furrowed. Now, shyness thawed, Nubians and foreigners communicate. John the Bold Boy has an army father too. Michele's boyfriend is a cowman. 'He's stayed behind in Aswan. Says he's seen too many temples.' Tony, one of the singles is a real estate man from LA. Harold, real name Peter, is a Pole. He's all right – he just drives everyone mad.

At midday, at last, we see the man-made mountain and the rescued temples, everyone hanging over the starboard rail as we leave them to our right and round the headland into Abu Simbel's port, a sandy beach. Nothing can describe the majesty and indifference of Ramses the Great's temples. Shelley of course springs to mind:

> 'My name is Ozymandias, king of kings:
> Look on my works, ye Mighty, and despair!'

Laudable Egyptian logic dictates the price of a ticket: plane travellers 6LE, boat travellers 3LE, students 1.50LE. The desert sun is ferocious. I'm too late with my filter milk. It's odd. Baalbek was big yet nothing. These temples are monstrous, their figures so huge you can't take in the whole, yet they move me. The carvings live and dance and do battle. Misery, joy, compassion – I look and I *do* despair. We seem to have gone backwards.

There are *dreadful* French and American tourists off the plane. One grabs the gold key from the Nubian at the entrance to the Great Temple and strikes an attitude – chewing gum noisily – while his giggling wife snaps him. The Nubian's face registers two emotions, surprise and contempt. My libation to Ramses – a Coca Cola – is sold to me by a man with a snake in a jar. He tells me a long story about the snake but I don't understand a word.

We spend the evening in port. I have upset Fatty in the white sheet by being the only person to have a return ticket. He took both my tickets by mistake, now has to amend his books; a loss of face which makes him grumpy. Sunset brings an ebb and flow to the top deck gang. The Half Humpers investigate the flotsam and jetsam; the French boys play frisbee with Arab bread; Bun, Fox, John, Moose and Tony play cards. Boundaries are down. The marvel of the temples and an afternoon in the Abu Simbel café with its weak tea, tins of baked beans, cold fried fish and fifth rate disco tape have made us brothers. We have shared cold nights and a miracle. All the clichés are true. At 6pm John announces that Abdul has made soup. We rise in a body and rush to the Ark. The soup is potent and heavily-garlicked. John, arriving 15 minutes later, finds not one drop left.

New cargo, passengers, sacks, crates and one white donkey are loaded. Standing near the top-deck Nubian I'm aware of his scowl. Suddenly with a flourish, he produces an orange from his robes. It's a present for me. He has the cabin so he can keep an eye on us. It's even colder tonight. I wear everything – sweatshirt, thick overshirt, sweater and anorak inside my bag. I'm still frozen. At 2am there are shouts of 'Wake up Abdul, wake up Sabri, wake up Muhammed!'

'Jesus!' wails Bun. The engine starts. We chug away.

Dec 7th, fourth day, the journey back

It's Tuesday. We're going downstream with the current, seem-ingly travelling at twice the speed, our tug pulling us through waters which the vicious North Wind has whipped into white stew. Bagged against the icy blast I read *The White Nile*. The new passengers are careless shitters. Nubians look so handsome in their robes, their long scarves wound carelessly round their heads. They put us to shame. Fox and Bun are sluts. They left their Gouda cheese open among the dirty socks and bags, a treat for inquisitive flies, and wandered off. The flies feasted for four hours on the cheese. Bun and Fox returned to devour it – and the fly eggs – with relish. I saw a man today I've never seen before.

John, Moose, Bomber and Goldie will be going back down the lake on the Wadi Haifa boat. John suddenly panics about bilharzia:

'I say! Look here! Have you lot been washing in the tap water?'

'Yes,' we answer absently.

'Well, someone says Harry gets it out of a side canal. It must be full of bilharzia.'

We make reassuring noises. John knits his brow. I'd have liked a son like him. The white donkey is lonely. It says so, frequently and noisily. The kids are interesting about life in a kibbutz and say the same thing: that the people inside are astonishingly unaware and uninformed. 'Money-grabbing and tight with their cash,' grumbles the fair girl, who's going back to her kibbutz. She seems lost. Drifting on the borders of sleep, I listen to someone describing the mosquitos of the Sudd – marshland of South Sudan: Harold, it *would* be Harold, lists the wonders of the ancient world. Another arctic night with an intrusive moon. Abdul the cook went into overdrive and dished up spaghetti for lunch. Supper is potato and aubergine stew. He looks more Italian than Egyptian and behaves like a character in a Mozart opera. I *wish* I was going to the Sudan with John and Moose and Co.

Dec 8th, back in Aswan

I feel as if I'd been on the Ark for a month. At crack of dawn we leave our anchorage with the usual yells. Read. Sleep. Read. Gaze. I shall never forget these five days. Bun is a graphic artist. The hours drift, broken only by rice and hot sauce for lunch. At the High Dam there's no train for two hours. Some leave to hitch, others take a taxi; a remnant, including me, sit in the station tea house and play cards. It's friendly, with good food and a telly. The small boys who run it are enchanting. Back in Aswan I move hotels to the Saffa beside the railway station, cheap, and with hot showers and a lovely soft mattress. The inside of my cupboard smells of something lost down the years.

Dec 9th, Aswan

Aswan is a frontier town, gateway to Africa. The faces are dark and beautiful. The music has the beat. First it was called *Abwa*, Greek for elephant, on account of its important ivory market; then *Swano* meaning market, then Aswan. It's a town of trees and flowers and tantalising, elusive scents, the Brighton-Eastbourne of Egypt (it cures rheumatism, says my leaflet). There's a colonial whiff to the promenade with its cafés and restaurants above the

Nile; the Rowing Club, the Swimming Pool. Aswan has every-thing for everyone: fun for the poor in the station-market quarter; comfort for the middle class; luxury for the rich in a clutch of hotels – the Oberoi Hotel with its own ferry service, the Old Cataract – as glorious as the New is horrible – the Grand and the ones which float.

Early morning and the dust lies douce. Later it will fly and bounce, churned by lorries, swept by sweepers, whirled into tor-nados by the wind from the north. Aswan has garrulous sparrows and hiccoughing pigeons. There's something unsettling about its sweet-scented flowers. Maybe they grew in Rangoon? I take my first *felucca* to Elephant Island and wander round the museum and its garden. Sexy Susie is the Inspector of Archaeology. After mint tea made by the gardeners, we tramp round very ruined ruins, Susie instructive and fond of saying, 'Look, my dear...' The building which houses the museum was the British Engineer's house. He built the first Aswan Dam in 1910. The garden, ineluctably English, is full of morning glory, phlox, roses, lilies, with a gazebo smothered in an ancient tree of jasmine. *Feluccas* are elegant. It's fun to watch the way they handle, their rig and effortless skim.

Now we all keep meeting, we of the Ark. Michele's cowman Steve is a lovely Yorkshire chap. The French coughers pop up in a tiled café in the market. John calls from across the street as I stroll back from lunch: 'Sara! Come and have *chai*.' Saying goodbye to the Two Bold Boys saddens me. Then Bomber and Goldie appear. Bomber has washed his hair which has lowered his brow, not lofty at the best of times. His last story shattered even my credulity: a plane crash followed by seven days in the Sahara without water.

'Goodbye, good luck, see you in Australia in two years' time.'

We go our separate ways.

The legal rate of exchange is 131 PT to the English £. There's a black marketeer in the market. Covert hissings among bolts of material – very Casablanca, Aunt Dot would have approved – got me 160. Exhausted by criminal activities, I spend the evening in the Hall of Culture watching Nubian Dancing. It's a splendid performance, more sophisticated than African dancing. Passionate, humorous, deeply moving. The men's clothes have the geometric design I keep seeing; the dancers spring like balls, leap like Cossacks, swing and dip with the casual fury of the American musical. Dignity, grace, pride – and intense homesickness. With their land drowned, dance is their last link with centuries of tradition and culture. The dancers are accompanied by a drum and two clarinet-like pipes. The drum is as eloquent as an orchestra. The Nubian language bears no relation to Arabic. Nor is it written.

Dec 10th, Aswan

They are a beautiful and dignified people in Upper Egypt. The Nubians especially are magnificent. The women, old and young, dress in black with a *mantilla* over the head. Farag in the tourist office was interesting about the re-location of the Nubians before the land was flooded. Though the Government moved villages with care, so says F, re-housing neighbours in the same street with the same street pattern, there were problems. The old houses had earth walls and floors or were stone with a wattle roof – cool in summer, warm in winter. The Nubians' new houses were reinforced concrete – hot in summer, freezing in winter. Nubians don't steal or rape. Those who moved to Egypt rather than to the Sudan found the locals had scant respect for anyone else's belongings; and that included wives. Nubian women working in the fields were molested. In Nubia the soil was very light, here in Aswan it's much heavier. The farmers found it difficult to adjust. Apart from that, imagine the trauma of your country vanishing under billions of gallons of water.

Aswan's market stretches from the station southwards, two blocks behind the promenade. My best discovery is a white-tiled Nubian restaurant with geometric designs in black, light green,

240

blue and pink. On my first visit I drank the national soup – a slimy concoction called *molohkia*. The potato and aubergine stew, peppered, is a wow. Fried fish stalls, sandwich bars (where an Arab glove ends up bulging with fried aubergine, egg, cheese, salad, falafel and swatches of parsley), spices spilling from sacks – here is life. Beautifully-woven baskets, platters and cottons clash with kitsch. The *chai* shops are nests of turbans and robes and hubble-bubble. Horse-drawn carts, donkeys, the odd garry, its brass glinting against the black coracle hood, negotiate the crowds. A lorry, trying to turn a corner without squashing an old lady and her cabbages, dithers and revs.

There are modern stores for the suspicious tourist. Farag says the Mineral Water Industry has done a great job selling people off the perfectly drinkable local water with bilharzia horror stories.

Dec 11th, Aswan

A Coptic church morning with Susie. Aswan has an abundance of Coptic, Catholic and Protestant churches. You can often smell incense. There are eighty million Copts in Egypt – can that be right? According to Susie, Sadat hated Copts and Christians. I have become fond of Susie. Her English is excellent with a slight Anglo-Indian twang and she's very intelligent. The way she holds my arm and gives affected laughs and tells me how clever I am is endearing. We meet mid-morning, look at a couple of old churches, then two modern ones. Modern Coptic is jolly, the interiors of the churches covered in wall paintings and ikons, a vast and friendly Pantokrator in the dome. The Coptic church was founded in Egypt by St Mark in AD 42. Copts are horrified if you cross your knees. It is disrespectful.

'Why have they three altars?'

Susie explains that the churches are built for grandeur. Their bulk needs three lots of supportive pillars which results in three altars. Suddenly she screams and rushes back to her office. I've decided Egyptians are the Irish Arabs – funny, philosophical, garrulous, good-natured, charming, *mad*.

My tiled restaurant in the market has spinach stew and tahini. The cook in the red shirt fancies me. He is 24, with four babies and a beautiful smile. He slips me some extra spinach, gazes at me worshipfully:

'How old are you?'

'46.'

'No, no!' He shakes his head vehemently. '30.'

I depart, my stomach much enlarged; also my ego.

According to Tourist Office Farag, Egyptian men have a great time bedding Western women. Farag's had Australian matrons in the sand dunes, New Zealand girls in the tourist office loo and Americans in their bedrooms. One woman with a rich, elderly husband who couldn't get it up fell in love with a boatman:

'He was becoming so tired, he had to tell her he was going to Cairo. Really he hid at home.'

Farag is obsessed with sex – and puzzled that I won't oblige. He refers to coitus as the *operation*. I suggested that it might be better if he said *making love* – it sounded less terminal.

The Saffa, my hotel, is a joy forever; the loos flood, the hot water heater leaks, but my green room is home. Travelling Sheet, the cotton bag inside my sleeping bag, is now a tablecloth. On it sits my Turkish glass, full of flowers. Sometimes at night, instead of the light, I switch on the fan by mistake. It's the size of a helicopter blade and much furred. The whistle and wail of trains mingles with my dreams; a lovely sound, redolent of journeys accomplished and those yet to come, of nostalgia not yet felt but inside one like a benign growth. The station is a recently-built magnificence. At night, its vertical fluorescent bars shimmering in the darkness, it resembles The Thing from Outer Space, newly landed, pondering its next move. Nearby *fahtirah* the Fantastic Pancake can be enjoyed. Three weeks and not a drop to drink.

The traffic police live in chalets up ladders. Striped chalets. They do nothing. Perhaps they're up there – 30 feet at least – to protect them from a lawless mob? On my last evening I take tea with the shoeshine boys outside the Continental and look at the Prophet's Eyebrow, the new moon, lying on its back in a guava sky. When the sun comes up it's the precise colour of jackets workmen wear at night. My list of Gods is growing:

Seth, Shu, Tefnut, Bes, Hathor; my favourites are Ra-Horakty and the Dog Anubis. Khnum is a ram. Sobek is the Crocodile God.

Likos, 2005

Is 'A day in the life of a pipe' still an essay subject for 11-year olds? My best effort was a day in the life of a pen. It fell out of Mrs Graham's handbag down a grating into a sewer which took it to a river where it was swallowed by a fish. The fish was caught by Billy Graham who took it home to his mother who gutted it and found, yes, her fountain pen. I got A+ for that. A day in my life here? Take yesterday…

At 6.30am a creamy light filtered through, brighter by 7am, blue by 7.30am. I got up, looked at the day which was fine, scowled at the cat, tea cosy on the balcony, and made a jug of espresso coffee. Reading out-of-date Spectators *and marvelling at the Tories is such a pleasure. Then I had a bath, tidied the office, hung my sheet and pyjamas from the balcony and started to work. It was now 9am. Two hours later, shouts from the street: Angelica. Did I want to eat octopus and spinach NOW? I retrieved my sheet and pyjamas which I'd forgotten about and flew down the road. As usual Greek Mama stuffed me like a goose so a walk in the hills was the only hope for the work ethic. So beautiful up there among olive and almond, the mountain lavender in first flower, the terraces dusted with daisies. An orchid, the first I've ever seen in Likos, hid behind a clump of sistus; pink on the edges going to dark at centre. Back in my room, I edited for another three hours, got Max's food from nearby Popi, fed him and returned the tin to her fridge. Then I sat by the open window of her kafenion and had my reward – ouzo. The evening was gobbled up by supper in the harbour and reading. I was asleep by 10pm.*

The last section of my Egyptian diaries is the stuff of nightmares. Can't find the station, the tourist office, the train, the shipping office, the hotel. Can't even find words to describe the not finding. Talk about amber lights. The competent, carefree traveller of the last five

244

years has turned into a neurotic. Travel fatigue, too much in one year, or something else? I'm not having the fun I had in Greece and Turkey; and bursting into tears is as out of character as not being able to find anything. Now, 23 years later, I watch the beginning of meltdown...

Chapter Eighteen

Luxor disliked – Alexandria
and the great ticket drama
1982

Dec 13th, Luxor

Luxor is wrecked. I hate it. Even 60 pelican flying up the Nile don't console. Mass tourism is here to stay and everyone is on the beast's back: 'Hello Madame…Change money Madame?...I'd like you to meet my mother (that means he wants to fuck you)…I have a donkey…I have a bicycle…Like a boat Madame?' on and on and on. There's sneering and staring. The place is a nightmare of cars, buses, lorries, litter and blue-rinsed Americans. Yesterday evening a man in the tourist office invited me to tea. When he started on homosexual/lesbian clubs and said how much I reminded him of his dykey girlfriend, I said that it wasn't my thing and did he proposition all female tourists and did his boss know? He fled.

Nothing can spoil the Valley of the Kings or the Temple of Luxor. I collected my bike and took the dawn ferry across the river – bicycling past villagers waving alabaster and plastic scarabs. The getting-lost virus pounced again, with wrong turnings and arrival at what looked like a hotel. Workmen chanted their way up a sweep of steps hauling a large object with ropes. If ever a fretful porpentine sought the Valley of the Kings, it was me.

'*Where* is the Valley of the Kings and *what* is this?'

'This,' answered the overseer in mild surprise, 'is the temple of Hatshepsut. Do you have a ticket?'

When I finally laboured up the hill to the resting place of the pharaohs I was not disappointed. The rich colour and magnificence of Seti's tomb; Tuthmosis III's with it's elaborate burglar traps of pits, gullies and chasm-like descents; a double Nut, Goddess of the Sky, in the tomb of Ramses IX; and Tutankhamen. Five tombs was enough. As Abu Simbel to temples, so Seti to tombs. Everything pales in comparison. I bicycled back to Hatshepsut's Hotel, looked at the Ramesseum and the Colossi of Memnon and took the ferry to Luxor.

I don't like the Temple of Karnak. It seems a muddle compared to the Temple of Luxor. Here, Ramses the Great's architects manage to keep faith with classical proportion despite the largesse of the schemes. The king's fourth right toe nail is the size of my clenched fist. So what's good about Luxor apart from its ancient wonders? The Cleopatra Hotel in the market; the New Karnak Restaurant with cheap and delicious food – spinach, bean soup, tahini, omelettes; the beauty of the river, though you have to scramble down the bank some hundred yards past the New Winter Palace to enjoy it in peace; my coffee man in the market, grave and courteous. I was his first customer this morning. He had lit his brazier of wood and was wiping the blue benches. Um Kulthum and the muezzin wailed in duet...

I'm tired.

Going back to Nov 23rd, Alexandria, excerpts from my diary on arrival from Greece

A fatal incapacity to find anything in this city of Cavafy and Durrell. A whiff of past splendours are the Hotel Grillon, Themistocles Sofianopoulou the Greek grocer, St Mark's Anglican Church, aloof and splendid in its dark garden, a second-hand bookshop full of Dornford Yates, the railway station which is the size of Buckingham Palace, the tram station with its fine blue and yellow rolling stock and two grand coffee houses – the *Delices* and the *Trianon* (this one has ants capering on the table).

I can't find the Tourist Office. When I do, they give me a map of Alexandria by Day and by Night, the print so tiny I can't read it with my specs on. I can't find the Black Sea Shipping Co; and even when I'm in the right street people tell me that I'm not. A surreal encounter with a shop called *La Vache qui rit* doesn't help.

'Parlez-vous français?'

'No,' they reply frostily. 'Arabic.'

I leave in despair. When I do find the Black Sea Shipping Co, a man says: 'Oh no! We're not the cheapest. You want the Egyptian Navigation Co.' He radiates loving kindness. I can't find the Egyptian Navigation Co at no 1 El-Horreya (alias Nasser) Avenue; and when I *do* find no 1, it's an art gallery full of pictures of dubious quality. 'Next door,' says a lady sewing below a picture. Five hours later I have a ticket costing 91 Egyptian pounds for the *Syria* on Dec 23, direct to Piraeus. Immigration says it's all right if I travel on the day after my visa expires. I took an hour to find *them*. Finally located, the place was full of handcuffed men.

Fin de siècle, Edwardian, and follies from the twenties and thirties line the Esplanade. Behind are markets and squalor, filth filthier than even the slums of Istanbul. Men pluck at my sleeve, a small boy mimes sexual suggestion. Well-bred Egyptian women are elegant. They wear 1940s turbans and long gowns of a furry velvety material. Others dress like Sahar's Circassian Mum in Amman in a kind of nun's getup – not just black and white but pale green and beige. And guess what? The Arabic for girl is *bint*. That's where it came from. Going along the Esplanade to the East reminds me of Beirut.

The museum, like the station, I discovered by mistake. It smells like school – a clutter of Graeco-Roman, Serapis, Apis and DREADFUL mummies with their dark toes sticking through hessian. A colossal bird with an Egyptian air comes from Thasos opposite Kavala. Very odd. Loveliest of anything is wooden Serapis, a target for the workmen above cleaning windows who send chunks of masonry crashing down. Serapis has a sad face. The female fashions of Hellenistic Alexandria are close to 18th century England – skirts falling from a ruched bodice, the hair styles Jane Austen.

Alexandria floats in garbage; and Pompey's column has nothing to do with the Roman general. A funeral passes, ignored by a football game. I plod from Pompey, westwards towards the tombs. An optimistic district, this: life, bustle, hope – God knows why because it's poor and squalid. At the tombs, closed due to electricity failure, I bump into a New Zealander staying at my hotel. We talk of NZ and Scots and my relations there:

'Invercargill is the arse-hole of New Zealand, so I'm told,' I say.

He comes from Invercargill.

A skeleton doesn't move for the horse and cart which – cruelly – just miss it. Crouched in dreadful dignity, the cat waits for death. It reminds me of a friend three weeks before he died of cancer.

Dec 18th – 21st, Alexandria

Where to start? After a hellish overnight journey from Luxor to Cairo, second class and 18 hours of freezing cold, I discovered that my boat, the *Syria*, leaving Alexandria on the 23rd, had been cancelled. Two days later I arrived in Alexandria to get my money back and find another boat. (Sadat's brother is being tried for corruption. He apparently made millions while Sadat was in power. Iran all over again.) Last impressions of Cairo, maddest and most endearing of cities: a red cart, piled high with creamy cauliflowers; small white donkeys; a frail old man with basket ware on his head carrying six pomegranates on a plate; the washing lines of the slums.

I'm back in the Hyde Park House Hotel in rue Amine Fakri. The hotel is on the 8th floor with an entrance of potplants and red-plush cosiness. Though dark and dusty, it exudes dignity and friendliness. Welcomed with smiles by the plump proprietor (he speaks English) I was given my old room back. It has a large basin, that rarity a bedside light and the loo is in the passage. The price per night is ridiculous; just under £2 sterling including breakfast of tea, two eggs, bread, cheese and jam.

It's now the evening of Dec 19th. Hysteria recollected in tranquillity. You would think being refunded for a ticket simple…

The day started well – it's lovely *not* to have to look for breakfast. The hotel dining room is shabby but grand. It has three sets of French doors, five chandeliers, a sideboard in which the elderly Greek-speaking Nubian waiter rummages and tables with white linen tablecloths. The chef coughs. After a rapturous reunion with the waiter and floods of Greek, I ate omelette, cheese, jam, bread and drank sweet tea. Suddenly the men at the next table cried out. The boiled egg given to the one in specs was raw, not boiled; his hands were covered in egg white. The chef laughed so much he stopped coughing.

At 8.45am I arrived at the Egyptian Navigation Co. Mr Sabri, the charmer who'd sold me my ticket a month ago, greeted me with smiles and tea. Then he summoned a boy to take me to head office in the port where my ticket would be refunded. 'Half an hour at the most,' said Mr Sabri, looking more like Maurice Chevalier than ever. At head office the game was *musical offices*: the first, where I surrendered my ticket, was full of women, a child and dust. Half an hour went by. One of the women filled in the form for me, chatted, went on writing; I was shown the child and offered a doughnut. Then my escort vanished with ticket and form, only to reappear quarter of an hour later. An error on the form. Back to the woman. Back to the escort. Once more he vanished. Ten minutes went by. Back came the escort. Then we went to another office where I was handed 75 Egyptian pounds.

'Not enough,' I said. 'You owe me 16 more.'

The man in this office was toad-like. He sent my escort off again, offered me tea, showed me another child and went back to his papers. I read *Let's Go*. Looking up half an hour later, there was my escort dozing in a chair.

SO WHAT THE FUCK IS GOING ON? I *really* lost it. Stamping and yelling I danced round Toad who sent me, still yelling, to the ground floor with the boy. Much whispering with a well-dressed managerial type while I muttered and fumed. Now to another office. 'Just five minutes,' beamed the Well Dressed One.

This office, the third, was full of men and women doing nothing. One of the men asked for my Thomas Cook receipt (the money change receipt necessary for the purchase of any ticket in Egypt), looked at it, then questioned its validity. I burst into tears. The response was endearing – horror, followed by cigarettes, coffees and teas; and after five minutes the 16 pounds. Fond farewells, then back to Mr Sabri inside the Palladian-porticoed, pale green splendour of the Egyptian Navigation Co. Such a nice boy, the escort. If nothing else, he had attended a short seminar on hysterical foreigners. Mr Sabri, wreathed in smiles, explained: the girl who had made out the form in the first office had been standing in for the usual woman ('It's a Sunday, you see'); and the clerks had thought the Thomas Cook money change receipt a travel agent's receipt, hence their unwillingness to produce the last 16 pounds (travel agents booking a ticket always take a cut).

'What news of the Black Sea Shipping Co?' I asked my protector. Gums furred with tannin, I was now calm.

'Ah, well. The captain who is Russian will only take Greek passengers, the fare is more than 120LE and the boat doesn't sail until January 7th…I think you had better fly. It will be the same price more or less.'

What a novel idea. Air travel never occurred to me. Clearly my grasp on reality was slipping. Who needs a nervous breakdown? Just go to Egypt for a month.

'Misir Airways will be the cheapest,' said Mr Sabri. Minutes ticked by while he tried to get a line, then: 'Look! *There* is Misir Travel, there on the corner outside. They will give you *all* the details…'

I crossed the road to Misir Travel – a pile of rubble. Its entrance was blocked by a large sideboard. Next door, not yet rubble, was the Misir Bank.

'Excuse me, but where has your travel office gone to?'

No-one had ever heard of Misir Travel. I felt hysteria rising again. Then the friendly cashier looked at a notice pinned to the sideboard. 'No 33. Down there. *That's* Misir Travel.' Down the road and up three flights only to discover that this – alas – was *not* Misir Travel. They knew nothing about flights to Athens. Feeling the last shreds of my sanity sliding away, I burst, once more, into tears. A woman took my arm. 'Please. I think the office is in Saad Zaghlul. But let me send someone with you.' Back down the staircase I fled. Deep breathing, put on your dark glasses, pull yourself together. It worked. I found the offices of Egypt Air in Saad Zaghlul, only a short distance from the Hyde Park House Hotel. They told me the single fare to Athens was 149LE – this meant changing another sixty quid. Cheerfully, I set off for Thomas Cook.

There I found a man and woman waiting by a caisse and the money changer sitting at the back of it reading *Newsweek*. Furious, I demanded action. To the dismay of the people waiting, I shouted. The money changer put down his Newsweek. At last my turn came. I handed my three travellers' cheques to the clerk. He looked at them. Frowned. Looked at them again. Then he announced that the signatures were not the same. One was a fake. My voice was deathly quiet: 'If you don't change these travellers' cheques *now*, this instant, I shall go mad, completely mad, in *this* office.'

By this time I looked bananas. Reluctantly, *very* slowly he gave me currency. Now I had *two* Thomas Cook receipts which confused the cashier back at Egypt Air; so I had to explain in detail about the cancelled boat for the second time. The Egypt Air cashier continued to protest that the two cheques together came to more than the price of the air fare. Too bloody bad. Who gives a fuck? In the end he gave up and issued me with a ticket on the 7am flight via Cairo to Athens on Tuesday December 21st.

I'm back in my room in the Hyde Park House Hotel drinking a bottle of wine. I shall probably drink two more. Does Egypt do this to everyone?

Dec 20th, last day and last thoughts

The sun is shining, the day balmy, the sea blue as a baby's bonnet. After breakfast, taking the stairs because the lift is unwell, I stroll out into the city with the *firm intention* of getting lost. On the corner of rue Amine Fakri the old man is polishing the apples and pears on his barrow with a feather duster. The cleanest street in all Egypt is the street of Alexandria's timber merchants; across from it the fish market, pungent and stacked high with gleaming baskets of fish, calamares, prawns, whelks and those things you pick off rocks. Little crabs wave weakly from their wicker prisons. Boys chop parsley. It's 9.30am, a good time to case markets: cuttlefish, cabbages and a large round basket of rabbits all eating furiously. Six black and white kittens frolic beside a stall selling saffron-coloured pancakes in icing sugar. Past vats of spluttering falafel I idle; past old gentlemen in quiet clock shops and grave tea makers; in and out of Alexandria's time machine.

The pace of the Middle East has an enviable dignity. May it never succumb to fast food, watery Nescafé or strident feminism. Mr Sabri gives me more tea and a signed photograph of the infamous *Syria*. With a bottle of dry white wine tucked under my arm I return to my room to write, feeling like a character out of the *Alexandria Quartet*. The hotel, like the city, has a pre-war flavour; a battered dignity. Suddenly a knock on the door and there are Fox and Bun from the Ark. What delight. We drink the wine and swap horror stories about tickets and vanishing boats. There are cobras in Egypt – thank God I didn't know. Fox and Bun have *fellahin* friends in Luxor who promised them pigeon

253

when they came back from the boat trip. Mysteriously, the pigeon which had been flying round the ceiling of the mud house wasn't there. Nor was it in the stewpot. Bun asked where it was. 'The cobra got it,' said the English-speaking child.

What is it about Egypt? My inability to find anything verges on the deranged. Aswan and Abu Simbel are freezing; Alexandria, 1000 kilometres north of the Sudan border, is warm. But everyone in Cairo says it's freezing in Alexandria and boiling in Aswan. The liftman in an Egyptian lift always holds a bunch of wires in case the lift has a seizure – it frequently does. On my last evening in Cairo I went and looked closely at the imperial lions at either end of the Tahrir Bridge and fancied I saw the same helpless bewilderment in their eyes as can be seen in the eyes of Egypt's tourists. Mad or not, the Egyptians are the friendliest, funniest, most charming people I've ever met.

A filling falls out during supper; the rest of my teeth will probably follow in the night. Am I insane to be flying Air Egypt? The flight is a mirage, we'll crash, my rucksack will explode... muttering *inşallahs* I sleep.

Egypt – dust, 'M'HAMED!', car horns, the Nile, very sweet tea, *kosheri* and cold, cold dawns.

Likos, 2005

'A fire, a woman and the sea' – according to a Likos saying, life's three dangers. For four months, from October to February, I've had the sea as a neighbour and the chance to watch her in all her moods. Someone once said: 'the sea is a place which unites memory with the present'. Perhaps, unknowingly, I chose my neighbour for that reason. It's extraordinary how a colourless liquid full of salt can assume so many different textures, colours and shapes; potter's clay for the sun and the moon and the sky – one minute wrinkled satin, the next, the hide of a spiny creature. She goes from silk to steel. She is more unpredictable than any woman, more ravenous than any pirate. A month ago – it was a dark day with driving rain and feral wind – she became her essence, the Kraken; grey, heaving, all-devouring. There was the sea of myth and sailor's tale, there the fury which tore the backs off the Miti houses in the winter storm of 1940.

My love affair with Greece began in 1961. Then, during the seventies, friends took me sailing on their wooden ketch. Summer after summer we explored Ionian shores, the Cyclades, the northern islands near the Gates of the Wind. We often night-sailed. That I shall never forget. To be at the wheel in the middle of the night is awe-inspiring: the moonpath, the wind in the sails, the groan of rope, the creak of wood, the hiss of the waves – and those voices. No wonder sailors are superstitious. Who are those voices and the secrets they whisper? Other memories: dawn on grey glass below Dubrovnik; 30 dolphin playing round our bows; the water spout from nowhere which smashed the mast in half and vanished before the captain, mending a sail, made it to the deck. During one winter I hitched a lift with fishermen from Astipaleia to Amorgos. A gale got up, force 9 gusting 10; on the last leg to Ayali we were running before the wind, the caique's beam lifting like

*a duck's bottom to let the mountains slide beneath us.
The waves looked 20 feet high. Fascinated I watched
them coming, convinced the next would devour us. The
Aegean looks like a pond but she is not to be trusted.*

*Here on Likos the mountain lavender is blooming.
It's February 22nd. Yet another north wind is belting
down the strait, banging Miti's shutters and making the
old men grumble. Max is a soldiers' dog now, with a
collar of his own. With his penchant for chasing goats
and eating turkey chicks, the hippie poet couldn't be left
on the loose. Though tied all day, he's got another dog
for company, a job to do and his food and drink provided by the Greek Army. May Saint Spiridion protect
him. The cat has started bringing his girlfriends to meet
me. How can a cat look like an oven glove?*

*Editing my diaries has sent me travelling again:
not only revisiting places in my mind's eye but smelling
them – dust, diesel, herbs, flowers, food, spices…to say
nothing of the ferries I took; the mindless pleasure of
leaning on a rail and watching land appear and disappear, the fluttering of flag over the wake, the hovering
gulls.*

*I returned from Alexandria to Athens just before
Christmas 1982 and spent the next few months on the
boat. I started a novel but couldn't make it work. Was it
time to go home? Home? What home? I didn't have a
home, I'd sold it. To postpone the prospect of what to do
next I went to Venice on the bus. March 1983. Venice
freezing and glorious. There I lost my passport and my
bus ticket back to Athens and ran – nearly – out of
money; only to be rescued by a combination of the
British Consulate, longsuffering as ever, and an
Athenian friend. If I went on losing everything and
failing to find anything I'd soon be invisible. In May I
flew to London to start the rest of my life. Clearly on the
way to losing my mind on top of everything else, I took
a job as a companion to an old gentleman in
Wimbledon. Then I panicked. What the fuck was I*

doing? I told the agency a pack of lies and flew back to Athens.

Amazing the capacity for self-deception. Another pleasant winter on the boat, friends, jaunts, the reassurance of old haunts lulled my angst. On a freezing morning in January 1984 I bought a ticket for the ferry to Haifa. The cardamom lands were calling...

Israel: a conundrum 1984

The essence of civilisation is to
respect the variety of life, and how
few of us do so...

Freya Stark

Chapter Nineteen

The boat to Haifa – Sister Juditha
and the hospice – Acre – unholy Zefat
1984

January 26th – 29th, by Sol Olympia to Haifa

We sail out of Piraeus at 4.45pm, first stop Rhodes. The Sol
Olympia is a friendly boat, cleaner than the average Greek
steamer. The alcove in the third class bar will be my bed. The
crew, whose relaxing alcove it is, don't mind; better than the
saloon which is full of pot-smoking backpackers eating chocolate
biscuits. People are loathe to sleep: a card game goes on till
dawn, middle-aged Cypriot ladies sew and chatter, old men
smoke and cough. A morning ashore in Rhodes, then south we
sail on the 20-hour run to Cyprus. My alcove has a reading lamp.
Life could not be better.

The second night is enlivened by an exchange of abuse with the
whisky-drinking card players and a storm which breaks most of
the glasses in the bar. The two Cypriot ladies scream. At 8.15am
we steam into Limassol. What an odd town. It looks as if
someone had played football with it. The road from port to town
is about three miles of dust, mud and lorries. No pavements. The
town centre has a bizarre small-corner-shop-in-Coventry-or-
Nottingham feel. Bovril everywhere. Drink coffee and go back to
the deserted ship to read. Cyprus looks dull.

We are a motley crowd. One young Jew in spectacles never takes
his hat off; nor does a burly Australian whose briefs are the
briefest ever. A Kosher family from Carmel eats and shouts and
eats. Two fat English girls plus a New Zealander who's been
living in Iceland are heading for a kibbutz. The Icelanders don't
speak much, says the Kiwi, but read, sing and watch telly. All the
food is boiled – fish, potatoes, veg. Alcohol is forbidden so
everyone makes moonshine. The winters are frightful, nobody

laughs, and nobody talks to foreigners. Three Cockney lads, truculent sparrows, swear and lark their way round the deck; a table of English sing and play guitar. Eavesdropping on the Greek crew is fun – they mock the passengers and boast about 'storms I have been through'. The card-playing Germans got off at Cyprus so the third night is quiet. I actually sleep.

Early morning and land in sight. Leaning on the rail and smelling the whiff of cardamom is traveller's joy. Haifa looks pleasant, its silo dominating the waterfront. So *this* is where the British once turned away refugee-packed boats from Europe after the war. As we dock, shepherded by tugs, I feel that inexplicable calm which means things will fall into place; not what I felt in my receivers on arrival at Alexandria…I'm booked into the St Charles Hospice in Jaffa Road which Kosher Granny says is in Carmel. Saying goodbye to the cockney sparrows, I shoulder my pack and set off to find bed and breakfast.

Jan 29th – 30th, Haifa

105 Jaffa Road is not in Carmel but a short walk from the port: a pleasant building with arched windows and a red-tiled roof. There is a white cross on the roof and green gates onto the street, one of which is open. Set among shady trees, a garden behind, St Charles Hospice – home to nuns of a German order – is too good to be true. Sister Juditha who confirms my booking is a female version of Nedo in Kusadesi: five foot, stout as a barrel, with eyes which twinkle like a water rat's. Like a nun I met last year in Venice, she is full of laughter. Instant love. Instant familiarity of the hospice which smells the same as my home in the north of Scotland – a mixture of polished wood, old stone, sweet laundry, flowers, overcoats and soap. My room looks over a tangle of fruit trees, cypresses and olives to the shrine of the Bahai faith. I digest my furnishings – a huge soft bed, a huge sofa flung about with cushions, large desk, wardrobe, small table and two easy chairs, bookcase with English books in it, bedside light, wash-hand basin and electric fire. It's Sunday morning. Outside pigeons coo and sparrows chirp. I realise how much I've missed the Middle

East, a nostalgia now assuaged by the whiff of cardamom mixed with the smell of trees and dust.

The sisters of Saint Charles of Borromeo have an unpredictable Mother Superior in Germany. She keeps shifting them from hospice to hospice. The nuns are old and gentle and the atmosphere tranquil. As for the breakfasts, they are a sinful temptation to stay the whole month here and go nowhere else. Sister Juditha is in charge and what you get is this: a tumbler of iced fruit juice, a pot of cardamom-flavoured coffee, good and strong, enough for eight cups, a plate of cheese, a plate of salami, a plate of peeled sliced tomatoes, a fried egg, bread, butter, marmalade and yoghurt. Ouf!

Haifa is pleasant. It's provincial, with tree-lined stone staircases climbing the hills. In the port a mixture of downtown Amman and England; Manhattan in Hadar, home to the tourist office and Haifa's Oxford Street; and St John's Wood crossed with Beverly Hills in Carmel. You can get *hold* of Haifa, walk everywhere, question, intrude, belong. The old men are straight out of *Fiddler on the Roof.* Others look as if they've walked off the Upper East Side. Bagels abound. Spend two days strolling and sniffing the air. Learn a bit about the Bahais and their faith which originated in Persia; mooch round Hadar with its tree-lined streets and plethora of snack stalls and the Arab souk; buy wine and goodies in take-away pots for supper. Inflation is dire. Over 60 per cent of GDP goes on weapons of war. Lebanon is 30 miles up the coast. The bay in front of the port must once have been lovely. It's now petro-chemical installations and cement works. Do a lot of sleeping and lying in baths. The English £ is 171.6 something shekels. Am uncomfortably aware that I haven't bothered to learn polite phrases.

Sister Juditha is a Palestinian Arab. Terracotta turtle doves hop in and out of her pot plants on the balcony. She confides that she can only fry eggs properly in one pan and keeps slipping me oranges and grapefruit and cups of tea. The lovely wild flowers on the tables in the dining room are her work. 'We have group on Monday,' she beams. Do saints like Sister Juditha start as they are, or do they have sainthood thrust upon them? On my second afternoon I sat on the balcony in hot sun watching old nuns weed the garden. Many are frail. No new sisters join the order. Later I walked to the Carmelite Monastery and met a kind-faced Italian father. He asked me if I was Catholic or Protestant.

'I believe in God.'

He took two of my fingers with two of his.

'God bless you,' he said. 'Pray for me.'

There is a longing in me to stay and dig the garden and prune the trees and talk German to the old nuns. Their singing is sweet and pure as that of young girls. Tomorrow I go by bus to Akka, Acre. Everyone, including St Paul has been there. All loos in the Middle East and Asia Minor should have 'St Paul was here' scrawled on their walls.

Jan 31st, Acre

The Turkish fortress built on Crusaders' foundations is home to the Arab population of Acre – noisy, cheerful, fishing, bartering, throwing their refuse onto the streets; swept, so the manager of the youth hostel assures me, four times a day. The sea laps at golden, crumbling walls. Acre has another fortress, a modern one, on the other side of a street called Ben Ami. Here, in neat rows of block houses, lives the new Jewish population. Acre's history is exotic. Although it kept the tribe of Asher and Napoleon at bay (Joshua allotted Acre to Asher but the inhabitants had other ideas so the Asherites never got their hands on it) the town also fell to diverse celebrities: Alexander the Great, Antiochus, Julius Caesar, the knights of St John – hence the name *St Jean d'Acre* – Saladin the Kurd; and an Albanian called Al-Jazzar known as *the butcher*. Oddly, the chief glories of Old Acre are legacies of the butcher – the Al-Jazzar Mosque and the Khan-el-Umran near the harbour.

The youth hostel, a 200 year-old Osmanli delight beside the light-house, is in the old quarter. It's elegant and beautifully main-tained. Sitting in reception, admiring the slender marble pillars which arch to the high, blue-painted ceiling, I could be in a hotel in Istanbul. The manager is five foot and called Alberto. A bed for elderly non-members costs £2.80 a night. God bless *Let's Go* and Harvard. The place is exactly as they described it. Only 10 of the 270 beds are occupied. Mine is damp but in a pretty room with four beds – it reminds me of my attic in Beirut except that it isn't up a ladder but a creaky wooden staircase. Someone really *thought* about this place. How intelligent to have split levels of four beds each instead of the usual claustrophobic ten or twelve to a room.

Acre offers the best of all possible worlds for the single traveller: the friendly society of the Arab quarter with its souks and alley-ways; old bastions to prowl; the tiny harbour with its brightly-painted fishing boats. For peace, privacy and no conversation there's tree-lined Ben Ami on the Maginot Line with its bars serving beer, coffee and cakes. You can read or stare into space undisturbed. On my first afternoon, I visited the Museum of Heroism. The British imprisoned many of the Jewish Underground here in the forties. Eight they hanged. Heroes or murderers, freedom fighters or terrorists – depends which side you're on as to how you react. Acre's Jewish community flourished in the 11th and 12th centuries. A Talmudic college was founded in 1260.

Feb 1st, Acre

The sky is an unruffled blue. What I thought was thunder as I dressed must be the heavy artillery on the Lebanese border. Smells, smells. Wonderful Middle Eastern smells. Cities, towns and villages are best at first light. You catch them with their pants down. 'Come fishing,' calls a fisherman in the harbour. It's 6am. Two minutes later he pops out of a coffee house and beckons me to meet his crew. What faces – clever, liquid-eyed, Levantine. A few are burly with fair hair. They are a handsome bunch, Sadi's fishermen. His English is adequate so I accept an invitation to eat fish and drink wine with them. Might learn something about the political situation. Back at the hostel, Alberto is in full cry: '80 per cent of Arab girls are lesbians...Englishmen are useless lovers...English women are wonderful once you break through their reserve...I like big people. Little people are greedy...' They don't come much littler than him. Alberto is half Italian, half French, brought up in Cairo and educated at Beirut's American University.

A lovely sight, the Mosque of Al Jazzar, green and white and set in a courtyard whose Roman columns were taken from Caesarea. After an underground city and small museum, I find a bastion and green grass spotted with anemones. Washing flaps on a nearby roof. Cats wail in triplicate. Soldiers fool about beside the slender cannons which kept Napoleon at bay in 1799. White-yellow orchids, curiously translucent, spring from the lush turf.

Sadi is the captain of the Acre fishing fleet. We rendezvous in a bar. After whiskies and beer, a secret agenda unfolds. 'Go with him,' says Sadi, pointing at a redhead. I follow the man through alleyways, labyrinthine, sinister. My guide unlocks a building, God knows where, and we stumble up pitch-black stairs. His grandmother must have been fucked by a Scot. Is he here to assist in my rape or murder or both? The door below clangs. Sadi climbs the stairs swiftly behind us. Too late to flee. Redhead opens a door and at once I feel better. No brothel this venue. The switched-on light reveals a comfortable Arab flat in excruciating taste – a king-size bed, a baby's cot, a vast telly, plastic flowers and a wardrobe like a garden shed. It's very respectable. Visions of doing the splits over beer bottles fade.

The morose redhead is sent for food and drink while Sadi and I make a stilted conversation. I invent a husband and a son at university. The husband remains a shadowy figure but the son I grow fond of. With a shocking lack of delicacy that puts my host in a huff I'm explicit about *no* sex. 'I'm interested in the state of affairs between Jew and Arab. You're an intelligent man and can tell me many things.' 'What about feelings?' he mutters. Sadi is good-looking, small-headed, delicately featured; a carbon copy of a friend in London. Even his mannerisms are the same. In silence we watch Sherlock Holmes quarrel with his aunt on television. After 40 minutes, Redhead returns with wonderful falafel, hot peppers, a bottle of *Carmel Rosé*, a bottle of cheap brandy and coke. Sadi drinks the brandy and coke. I sip the wine. Suddenly he laughs, claps me on the back and stops sulking. Redhead, now even more morose, is sent for another bottle of wine, most of which – idiot that I am – I drink. (Anything said about politics I couldn't remember due to a massive hangover.) With the wine arrive two friends and hashish.

Sociably we pass a joint around. I am now one of the boys. Batty but harmless. At least I stay sober. The captain of the Acre fishing fleet is so pissed Redhead and I have to help him downstairs and along the street. Alberto is furious. It's ten minutes after closing time when I reach the hostel.

Feb 2nd, Acre

Feel DREADFUL. Swallow aspirin and walk to the garden where Baha 'ullah lies buried. It's very near the Lebanese border. The Bahai faith is most attractive – human, tolerant, unnationalistic. No priests. Baha 'ullah said that religion and science must proceed hand in hand because religion without science is superstition and science without religion is dictatorship – something like that. Despite my banging head, I'm bewitched. This is a Garden of Eden: eucalyptus – their branches smooth as limbs, swirl-striped, mottled; warlock olives; a view down a walk edged with cypresses, the line interrupted by small trees sprouting between.

A gardener is mowing grass and the smell makes me homesick. Every bloom, every tree, every shrub is perfect. There are hillsides of rosemary, nets of white broom. The birds – beautiful creatures with russet patches and zebra backs – are tame. Endearingly, molehills mar the perfection; obviously Persian moles. I eat more aspirin and walk back to Acre. A storm has got up making the wind whoop and howl. To be snug in bed when the wind howls is delicious.

Feb 3rd, from Acre to Zefat

It's Friday. Before catching the 10.45am bus to Zefat, I consume a breakfast of pitta, hummus, raw onion, tomatoes, hot peppers, half-sours and coffee; encouragement for the convalescent stomach. 'The coffee is on the house,' says the proprietor. Nick a postcard from Alberto and catch the pre-Sabbath 361 bus: standing room only but a boy gives me his seat. Zefat is one of the holy cities. We roll through lovely country, hills, pine forests, lush meadows. The Jewish Sabbath begins at 3pm this afternoon. Nothing opens again until 6pm tomorrow.

Zefat is ugly, a disappointment. My first imperative is wine, dates, cheese and somewhere to stay for two nights. The family Pinko – between Snir Jewellery and the bus stop – takes in paying guests. Avram and Molka have six children: Sara, Ester, Liora, Dorrit, Svikam and Shaoul. It's an old house, small, clean and jammed with status symbols; centre lights like flying saucers and a huge telly. I'm put with Sara and Dorrit. A puppy tied to a drainpipe cries its heart out. The family are friendly. Frau Pinko and I communicate in German. This Jewish Sabbath is no joke. Out on the streets, silence; nothing, no-one. No buses, no cars, no cats. No humans except for me and then, suddenly, three frockcoated gents in *streimels* (fur hats) and three rabbis. All six glare at me. One carries a green cushion.

I am becoming depressed. An ugly town, a heroes' park, acres of graveyards and an artists' colony full of rubbish. Zefat's Arab population was 'gloriously' conquered in 1948. Their quarter lies in ruins. It's evening. Back at Maison Pinko candles burn and a dish of moles in batter circulates. Sara and Dorrit are asleep by 8pm. There's no reading light. They both snore.

Feb 4th, Zefat

It's interesting to observe a Jewish family at close quarters; they couldn't be kinder. There are no flies on uxorious Avram. Breakfast – a small piece of omelette, bread and yoghurt, carrot and tomato salad and milky coffee – is 300 shekels. I feel wrongs have been done here. Spend the day in a forest on Mount Sion looking at the Golan Heights. The weather is lovely. I can just catch a glimpse of the Sea of Galilee. Back in Zefat, on the dot of six, the town awakes. Crossly I buy hard-boiled eggs. Each egg contains a Jewish soul.

Likos, 2005

'August is on the edge of winter,' observed my friend. We were sitting in the harbour at Psara, the caiques bobbing at their moorings, fishing nets spreading pools of colour on the quayside. They are fine men, the Psariot fishermen: Miltiadis and Vassilis, the two elder statesmen and brothers; Haralambos and Pavlos, also brothers, and Pavlos' son Stefanis; Adonis with his two sons Pavlos and Stefanis; and Popi's Dionysis, much younger and fishing alone. I have the greatest respect for fishermen. The work is skilled, backbreaking and dangerous; the small profit achieved no recompense for the hours at sea and the wear and tear on the body. Yet Pavlos' son Stefanis refused to consider any other life; and I doubt whether the others, despite their grumbles, could ever work on land. During that long, hot summer of 1981 my sleep was often disturbed by the chug of boats going out. In my cot above Aphrodite's taverna, the small room full of her pots and pans, the household lamp burning in the passage, I would silently wish them luck.

'Beware the Westerlies. The Wolf will have you by the tail.' Fishermen's lore runs deep as their superstition. The Psariot fishermen are also masters of wit and delicacy of compliment. I remember the following exchange with Haralambos:

'Sara! You are always walking about. You are a mule.'

'No, I am a donkey.' (Meaning not just the animal but someone who's stupid.)

'No, you are a mule. Mules have principles.'

The boys of 1981 are now the fishermen of 2005. The winds blow round in the same old circle. The sea still changes her moods. The quayside scene is timeless: men sorting and selling their catch, sorting and mending their nets, tinkering with the boat, watching the weather. Miltiadis is a legendary figure to the young. They say he could 'smell' where the fish were.

Miltiadis' father was a fisherman and his father before him. It's in the blood. Or maybe something stranger? My old friend told me the other night how, for years, his dead father would appear and tell him where to fish. The fish were always there, the catch always good. He said: 'I never spoke of this to anyone. Then one day when my catch was enormous I told Angelica and the priest. I never saw my father again…'

I remember the day spent fishing with Dimitris and Jannis before we made for Amorgos – the nets coming in over rollers, the fish immediately sorted, cleaned and crated in crushed ice, the boys' hands raw and purple as they manhandled fish and ice blocks, the boat dancing like a dervish. I remember a storm on the Sea of Galilee; and the fishing boats making for the shore while the wind moaned and wailed and tried to break every window that wasn't already broken in the monastery beside the church of Saint Peter. Terra Sancta, Sebastian Flyte land…

Chapter Twenty

The guest farm of Yehuda Agni – the Sea of Galilee – Terra Sancta at Tiberias – Nazareth – ten days in Jerusalem – reflections on a city
1984

Feb 5th, to the farm above Galilee

A clear blue day. The bus from Zefat drops me at the entrance to a 'guest farm' praised by *Let's Go*. If Christ is absent in Zefat he's powerfully present here, in the fruit groves of the Hill of the Beatitudes and by the shores of the Sea of Galilee. Mark Twain, for one-upmanship cracks about this part of the country, should be ashamed of himself. On entering the main building with its wooden bar and restaurant of people eating breakfast, I am welcomed by the wife of the proprietor. The ranch house is set among gardens, the stables, paddocks and bunkhouse nearby. Tucked here and there among coppices and climbing roses are stone cottages, self-contained dwellings for visitors. Budget travellers sleep in the bunkhouse. My hostess – Austrian I think – works out that I can ride for four hours, spend the night in the bunkhouse and have breakfast for the equivalent of £26. She is charming. If it had come to double I would have stayed. 'You're lucky,' says my host with his slow smile. 'Chico's going out in half an hour. You can make a fourth.' It's ten years since I last rode. Hope I don't fall off.

Chico, 22, was raised in a kibbutz on the Golan Heights. He's a curly-headed, light-hearted soul who knows horses, rides beautifully and flirts with his customers. Eyelul is my horse, a good-natured chestnut of 16 hands who doesn't look where he's going. We set off, Chico cocking a wary eye in case I've told him a pack of lies about my riding. After five minutes, to my great satisfaction, he ignores me. It's wonderful when an old skill returns. I don't even bounce. Riding through spring growth of dockens and wild fennel, orchids, anemones as big as dahlias, the crushed grass and weeds, I fancy myself a child again. Below the Sea, a coppery glint, merges with sky. Everywhere blackbird and thrush are singing.

Horses smell so nice. We stop for a coffee with Bedouins near the lakeshore, then start back, skirting the orange, lemon and grapefruit groves and letting the horses have their head. The girls are a nice pair; both work on and off in the bar and restaurant in return for riding lessons. To ride beside the Sea of Galilee on an early February morning – the sun shining, the birds singing, the air warm enough for shirtsleeves – what's this if not a miracle?

The ranch appears to run itself which means that Yehuda and his wife and staff never stop working. After watching Thelwell children being taught to canter and a snooze in the bunkhouse (I'm the sole occupant), I take my wine, dates and cheese to one of the tables on the terrace and watch the sun set. Yehuda wanders over. He came from Chicago just after the war, was one of the first kibbutzniks, had this dream that one day he would have a ranch and breed Arab horses. He and his wife built the ranch themselves, including the exquisite gardens. I make a silent vow to come back one day, with *lots* of money, and stay in a cottage and eat wonderful meals. Two of the cottages are occupied – one by Carol, a Hohenzollern prince, and the other by a man called Gordon who's waiting for the Messiah.

The buildings are attractive, the gardens lovely, the hospitality marvellous, the kindness to a middle-aged backpacker endearing – 'of *course* you can eat your food on the terrace.' These two Israelis run the best outfit since Captain Hunt and the Invergarry Hotel.

Feb 6th, to Tiberias and Terra Sancta

Sleep like a log. Enter the dining room mad with hunger, say good morning to the prince who is eating a boiled egg and am served the following: six cups of coffee, not all at once; an enormous grapefruit (quite unlike any grapefruit I've eaten before); two fried eggs and five thin square rashers of bacon; thick toast which appears two slices at a time; butter in a lordly dish; a plate of raw vegetables; a plate of olives; a plate of cheese and salami; a bowl of thick whipped yoghurt and home made strawberry jam. I make a pig of myself. Vagabond habits die hard. I squirrel the cheese and salami between two chunks of hot toast and slip them into a pocket.

It's Monday, another lovely day. (With Sunday being Monday I'm confused.) Time to leave the Mount of the Beatitudes and descend to the Church of St Peter and its monastery, Terra Sancta... '*the Franciscan Church of St Peter, commemorating the miraculous catch of fishes, stands upon the lake shore. Built in the 12th century by the Crusaders, it became a mosque under the Moslem, then a khan, then once more a church. Rebuilt in 1870, enlarged in 1903, then restored in 1944 in its present form, St Peter's Church shows an east-orientated nave in the shape of a boat. In the courtyard is a monument put up by Polish soldiers quartered in the hostel during World War II...*' No repairs have been done to the monastery's hostel since the Polish soldiers. No-one, including me, cares. Shabby, paint-cracked, this place of broken windows breathes serenity. I share it with Fathers Francis and Philip, Martin the mystic, the Arab family who are caretakers, Steven the Cockney waiter and Mike. Mike's eyes look bruised. He's recovering from a divorce, two children, all that misery.

The bedrooms are dusty but clean, the beds the ones the Poles slept in. Sun, dust, broken windows, swallows swooping in and out. An extension on the second floor is our kitchen and eating area. The loos and showers are next door. The loos have the old notice 'closet' above them. They don't smell. Nothing smells. Ants trot about. The main room has a wooden table and chairs, a bench, cupboards with food people have forgotten about and a gas stove with one half-working ring. Above the stove is a notice: '28 people use this area. Please leave it as you find it. Thank you. The Pope.' Two doors lead onto roofs, terraces and ledges. There you can sit, read, look. Looking at the Sea and the hills opposite is best. Never was there such a place for vacant contemplation. The Arabs call it *kaif.* Mount Hermon floats to the north.

Spend most of the day on the roof and by the lakeshore. The sweet-water sea is limpid, shimmering, blue. Herons stand on one leg at the water's edge, coots dive, gulls mew above the fishing boats, swallows play war games. On an outcrop of old wall boys splash and shout. When evening comes, the mood changes. Fretted by blustering rain, the sea becomes a wild thing, empty of boats and birds. Solid downpour. Then wind, wailing and moaning, banging doors and windows. Lulled by this fury, I fall asleep.

Feb 7th, Tiberias

The resident cock crows not thrice but all night. The storm has blown itself out. A bell tolls for devotions at 6.30am and, as if summoned, the sun comes over the hills. Birdsong is wonderful here – they've been at it for an hour or more. Terra Sancta is on the edge of a pit, a monstrous maw for another new hotel. Poor Tiberias. It's a mess of diggage. After coffee and a hot pastry I marvel at the destruction. I don't understand why the Israelis want to spoil this historic town. The highrises like the Plaza are crass, monuments to money and bad taste, out of proportion with their surroundings – the old Roman wall, the mosques, the Greek monastery, Terra Sancta, the Scottish hospice. Bulldozers gouge. The sky is full of cranes.

Despite the shambles and a couple of impersonal supermarkets, lakeshore Tiberias manages to keep charm and bustle, a blend of Jew and Arab. There are rows of falafel shacks, bars, cafés, fruit stalls, old-fashioned grocers buttressed behind pulses and rice, pasta and spices. A few kilometres down the Sea bubble hot springs ancient and modern (the water is supposed to have purgative qualities); there's also a tiny museum and pretty mosaics in the ruins of an ancient synagogue. At the south end a kibbutz and palm trees. The eucalyptus hang down over the water's edge, giving an impression of swamp and everglade.

Feb 8th/9th, Capernaeum and Nazareth

As the swallows through the broken window, so my emotions

hightail and swoop. Music. Laughter at travellers' tales. Confidences. We are respectful of each other's space which makes our meetings good. Steven the waiter talks of the political brain-washing which goes with *Ulpan* – a government-paid scheme to teach immigrants Hebrew and acclimatise them. Another boy passing through had worked in one of the kibbutzim on the Dead Sea. He said they were pioneers, their dedication absolute…

'Lots of people can't take it. There were three suicides among the volunteers while I was there.'

Spend a tranquil morning at Capernaeum and Tabgha. At her north end, lapping at the shingle beach where the Church of the Primacy stands, green fields and orchards behind, the Sea of Galilee feels European. I picnic in a grapefruit orchard, feasting on windfalls for pudding. Their taste is sublime. I shall never eat grapefruit out of a shop again. The weather is black and blue, chasing shadows across the land. Then thunder and lightning erupt, the sea turns to aubergine, solid rain again. I bus to Nazareth – a cheerful place with Christian Arabs and not so much rain. A Franciscan monk, Spanish sceptic, takes me round his unopened museum and leaves me to rootle in the caves of the ancient town. After an hour he reappears – he's a jokey man – and waves at a boulder.

'Supposed to be used by John the Baptist. Well, you know, *supposed…*'

Together we gaze at a carved half wing said to belong to the Angel Gabriel. 'Sounds like a position on the hockey field,' I say. 'Where's the other half?'

'God knows,' sighs my companion.

A group of Austrian pilgrims are holding a service at the altar of the Basilica of the Annunciation, a complex built only 17 years ago by the Franciscans. They own vast tracts of real estate in the Holy Land. It's rather magnificent. After drinking water from

Mary's well and investigating the Arab quarter, I board a bus for home.

I should have learnt by now *never* to buy a return ticket. Foolishly I'd offered both tickets to the Tiberias-Nazareth driver who, equally foolishly, had punched holes in both. The Nazareth-Tiberias driver is incensed by this piece of carelessness. He demands I buy another single ticket. I refuse. He insists. I am unmoved. 'Can you speak no Hebrew?' he asks pathetically. Finally, a small garlicky man beside me says he speaks English. I explain all. 'Please tell the driver that it was the other driver's fault and not mine.' After much waving of hands the driver is mollified. The bus can depart. I am told NEVER to take a return ticket and to report the driver of the other bus. I promise to do both, with no intention of doing either.

As we bowl through Cana of water-to-wine fame, my interpreter tells me he's an Arab typesetter working for a Moroccan Jew in Tiberias.

'At school we read *Moonfleet, Cloister and Hearth* and *King Solomon's Mines*. Then we make précis of her...'

Emboldened by my genuine interest, he chatters on, his English becoming more fluent. He's a sweet man, untidy and shabby. He was educated by the British in Palestine, learnt English for nine years. With the hospitality of the Arab, he offers me half his frugal lunch. His great dream is to go to Greece and see the classical temples he's read about. As we approach Tiberias, he gazes intently at me, touches my arm:

'Do you know who you look exactly like – your eyes, your mouth?'

I preen myself. Ingrid Bergman? Elizabeth Taylor?

'Margaret Thatcher.'

For the rest of that day I have Terra Sancta to myself. The rain has cleared, the crickets whirr, everyone has gone. *Kaif* overwhelms me and I sit on a wall and look at the Sea and the mould of Mount Hermon, a jelly topped with evaporated milk. Occasionally dotty Father Francis hoes the vegetables or rings a bell. This place will haunt me for ever – the monastery and the Sea, the fat little birds with blue bottoms who flit in the palms, my white heron. The moon sails in a cirrus sky and I am queen of the castle.

Feb 10th, to Jerusalem

So now I go up to the Holy City of Jerusalem via the West Bank and Jericho. The bus is full of exhausted young soldiers, some looking only 15 years old. Am horrified by the way Arabs are treated when they get on at the different stops – as if they were aliens, a sub-culture. A recruit falls asleep on me; a girl soldier talks to me. Orna has only six more months of her National Service – boys do three years, girls two and a half – and a boyfriend called Mordechai, Motti for short. She shows me a white chocolate rabbit he's given her. Constant manoeuvres keep the boys slim as matchsticks. Orna says the girls get bored and fat. Up up we climb into the high hills. As the bus enters the outskirts of Jerusalem the radio plays 'We all live in a yellow submarine.' There are rockets on the West Bank. What a weird journey. What a weird country.

'Go and stay at the Rag and Bones Hotel near the Damascus Gate,' said Martin the palmist. 'You'll like it. They say its owner, the Mr Big of Jerusalem, won it in a crap game.' The Raghadan Hotel is clean, cheerful, full of backpackers and run by Scottish Aggie in her early twenties. She could very likely run the world. Aggie doesn't know what to charge me. We finally agree on a double for 300 shekels a night. I suggested paying twice as much as the kids since I'm twice their age. Aggie vetoed this.

Ten Days in Jerusalem – reflections on a City

She came as a shock the Holy City. Not a city as Europe uses the word but a sprawling town built on hills, at its centre a religious heart. Why is Jerusalem familiar? Did I know it in a previous life

GOING WHERE MY PIG IS HEADED

with a bloodthirsty crusade? Mystic Martin who fell down the Damascus steps one day and landed at my feet said I had been a jester...This is a snakes and ladders place, blue with forests of rosemary. Its religious extremes are equalled only by its climatic ones. Air crackles as in Austria. Sun burns. Wind bites. Sweating and peeling during the day, I froze at dusk and dawn.

Ah, those Jerusalem dawns, rat grey at 5.30am, soft with the hic-coughing of turtles and gurgle of thrush and blackbird; the call of the muezzin, squawking chickens, the wail of a woken child, the rumblings of my stomach. My *Zachlab* man would be in the street, his hot thick drink dusted with cinnamon and raisins. Solace for my emptiness. Sometimes I met curious stares from Arabs going to work, neatly if shabbily dressed. The poor rise early. Only the rich lie abed. Dawn is the time to go snooping; in souk and church and chapel, with no crowds or merchandise to blur the edges. You must catch Jerusalem unawares – before she puts her make-up on. She is the oldest tourist trap in the world. Her cynicism is fearful; oddly, she still inspires faith. Her pilgrims, singing in groups outside this or that church, are touching – however gullible or naive the unbeliever may think them. Virgin and whore, Jerusalem has been fought over, taken, killed for, possessed and re-possessed, held with jealousies so frantic that those in control would have her destroyed rather than lose her. There's a coldness, an indifference about the lady.

Where is Golgotha? There are two. One is in the Holy Sepulchre Church, the other over the wall from the ground said to be Joseph of Arimathea's garden, site of the Garden Tomb. The Arab bus to Jericho goes from this Golgotha, making the last station of the cross a bus station. The Garden Tomb is a piece of Old England. When General Gordon in a Thatcher-like way decided that this, without *any* doubt, was where Our Lord died, the British bought the land. That was in 1880 and they still own it. Flocks of elderly American, French, British and Japanese pilgrims pour in to be lectured free of charge by polite Englishmen with loudspeakers. I found it touching and quite mad. For instance, why would a rich man like Joseph of Arimathea buy land for a garden beside a public gallows?

Father Francis lent me a guide which says the Crimean War started from a row between the Russians and the French over the Holy Places. The Holy Sepulchre Church – the alternative Golgotha – is divided into six parts, the three main portions shared between the Franciscans, the Greeks and the Armenians. The second eleven who don't seem to have much of a say in matters are the Copts, the Ethiopians and the Syrians. If the Garden Tomb is mad, this place is madder. Two Muslim families hold the keys to the church and have done so since the days of Saladin the Kurd. No Jew was allowed to enter the Holy Sepulchre until 1967. No Protestant faith is represented. What I want to know is this: what malign power impelled the three great faiths of the last 2,000 years (longer in the case of Judaism) to establish the Wailing Wall, Dome of the Rock and Holy Sepulchre in the same place? Especially when they disapprove of each other so much? Jerusalem is a holy hotchpotch.

On my first morning in Jerusalem the Greeks were singing in the Holy Sepulchre, on my last the Franciscans. An Armenian floor-sweeper showed me a beautiful mosaic and another asked for my prayers. Father Francis worked here for twenty years. No wonder he's dotty. Up on a roof behind the Holy Sepulchre is a village of Ethiopian priests.

For days I walked the labyrinths of the old city and the leafy roads of twenties/thirties Jerusalem; reminded of Amman, tickled by a Britishness lurking here and there, obstinate ghosts of forty years ago. The letter-boxes are still red. My first morning, just outside the gateway to the Dome of the Rock, a pigeon shat on my head. 'In my country, it's good luck,' I said to the Arab guard, shaking the soft blob out of my curls. 'With us too,' he replied. What a wonderful mosque. Afterwards I strolled and became annoyed by the rudeness of the whey-faced Hassidim in their frockcoats, prayer shawls and tassels. They barge through everyone. Beside a notice saying 9th Station boutique I found a hole in the wall where the coffee was sweet and strong.

279

A walking tour of the Jewish Quarter was interesting – most of it carefully rebuilt or in process of being. There are rumours that, during the bulldozing of the foundations, many early Christian churches were uncovered and hastily built over. You can hardly blame the Israelis for this. If every early Christian ruin were sacrosanct, the new Jewish quarter would never get built. As it is, great chunks of the Cardo, one of Hadrian's cross-streets, have been excavated.

One evening I got lost on Mount Sion, floundering about until a Hassid with ringlets, carrying a plate of cakes, rescued me. Mount Sion is a favourite spot. It's owned by Lutherans and Greeks. The church is hideous; but music students practise there in the afternoon so free concerts of Bach or Handel are on offer. The coffee in the cafeteria with its cushioned wicker chairs and good pictures is delicious. A benign refuge. Not many places in Jerusalem feel benign. The Mount of Olives is an exception; also St Andrew's church beside the railway station. The careful rebuilding of the Jewish Quarter is like the restoration of Yemin Moshe, the artists' quarter below the windmill of the Mad Montefiore. Tasteful, but dead; all the squalor and racket and life and fun gone. I prefer the pungent odours of the souk.

The souk is like every souk – I am spoiled by Aleppo's. Here you find the dropscone pancakes soaked in honey; also wonderful hummus, spiced with bowls of red sauce, served with raw onion and pitta. Sesame rolls of *zatar* and hard-boiled egg make a satisfying breakfast. The chopped vegetables on the falafel stands are like herbaceous borders. An unforgettable sight: a Crusaders' alcove in the old quarter, tiny, stuffed with brand-new TV sets and eight Arabs drinking coffee. 'Today you are even *more* beautiful!' wails the fat moneylender near one Station of the Cross. It's not my body he lusts after but my wallet full of crisp pounds sterling. One day I went down to Masada on the Dead Sea and hated it – the place, the ethic, the lemming fanaticism of the sacrifice. People from a nearby kibbutz stopped the bus and asked if anyone wanted to join them. Rectitude and determination make a formidable combination.

Of all the geese which jealously guard this golden egg, Jerusalem, I like the Armenians best. They are so dignified and sad, having lost their country. They claim to be the earliest Christian Church, beating the Copts to it by a short head. Their museum is heartbreaking, mostly photographs of vanished artefacts. Its curator told me the Armenians are still the silver- and goldsmiths; were the great shoemakers. They also had the first printing press, photographer and girls' school in Jerusalem. Their liturgy makes you cry. One morning on Mount Sion, eavesdropping on an English cleric from the pages of Trollope, I saw an Armenian funeral procession. The corpse was only 33, so my friend from the museum told me later. He was fat and smoked. It was a good send-off: scouts, slow drums, cowled priests and mourners and a trumpeter playing the Last Post.

Secret gardens full of ivy and golden stone. *Jerusalem Walks* by Nitza Rosovsky is a treasure, its routes flushing out goodies like Conrad Schick's house from the turn of the century and twenties and thirties stuff. (Note the public lavatory on Kook and Yafo and Ethiopia Street). It also has great stories:

Two Mithnagdim were walking down a street. Said one:

"I have thought and thought and have reached the conclusion that in the eyes of the Almighty I must be a *gornisht*, a nothing..."

"Amazing," said the other; "I have been pondering the very question, and have arrived at the same conclusion. In the eyes of God I too am a nothing."

A Hassid who was walking behind them joined the conversation. "Gentlemen, I couldn't help but overhear you, and I want you to know that by some incredible coincidence I have also thought of God and the Universe and decided that in God's eyes I too must be nothing, a *gornisht*..."

"Ha," said one Mithnaged to the other. "Who is he to think that he is a nothing?"

…The railway station was inaugurated with pomp and circumstance in 1892…The train made life easier for all travellers, and after a few years it even ran fairly regularly. There were exceptions, though, as evidenced by contemporary humour:

"Why do you complain about the service?" a young man asks his friend. "It is now three-fifteen and the train is here, only fifteen minutes late."

"This is yesterday's train. Today's will arrive in twenty six hours."

…A story is told by Dov Yosef, the military governor of Jerusalem during the 1948 siege, about the Christian Arab families who lived in Abu Tor (The Hill of Evil Counsel). In anticipation of the Second Coming these families always took along an extra plate when they went on picnics, in case Jesus should suddenly join them; on their houses they hung signs saying "Maybe Today".

The YMCA, built by the man who designed the Empire State Building, was the scene of a surreal encounter with a physical training instructor. He stopped me at the door.

'What are you doing here? Are you a member?'

I said I just wanted to look around. 'Fine,' he said. Half an hour later he stopped me again. 'There is a concert.' By this time I was beneath the concert hall where the gym work-out rooms are. A ballet class tinkled and squeaked in one. The instructor was becoming a bore.

'*You* would benefit from physical training. You would lose weight here' – he prodded my bum – 'and here,' prodding my stomach. Then he looked puzzled:

'You *have* no weight to lose.'

'No,' I said.

'Yoga is good.' The idiot was off again, massaging my shoulders and back.

'Don't!' I snapped, dumped him and persuaded a kind man who'd sold all his tickets to let me in to the concert without one. It was wonderful: a talented girl playing Beethoven, Rachmaninoff and Chopin. Afterward, I went and read the *Times* in Jerusalem's very gloomy but centrally-heated British Council.

Bethlehem is bizarre, its Manger Square impossible to take seriously. I arrived there early one morning and caught the different denominations at their devotions; first in the Manger Basement of the Church of the Nativity where three old things – either Greek or Armenian – were chanting Mass; then in the gingerbread splendour of the Milk Grotto Church where a well-fleshed Italian priest was going through his paces. He struck me as pretty cavalier in his observance of the rituals – I was his solitary audience – drank an enormous goblet of wine and munched the Host like a breakfast cereal. No ascetic, he. Finally he turned round, blessed the empty church, gave me a dirty look and vanished. Bethlehem is unreal. Not so the nearby Herodion which towers over the Judaean desert. Talking of reality...the Shiites and the Druse have taken back West Beirut and the Americans are pulling out. What the Israelis will do, God knows?

The other day I watched a boy in the Rag and Bones carefully slicing packaged bread. Fancy buying that muck when you've got sesame glories on the bread barrows. Middle class hygiene runs deep as toilet training. Greek came in useful in Jerusalem and wheedled the keys to two churches from Kyria Lela. One day I climbed the tower of the Church of the Redeemer. Another day I wandered on the Mount of Olives, empty of life except for two brown sheep and a crocodile of camels. Jerusalem is a city of peachy sunsets and apricot dawns and wind; a city of green open spaces punctuated by cypress, olive, carob, fir and pepper tree; a city full of beauty – the Dome of the Rock at sunset and the view from Mount Sion. One evening an ancient produced delicious food in his tiny restaurant – *shishlik*, a mole-shaped hummus in batter, cakes of meat and cracked wheat. The brown dog in the Rag and Bones peed with delight when she saw me. Another evening as the sun went down I lay on the city walls and looked at Jordan and wondered if we, the British, would ever be forgiven for the mess we've made in the Middle East.

Feb 20th, Jerusalem

My ferry for Greece sails from Haifa in six days' time. Tomorrow I shall say goodbye to the Rag and Bones and Aggie and the little dog, bus down to Terra Sancta for two days of *kaif*, then on to Haifa and Sister Juditha's breakfasts. It's been an odd, uncomfortable month. Israel is an uncomfortable country. This new state, a European interloper in the middle of Arabia, is a raft of contradictions: vulgarity and beauty, surliness and kindness, conviction and doubt, extremists doing battle with the beginnings of a Peace Movement, the hilarious self-deprecating humour. I find the exclusivity of the Jewish religion depressing. Why should I be made to feel unwelcome in a synagogue? No Muslim, Hindu or Catholic would rebuff an interested visitor. I am at fault too. Not learning polite phrases in Hebrew didn't help and I did arrive – and leave – pro Arab. How can anyone not be? The intransigence of Zionism and its rectitude cannot be right. How can you take a country from its indigenous people without suffering consequences? The Israelis suffer, the Palestinians suffer. And always the slaughter of the innocent. I will never come back.

Postscript

Likos, 2005

*Carnival is over. From today, Clean Monday, the first
day of Orthodox Lent, there will be no more children in
mask and costume roaming the streets. Over too is the
shaping of my 1977-1984 diaries. So what, you may
ask, happened after 1984? Did the cheerful adventuress
go home and live happily ever after, become a published author, marry the lover left by the wife, cultivate
her garden? Well no, she didn't. There's a different
ending; and to understand it you must consider again
the question posed by Kundera: 'what happens when a
person rejects what he previously considered his
mission?' Now, nearly 30 years later, I think I know.
Call it speculation. Call it guesswork. At some point in
our lives we take the right or the wrong turning – and
we either survive or we don't. One side effect of
breaking a pattern is a shock to the system; and if the
system, as mine did then, relies on a child-erected
defence mechanism with its concomitant fragilities,
there are consequences. Mine took time to mature. For
five years it was fun and adventure. In 1982 things
started to fall apart.*

*It's there in the diaries if you can see it. In 1984 I
went back to England, tried to write another novel,
looked after friends' houses and drifted into despair.
Xmas morning 1985 tipped me over the edge. Sitting in
a rented flat in Red Lion Square I opened my three
Xmas presents. The first was an oven glove. The second
was an oven glove. I started to laugh. With trembling
fingers I opened the third parcel. It was an oven glove. I
burst into tears. Now I knew I was not only lost but
invisible. Sara Sharpe had vanished.*

*Trapped in a dark wood, I confronted monsters I
could neither understand nor cope with. It's all very*

well Kafka saying you can only see in the dark. Without someone to hold your hand you may die in the dark. That's where luck intervened. A Jungian psychotherapist took me on and over the course of four years guided me out of the wood. I have no idea how they do it. A friend once asked, rather shyly, what analysis was like. 'Reading enlightenment,' I replied. In 1989, unprompted by my analyst, I rang up my father's regiment and asked where he was buried. The archivist was horrified. 'You mean you haven't even read the obituary? But I knew your father. I served with him in India.' A few weeks' later, I took a bus to Hanover to say goodbye; after 40 long years, to let go. My father lies in a war graves cemetery among his peers. Great trees shade the graves. Gardeners tend the flowers. Birds sing. I cried for a week.

Doors began to open. At last I understood how our family had been wrecked by my brother's death; the tragic effect on my sister; the loss I'd absorbed as a two-year old; then my father's death; my sister's stroke and depression. I saw the defences I'd erected as the prison they had become; was amazed at what I had never asked my mother; realised how much of myself I had locked up, that September morning in 1949. My theory is this: that without those seven years of wandering – an unconscious quest, the beginning of a path to Hell – I would never have been free. Packing away the diaries on this spring day in 2005, I salute the writer for following her pig. Rejection of a mission is a hazardous business. In my case, lost and found – but a very near thing.

These five months have been dreamlike, a drifting in and out of times. The other day a capricious deity planted my old love, the sea captain, at the bottom of the post office steps. 'Is it really you?' I exclaimed. A bit older, a bit stouter, but still a handsome man. No, he said, he wasn't retired but skippering the freighter at anchor in the port. 'See you this evening at Popi's,' he said.

I never went – and I have no idea why not, none at all. An embroidered picture called 'Unknown Love' hung on the wall opposite my bed; a flesh-coloured Eros with yellow wings, his arrow drawn back in the bow preparatory to shooting a red heart. I lay and looked at it and mourned my old friend and the offence I must have caused; and wondered if I could ever relearn the qualities the picture possessed – artlessness, innocence, a joyful seizing of the moment.

Max ran away from the soldiers and took to the hills. He'd run away twice before and I'd taken him back. When I looked in a few days later to see if he was alright, the young soldiers told me that the other army dog had savaged him. What they didn't tell me was that he had slipped his chain yet again. Poor Max. He knew better than to come back to me a third time. I feel I've betrayed a friend – nor do I know what to do for the best. He was always free to wander, a vagabond. Perhaps he should live and die as one? No one wants him and in Miti most people's hands are against him. As for the cat, it is clearly gay. Sometimes the gang rape below my balcony is so ear-splitting I empty a bucket of water over the lot of them. 'Have you no shame!' I roared in Greek the other day. Adonis, painting the roof struts of his taverna, nearly fell off his ladder. Cats are bizarre; the male confrontations and the wails and the body language; the eye flicked which yields an advantage, the elaborate slow-motion of the backdown. They are weirdest when sitting together, male and female, plotting the downfall of the human race.

The island is getting ready for Easter and the first showing of tourists. A middle-aged group from Switzerland have arrived and live in one of the old houses in Mavro Klima. Some are still as they were 50 years ago: painted apple green inside, with fireplace, wooden ceilings, small glass-fronted cupboards, wooden settles. In Miti every builder, painter and carpenter is at work; the cement everyone has been waiting for has finally arrived. Council workers plant trees – in the squares, by the sea, even along the new path across Boulder Beach. Round this western flank grow cabbagey moonplants, six foot high, their arms covered in yellow bobbles. Red and black butterflies feast on the pollen. The other day I was sitting in Harbour Popi's watching her son Michael touching up paintwork. A Greek song played. Popi was stacking plates. The roof struts patterned black design on the white road. Suddenly, onto this Bridget Riley background flashed the essence of the Mediterranean: an apple-green open three-wheeler full of gas cylinders, driven by a dark-haired boy in bright blue sweater and primrose yellow trousers. Colours of Benetton.

My old friend, homesickness, ails me; a regret for things soon to be lost – routine, smells, noises, people and patterns. The knowledge that small island life would drive me mad after another few months neither lessens the regret of leaving nor diminishes the love I feel. Here is such beauty of countryside, terraced, treed, with flowery hills climbing to peaks and eagles. Nor have I seen abundance of wild flowers on any other island – squills, cyclamen, anemonies, mandrake, narcissi, sistus, orchids, hyacinth, lupin, viper's bugloss, mountain lavender, oxalis, corn marigold, asphodel, daisies, poppies, broom, gorse, lavatera, sea stocks, cornflowers, campanula, fresia, scabious, hollyhock, honeysuckle, lily, wild rose...that's just a taste. Last week I walked the cliff track to a headland of euphorbia and sat there looking at the sea and the shadow of the horizon. Below a white ship passed, engines just audible. It was a picture from a child's book. Above two eagles circled.

Likos is not the real name of my island; but anyone who loves it will know it and anyone ready to respect its way of life will find it. The geography, the number of villages and their names have been changed. The people, their names and their lives are true. As to my friends: if I lived for another hundred years I could never repay their kindness. I shall miss them and the grey rains blowing in from the west and the old track over the hill and the road that leads to nowhere. And this coming September I shall take my road again: to Rangoon and Kalaw in Burma by way of my grandmother's home in the south island of New Zealand, Sydney, the Blue Mountains, the moonscape of the outback, Alice Springs, Swan River. And on again to Calcutta, Darjeeling, Delhi, Mussoorie, the high places of Kashmir...